# CHEATING HITLER

## ALLIED AIRMEN WHO EVADED
## CAPTURE IN WW2

# CHEATING HITLER

## ALLIED AIRMEN WHO EVADED
## CAPTURE IN WW2

## MARTIN W. BOWMAN

AIR WORLD

**AIR WORLD**

**CHEATING HITLER**
**Allied Airmen Who Evaded Capture in WW2**

First published in Great Britain in 2023 by
Air World
*An imprint of*
Pen & Sword Books Ltd
Yorkshire – Philadelphia

Copyright © Martin W. Bowman, 2023

ISBN 978 1 39907 325 7

Typeset by SJmagic DESIGN SERVICES, India.

Printed and bound in the UK by CPI Group (UK) Ltd.

Pen & Sword Books Limited incorporates the imprints of Atlas, Archaeology, Aviation, Discovery, Family History, Fiction, History, Maritime, Military, Military Classics, Politics, Select, Transport, True Crime, Air World, Frontline Publishing, Leo Cooper, Remember When, Seaforth Publishing, The Praetorian Press, Wharncliffe Local History, Wharncliffe Transport, Wharncliffe True Crime and White Owl.

For a complete list of Pen & Sword titles please contact

PEN & SWORD BOOKS LIMITED
George House, Units 12 & 13, Beevor Street, Off Pontefract Road,
Barnsley, South Yorkshire, S71 1HN, England
E-mail: enquiries@pen-and-sword.co.uk
Website: www.pen-and-sword.co.uk

Or
PEN AND SWORD BOOKS
1950 Lawrence Rd, Havertown, PA 19083, USA
E-mail: Uspen-and-sword@casematepublishers.com
Website: www.penandswordbooks.com

MIX
Paper | Supporting
responsible forestry
FSC® C013604

# Contents

*His crew was hit over France near Paris. They bailed out, hit the ground OK and were grabbed by the Free French. Instead of being hidden in a farmhouse, six of the crew were taken into Paris and hidden in a house of prostitution. This fellow said that when he was twenty years old, he weighed 160lb. Several months later, when they were moved, he weighed 140lb. He said they could not be confined without sampling the merchandise.*

**Staff Sergeant Larry Goldstein,**
**B-17 radio operator, 388th Bomb Group**

# Acknowledgements

I would like to offer my grateful thanks to the following British and American airmen and friends for the kind use of their stories and anecdotes used in this book, which they related to me in correspondence and fascinating interviews that began over 45 years ago. From America they are Frank McGlinchey; Benjamin C. Isgrig Jr. and Robert (Bob) Starzynski. From the UK have come W. 'Steve' Bostridge, Tommy J. Broom DFC\*\*; Sergeant 'Jack' Pearce; Flying Officer Reginald 'Reg' William Lewis; Sergeant Harry Simister; Cyril Penna; Sergeant John Goffin 'Jack' Pearce and Reginald 'Reg' William Lewis. I am equally grateful to Dave Cole for his kind permission to quote freely from his article, 'See You At Breakfast'.

And last but not least, the following sources: *RAF Bomber Command Losses of the Second World War: 1943* by W. R. Chorley; *First Over Germany: A History of the 306th Bombardment Group* by Russell A. Strong (Hunter Publishing Co., 1982). and *Memories of Witchford* by Barry and Sue Aldridge (Milton Contact Ltd, 2013). *Free To Fight Again: RAF Escapes and Evasions 1940–45* by Alan W. Cooper (Pen & Sword, 2009).

Martin W. Bowman, 2022.

# Chapter 1

# Stirling Escapade

*Twenty-one-year-old Sergeant Cyril Penna, who hailed
from a little mining town called Willington in the County
of Durham, was posted to Operational Training Unit
Lossiemouth in Scotland and arrived at that station on
Tuesday, 19 May 1942. Penna's father was a miner and
had suffered very badly from wounds he had received in
the Great War. He had been savagely bayoneted near
Arras, France, along with many others in his regiment,
the Durham Light Infantry. His life had been saved by
a cavalryman, who on seeing him move, lifted him onto
his horse and took him to a field hospital. His rescuer
turned out to be an inhabitant of a small hamlet 4 miles
from Willington. Cyril had been summoned to report
to St John's Wood in July 1940 to start life in the RAF.
Now, two years' later, at Lossiemouth, he was greeted
with the news that the intake was to be crewed up as
bomb aimers, a classification that had been introduced
because of the four-engined bombers coming into
service. However, whilst at Lossiemouth, they would be
crewed up to man the Wellington bombers on the station.
This being so, Penna was crewed with Flight Sergeant
Frank Ellison Gatland DFM MiD of Drury, New Zealand,
where, on 14 April 1917 he was born at Onehunga,
Auckland; a wireless operator from Manchester; a rear
gunner from Cardiff – all sergeants – and Pilot Officer*

*Pat M. W. Butler, the navigator, from London. The five of them were to fly as a crew, working as a team and eventually would be posted to a squadron for operational duties. Their skipper, a farmhand, joined the RNZAF in March 1941. The excellent visibility over Italian cities, with their relatively lighter defences, meant crews were able to go down low and more readily locate the aiming points. During one raid on Genoa Gatland startled his crew by 'flying between the cathedral tower and the top of a high building'. His machine was hit by fire from the ground but he managed to get it clear of the area and return safely. Losses during these raids on Italy were comparatively light, although there were occasional interceptions by night fighters.*

'Two months elapsed, during which time we had flown on daylight and night exercises,' recalls Cyril Penna.[1] 'On 24 July 1942, after a brief period of leave we reported to 214 Squadron, Stradishall in Suffolk. We were told that we were to fly the new Stirling four-engined bomber and have our crew increased by the addition of a flight engineer and a mid-upper gunner. This transition would entail a conversion course at a nearby conversion unit and so we were sent to 1651 Conversion Unit, Waterbeach, and met our two new crew members [Arthur Goldsack Short MiD[2] and Herbert Allenby Harris[3]], both sergeants. Now, as a crew of seven, we were introduced to the Stirling and for the next four weeks we flew day and night, weather permitting, to acclimatise ourselves to the aircraft and to get to know the new members of the crew. Having become very much attached to the Wellington, it was indeed quite daunting to fly in the biggest

1 *Escape and Evasion* by Squadron Leader Cyril Penna DFM (United Writers Publications Ltd, Cornwall, 1987). See also, *Escape – The Best Sport Ever!* by Frank Gatland DFM.
2 KIA 29 November 1942, aged 21.
3 KIA 3 December 1942, aged 26.

aeroplane in service at the time. A great deal of skill was necessary to take off and land the aircraft, which when the wheels were down stood 22ft from the ground. The undercarriage was so delicate that any 'cross' landing invariably meant that the aircraft would come to an ignominious end on its 'belly'. Fortunately, Frank was a very capable airman and in a very short time he had mastered the intricacies of the Stirling and proved to be an exceptional pilot.

'Life at Waterbeach was very pleasant and when we had time off from flying, we visited Ely and the neighbouring towns. I can well remember a daily occurrence to which we all looked forward. When flying in the afternoon we usually had time to sit on the grass outside the aircraft, which was parked in the dispersal circle by the side of the road that ran from Waterbeach to Ely. We soon made friends with the driver of a bakery van that used the route to Ely each day and inevitably it became a habit for the van to stop and watch the preparations for the aircraft to take off. An introductory wave was followed by conversation and from then on we always had a bag of buns and cakes to enjoy when our flying ceased for the day. I often think of that van and the kindness of the driver, and no doubt the custom would continue after we had gone and the new crew to occupy that dispersal point would be treated in a similar fashion.

'Our last flight from Waterbeach was on 5 September and on the 8th we flew Stirling R9350 to the 214 Squadron airfield at Stradishall. We were very elated because we were now among operational crews and knew that we would be detailed for raids over enemy territory almost at once. Despite this feeling of apprehension and excitement I secretly had sadness in that my hitherto inseparable friend, Dennis Rushton, had remained at 218 Squadron, Marham, and for the first time we were parted.

'On 10 September we took off to bomb Düsseldorf. With mixed feelings we arrived at the aircraft in the crew bus. We were excited, apprehensive but carried along on the wave of enthusiasm that seemed to exude from the more experienced crews round about. We took off at 2120 and I will always remember the green light that flashed to give Frank permission to start his take-off run. I was in the 2nd pilot's seat to assist take-off and I also recall the pride that we felt as we moved forward and saw the wave from the CO and several others who were always at take-off to wish the crews Godspeed. We were soon airborne and with our load of incendiaries we made from Cromer and then set course for our target. There was no idle chatter over the intercom now. Silence was golden and was only to be broken when any member had some urgent report to make. The front, mid-upper and rear turrets were now the eyes of the aircraft and a vigilant watch was kept for marauding enemy aircraft, about which we had heard much from those well versed in operational flying. We saw several other bombers on the way to the target but as luck would have it, no enemy fighters.

'It was not long before we saw ahead a virtual cauldron of fire and light. The Pathfinders had illuminated the target and earlier aircraft had dropped their bombs and the glare from the ground, coupled with the numerous searchlights and streams of tracer bullets and flashes from exploding anti-aircraft gun shells, mesmerised us all. It was the first sight of action and the enormity of it killed any sense of fear. We were approaching the target and ready to make our bombing run. I was lying on my stomach gazing down on all the action below, feeling very elated. Somewhere below there was a factory that we had to hit and put out of action. I had set the height, speed and wind direction on the bomb site, had muttered 'bomb doors open' when a cone of searchlight hit me full in the face and the aircraft seemed to be 'frying'. The heat seemed to be intense and the natural reaction was to get out of it as fast as possible. This we did. The pilot banked sharply to port and away from the inferno.

'This was not the answer, however, and we soon realised that we had to go through the 'flak' and searchlights, drop our load and get off home. Again, we turned into the target, only to be coned again and evasive action took us away from the area. We were now all at sea and confused. Frank now took control and said we were going in.

4

This we did and I was amazed how coolly I followed the target along the bomb sight and at the precise moment pressed the bomb release. This sent hundreds of small incendiary bombs on their way to the ground: activated the switch that sent down the flare from the rear of the aircraft and started the camera in motion to photograph the point of contact of our bombs. With our load discharged we turned for the safety of the comparative darkness outside the target area, but we were again coned. This time we could not escape and it seemed that, despite the evasive action taken, the searchlight crew were intent on keeping us in their sights. Eventually and to our intense relief, we were in darkness again and it was a time to reflect on what had happened. Quietness reigned again and I know that we all thought of the crews that had not been so lucky and had not survived. We saw several aircraft in flames and noted one or two parachutes silhouetted against the fires on the ground. One could only surmise that, with the shells exploding all around them, they had a very poor chance of reaching the ground safely.

'We landed back at base at 0130, clambered into our crew bus and were driven back for debriefing. Even then the enormity of the happenings of the past few hours had not been realised by us. The more experienced crews reported that the enemy defences were very strong and said that they had had one of their most difficult operations. We had no other trips to judge the truth of this, but all felt that if things were no worse in the future, then we would survive. It appears that 479 aircraft were used on this raid and 33 aircraft were lost. There was much damage done to Düsseldorf and the surrounding area and 52 firms were obliged to cease production for various periods of time. Many houses had been damaged and many people were killed or injured. We were not to know of this at the time and so the results of our bombing seemed to be so remote that we were not aware of the carnage, damage and suffering we must have caused. We were aware, however, of the number of airmen who had been lost and it was very personal when I learned that Dennis Rushton had been one of the casualties. His aircraft had ditched in the sea off the Dutch coast and though some of his crew had been able to get into their dinghy and were picked up by rescue boats, no trace was ever found of him and he went down with the aircraft.[4]

'We returned to our quarters after a meal, weary but thankful that we had survived our baptism of fire. The night had been too eventful for us to fully comprehend what we had been through. Sleep did not come, however, and one by one we realised that the older hands had been right in their assessment of the situation and that our inexperience had possibly played a great part in our survival, and I can say that future operations were always approached with more caution and trepidation.

'Other targets quickly followed, of which Essen and Hamburg were the most heavily defended. Kiel, too, was quite a hot spot, since the latecomers were fired on, not only by the static defences, but by the warships that were in the base but that had hitherto not announced their presence until the raid was well and truly under way. What was most noticeable was the contrast of the searchlight batteries in England and Germany. It must be said that our searchlights were as candle in comparison and the numbers and their intensity had to be seen to be believed. It was a common occurrence for an aircraft to be handed from one cone to another and to be so held for a considerable time despite evasive action. This was extremely disconcerting and dangerous, because the fighter aircraft were invariably lurking around and attacking those unfortunate enough to be pinpointed.

'The bomber offensive was now gathering momentum and various moves were afoot to increase the number of conversion units, and on 1 October 1942 Stradishall became the base for the newly formed 1657 Conversion Unit. This meant that 214 Squadron had

---

4 On 10/11 September, returning from the raid on Düsseldorf, Flight Sergeant E. B. Cozens ditched Stirling R9357 HA-E off the Dutch coast. Dennis John Rushton and Sergeant Douglas Alexander Watt Innes were lost without trace. Their names appear on the Runneymede Memorial. *RAF Bomber Command Losses, 1942* and *Vol 9. Roll of Honour 1939–1947* by W. R. Chorley (Midland Publishing, 1994).

to move to a satellite aerodrome at Chedburgh, ten miles north-east of Stradishall and on the A143 towards Bury St Edmunds. We were very sad at leaving Stradishall because it was a pre-war station and the accommodation and amenities were first class. It had opened in February 1938 and became the 'home' of 214 Squadron from February 1940. Many raids had been mounted in that time and, of course, many losses had been incurred. It was with mixed feelings that we took off at 1410 on Thursday, 1 October and flew the short distance; a mere 40 minutes flying time from take-off to landing, to what was to be our new airfield. Chedburgh had opened on 7 September and was to be the base for 214 Squadron until late in 1943. We were not enamoured with our new surroundings. After leaving such sumptuous accommodation Chedburgh provided a very spartan alternative. As I recollect, mud was everywhere and it was imperative to keep to the concrete paths while moving from building to building. We had little time to indulge in self-pity because of the task of settling in and local flying to get used to the new approach and landing features of the airfield. On 6 October we were detailed for the first raid from our new station. That night we took off at 1927 hours for Osnabrück and after a fairly uneventful trip landed back at around midnight. A couple of minelaying trips followed in quick succession, one of which was to the Baltic Sea and which was undertaken by a small force with relatively few casualties.

'Towards the end of October, the targets chosen were in Italy. This strategy coincided with the successes the armies were having in Africa and so the attention of Bomber Command was turned to the cities of Italy, one could only surmise as a 'softening up' preparation before an assault by land was made. Our first target was Genoa. On 23 October we set off at 1845 hours on the long haul over France, the Alps and into Italy. A force of 122 aircraft was employed and the flight across France was uneventful. There was good cloud cover but the experience of crossing the Alps was rather daunting. There were times when it appeared that the aircraft would never clear the next peak and I am sure that this fact, together with the extreme cold, accounted for some of the losses we sustained in attacking Italian targets. Having reached Genoa, we found that the city was covered with cloud, which extended over the sea. We decided to go down low to try to pierce the cloud base and so we approached the city from the sea. Laying on my stomach in the customary bombing position, I suddenly saw looming up ahead a tall obelisk, perhaps a lighthouse. I was sure that we would hit it but with great dexterity Frank tipped the wing and just avoided it. The violent movement of the aircraft was not appreciated by those of the crew who had not seen the obstruction, but this was yet another occasion when we had just cause to be grateful for the skill and courage of Frank. We swung to the starboard and at a height of about 300ft we flashed over the marshalling yards of Genoa. We were assisted in our identification of the target by searchlights, situated on the hills surrounding the city, who tried to pick us up and in doing so lit up the terrain below. Our bombs were released and, with parting shots from the mid-upper and rear turrets, we turned out into the cloud again. It was all over in seconds and exhilarating it was to flash over the ground at such a low altitude. I may say we never did it again, on the advice of those at base who had the planning and organisational responsibility. The aircraft received several hits from light gunfire and we had to land at Duxford on our return, being short of fuel and in difficulties. We were able to take off again next day and after fifteen minutes' flying landed at base.

'Luck had been on our side up till now and apart from being peppered by fragments of shells and coming home with numerous holes of various sizes in the aircraft's fuselage, no great trauma was experienced. On one of these raids Gerry, our mid-upper gunner, had received a piece of shrapnel in the back of his head, but we were able to get him back safely and he recovered fully after a spell in the sick bay. November had been a very quiet month for the squadron and minelaying trips had been the main activity. On 28 November we were detailed for another raid on Turin, this time to attack the Fiat motor works. We were told that it would be mounted by only a few aircraft and as take-off time approached we were concerned about the weather conditions at base. We had been warned that the weather forecast was bad and that the route over the Alps could be fraught with icing conditions. We took off at 1830 and climbed steadily to 6,000ft and set course for Italy. The journey to the target was indeed uneventful and we met little opposition. The weather it seemed was too bad for much flying. We did experience bad conditions over the Alps, but having negotiated this obstacle nothing stood between us and the target. The Pathfinders had done their job and, having pinpointed the target we ran in at about 1,500ft. We tried another run because our first was well off line and because of the height we had little time to correct our error. At the second attempt we were able to discharge our load and we began the slow climb back towards the Alps and home. We found this period of climb quite worrying because we were sitting targets if attacked by fighters. We were struggling to gain height and therefore sacrificed speed. Nevertheless, we were successful and eventually reached the comparative safety of France and, in our opinion; we had surmounted the worst obstacle.

'We were all feeling very cold and uncomfortable. These flights into Italy from UK certainly taxed the stamina of the crews. On this occasion we were more than usually concerned because we had taken as our rear gunner and mid-upper gunner two new members with whom we had not flown before and to my recollection were making their first trip to Italy. I think that most crews were rather superstitious about a change of personnel and I have often thought how much worse it must have been for the new members who were also flying for the first time with a new crew. Silence was, as usual, observed and apart from a few shells being fired from the ground we were lulled into a false sense of security by the lack of enemy opposition.

'We were just north of Paris [at Couvron-et-Aumencourt], the time around midnight, when the whole aircraft shuddered. A loud bang and instantly we were enveloped by tracer bullets.

[The Stirling had been intercepted by Leutnant Helmut Bergmann and Unteroffizier Günter Hauthal of 7./NJG 4, who were flying a Bf 110F-4 from Juvincourt airfield. Both aircraft collided, the Luftwaffe crew limping back to base.] 'I heard a scream over the intercom and instantly went to the 2nd pilot's seat in case the skipper had been the one to need help. I found him quite unhurt but struggling valiantly to take evasive action. The controls were limp and still the shells were being pumped into us. He gave the abandon aircraft order and we acted on those instructions. Fire had now broken out in the aircraft and before leaving his seat Frank opened the throttles to try to keep the aircraft aloft as long as possible to allow us to get out.

'I clipped my parachute to my harness and tumbled into the inky blackness from the forward escape hatch, closely followed by two other members of the crew. I found myself suspended in air with nothing but the silken cords of my parachute to see me down safely. I saw two other parachutes, but soon became engrossed in looking below to see what my landing area would be. The aircraft had by this time disappeared and suddenly the sky was lit up as it crashed some distance away and all was quiet except for the wind rushing past my ears. I was able to see quite clearly that I was going to land in some water. I had looked down, and in the moonlight had seen what I thought were waves. This did worry me because I was no swimmer and it was bitterly cold. Had I been in command of my senses I would have realised that I couldn't be over the sea and that whatever I was seeing below was therefore not water. Indeed, I nearly did panic and inflate my Mae West, but thought better of it since it might have been damaged by the webbing of my parachute. I was so busy with these thoughts that I was totally unprepared for the sudden landing. However, on reflection I concluded that it was a good thing because I hit the ground completely relaxed and escaped injury. True I was winded for a while, but above all I was very bemused and uncertain as to what lay ahead.'

Cyril Penna was the only member of the crew to evade capture. Three of the crew were killed and three others were taken prisoner.[5] Cyril made his way, often painfully, through France, helped every step of the way by villagers who risked everything to assist him. Gilbert Biguet, from Warlus near Arras, allowed Cyril to stay for two weeks in his house with his parents before they entrusted him to the French Resistance network. And in Andorra in the Pyrénées locals tended him and helped to rehabilitate him mentally and physically from the effects of being a fugitive and having his feet and one of his hands becoming badly frostbitten crossing the mountains. He finally crossed into Spain and then to Gibraltar. He arrived home, appropriately, aboard the *Stirling Castle*.[6]

---

5 Frank Gatland bailed out safely and was captured by the Germans ten days after the crash and taken into captivity. So too were Pilot Officer P. M. Butler and Sergeants' G. Booth. Arthur Goldsack Short MiD and John Stammers, the 18-year-old rear gunner, were killed. Sergeant H. A. Harris was taken prisoner but died later. *RAF Bomber Command Losses, 1942–1947* by W. R. Chorley (Midland Publishing, 1994).

6 For his gallant evasion and return to the UK, he was awarded the DFM. Cyril died on Wednesday, 2 July 2014 aged 92.

# Chapter 2

# Escape to England

*Thomas ('Tommy') John Broom was born in Portishead, Somerset, on 22 January 1914 and educated at Slade Road School. After leaving school Broom got a job in a local garage. He soon grew bored and, in 1932, aged 18, he joined the Royal Air Force, where he trained to be a navigator. Mobilised to France at the outbreak of the Second World War, during 1939 he was assigned to 105 (B) Squadron operating Fairey Battle light bombers. He continued to serve with 105 Squadron until November 1940, a period that included the disastrous Battle of France and low-level attacks on the Channel ports to destroy invasion barges, in both of which actions the squadron suffered severe losses. During a raid on Cologne in November 1940 Broom's aircraft was severely damaged by anti-aircraft fire, but the crew managed to struggle back to England, where they were forced to bail out as they ran out of fuel. Having completed more than his share of front-line flying, he was transferred to 13 Operational Training Unit at Bicester, to teach navigators the skills required for combat. He returned to 105 Squadron in January 1942 and completed another tour, after which he was posted to 1655 Mosquito Training Unit in August where he remained until May 1944. Broom was awarded the first of his three DFCs on 3 October 1944. Subsequent to this he returned to front-line flying*

*until the end of the war, with Nos. 571, 128 and 163
(Mosquito) Squadrons. The citation for his second DFC,
reads: 'Flight Lieutenant Broom DFC was a navigator in
a Mosquito aircraft of 128 Squadron detailed to place
a 4,000 lb bomb up to the mouth of a railway tunnel in
the region of Kaiserslautern on the morning of 1 January
1945. This operation required great skill, determination
and the utmost precision.' His third DFC award followed
on 26 October 1945.*

On 25 August 1942 two of the three 105 Squadron Mosquito IV
crews at Horsham St Faith near Norwich that were detailed to raid
two electric power stations and a switching station at Brauweiler near
Köln had returned safely. The exception was 'O-Orange', flown by
Flight Lieutenant Edgar Alfred Costello-Bowen of Paignton in Devon
and his navigator, Sergeant 'Tommy' Broom, who recalled. 'We took
off at 1930 hours and went in formation to the Dutch Island at the
mouth of the Scheldt, where we split up and proceeded individually.
Not long after crossing the coast and the islands, we were very low
and brushed the tops of the trees. A few minutes later after crossing
another small wood, an electricity pylon suddenly loomed in front
of us. We pulled up but the starboard engine struck the pylon at its
top. Immediately the engine and the propeller stopped. The action of
hitting the pylon jammed the controls. We were 80ft up and there was
nothing we could do. We were doing about 250mph and just had to
wait until we hit the ground. I said to Costello-Bowen, "Well this is
it." It's a funny thing, but neither of us was worried and we were very
calm, although death stared us in the face. We lost height steadily and
crossed a couple of fields. Then the pine woods loomed up in front.
We were bound to crash into them – this was about half a minute after
hitting the pylon. Just before we hit I instinctively released my safety
harness; why I don't know. Then we hit and everything went black;
no physical pain, just darkness and I felt myself rolling over and
over like a ball. I must have been unconscious for a time. [They had

crashed in Paaltjesdreef Wood at Westmalle in the Belgian hamlet of Blauw Hoeve].

'When I awoke, I was covered in branches and bits of aeroplane and there was a strong smell of petrol. I was amazed I had no injuries; not even a scratch. I must have been flung out of the top of the cockpit as I was right in the front with the nose of the aircraft. It was amazing that the aircraft did not catch fire or the bombs explode. The nose of the aircraft must have passed between two trees. How lucky can you be? My next thought was Costello-Bowen. Although it was nearly dark, I found him in some wreckage about 20 yards away. He was unconscious and looked in poor shape. The rudder pedals had torn off both his shoes. After talking and patting his face for a few moments, he finally awoke. I lifted him up and half carried him about 400 yards away, where we both sat down. He gradually recovered and we were soon talking. We both felt very despondent at the thought of being made prisoners of war.

'We knew we were in open country and it would be a while before any Germans or locals found us. Costello-Bowen's ankle was very bad and he was severely shocked. I felt reasonably well, although I was "browned off". We decided to try and get away and see if we could get in touch with an escape organisation. This was a natural thing for any aircrew to do; in fact, it was our duty. We chatted. Costello-Bowen didn't feel as though he could make it and told me to go it alone. I went a few yards and then thought "I can't leave him". We both had our emergency rations and knew that in this state a Benzedrine tablet would do the trick and give us a lift. With Costello-Bowen clinging to my arm, we started off and had reached a road when we heard someone approaching. Instantly we dived into the hedge and he passed without noticing us. We set off across fields. It was now dark and we made our way steadily. (Costello-Bowen now felt much better and was able to walk alone.) We knew we had to find a hiding place before dawn. It was no use being caught in the open in daylight. Eventually we came to a small wood about 100 yards square (small firs, Christmas tree size, about 5ft). We settled down and slept a little. I could hear a clock striking in the distance. We were thirsty and we found a small ditch at the side of the wood. The water didn't look too good but we had rubber bags and purifying tablets, which we used and we had a drink. Not very appetizing. We wandered around inside the wood so we could not be seen from the tracks and discovered a hutted camp. We lay down and for about two hours we kept the entrance under observation. We saw no German soldiers, only nurses going to and fro. It must be a hospital of some sort [it was the Lizzie Marsily hospital, which was used as a sanatorium for tubercular patients] and we decided to take a chance. We walked over and knocked on a door of what appeared to be an office. A nurse appeared and was somewhat startled to see us. We walked in and one of the nurses recognised the RAF uniform. She fetched a doctor [Dr Debaudt, a veteran of the First World War] who spoke English. He knew about the crash and that the Germans were searching for us and he wanted to know what we required. We told him that there was an escape line but the only way we knew how to get in touch was to go to the cafes and restaurants near the railway station at Antwerp and with a quiet word here and there, perhaps something might happen.

'He and some friends would see what could be done. We were given a boiled egg and a hot drink and it was arranged we would go back to our hiding place (which we showed them). At 6 pm each evening an English-speaking nurse would pass the edge of the wood and whistle a few bars of a well-known tune. This would be our signal to go to the edge. She would give us a bottle of water and a tomato sandwich each and give us the news. The days were very hot (cloudless sky) but quite cold at night. We each had a small pack with about twelve Horlicks tablets and some chocolate. I had a pullover, which I wore for half the night and then passed it to Costello-Bowen for the remainder of the night. The days were long and we often heard German soldiers passing along the paths. This routine was kept up from Wednesday evening to Friday evening, when we were told that no contact had been made and that it would be dangerous if we were caught as the local inhabitants would be suspected of harbouring us and reprisals would take place. We said we would wait for darkness and then move off. As darkness fell, we made our way and had only got about 50 yards down the road when the nurse returned and said that contact had been made. At 6 pm the next day (Saturday) someone would come and start us on our journey. It was rather queer that neither of us felt any elation. So far life had been taken for granted, but all that was about to be altered.

'We slept well that night. Saturday seemed to drag on but at about 6 pm we heard our tune and went to the edge of the wood. There was our nurse with another young woman (possibly Dédée De Jongh whose father, a doctor, ran the Comète escape line that had established 'safe houses' along a route that led from Holland and Belgium through France to neutral Spain. Later, with the demise of the "Comète Line", the "Marathon Line" took over.) We could only thank her and ask her to thank all those who had helped us. They had taken a tremendous risk and we were very grateful. We returned to our little den in the woods. We didn't ask her name because if she was captured it was best not to know. If one should reveal a name a chain reaction could start and the line would be wiped out. We were questioned to try and establish that we were bona-fide aircrew, and looking back it would appear that they knew all about us – squadron number, station commander, where our home address was, etc. The lady had a suitcase with her, and this contained two suits, also a shirt and tie, bottle of water, a lather brush and razor, and a trowel. We shaved and changed and then buried our battledress. We were given a small attaché case each with a few items in it (this came in useful later on the outskirts of Antwerp). She told us we would be going about a mile down the road, have a drink in a small restaurant and wait for a train to Antwerp. She would do the talking and we must not speak. I asked if there would be any German solders around. "Yes", she said, "but behave just as though you are in England in a strange town where you know no one." I wondered what my reactions would be and said I thought I might colour up and become nervous. She said, "You'll soon get used to it."

ESCAPE TO ENGLAND

'Away we went and had a beer at the restaurant at the Hotel Beukenhof. On the balcony there were German soldiers around and to my relief I felt quite normal. Eventually we boarded a train and had to stand. She bought the tickets. At the outskirts of Antwerp, the train stopped and the police and Germans boarded and carried out a search (not inspecting papers, for we had none) but for the black market. We reached our destination and discreetly followed the lady to a doctor's house, where she left us and said she would return the following morning (Sunday). The doctor was very kind and after a cold bath (no hot water available); we had a small meal, boiled egg and bread and butter, to get our stomachs used to food again. We sat around chatting and had a beer, then off to bed. After breakfast next morning, our guide arrived and we went to the station and caught a train for Brussels – no papers, but no trouble on this short journey.

'We were taken to a house about five minutes from the station to a grand old lady who lived alone and told that we would be fetched the following afternoon to go to the "Bon Marche" to have our identity photos taken on the machine in the store. The grand old lady told us that we would be quite safe as the Germans had the week before raided that street and taken all Jews and suspects. There we had our first taste of black, doughy bread and acorn coffee.

'We were fetched about 1700 hours on Monday and walked to the "Bon Marche". As we were just inside, I was in front, a German put his hand on my shoulder, said something I didn't understand, and took his hand away, and turned away. The guide was now by my side and whispered that he said the store was closing, and to leave. It didn't frighten me; it just took me by surprise.

'We went back to the house and returned the next afternoon, when all went well. The next day we moved to another house, which I now know to be Carl Servai's (because in 1944 I received a postcard from him). There we were introduced to our guide for the journey to Paris, who gave us our identify cards and said he would fetch us the next day, in the morning. We were staying with a very happy family with young children and we gave him the nickname "Chumleigh". We were

17

sorry the next morning when Albert Johnson, our guide (I found this out in Ste-Jean de Luz in 1962) came for us. I was "Pierre". At the station the guide bought books similar to *Picture Post* and said that looking and pretending to read these would dissuade our fellow passengers from having a conversation with us. He told us we would go alone. We should follow him to the train and sit as near as possible to him. This we did. The carriage had a central corridor with four seats (two facing each other) each side of the corridor. Costello-Bowen sat next to the guide and I was opposite, next to what turned out to be a Belgian with a black army uniform on. We had booked to Lille (the guide had obtained the tickets). They wouldn't expect evading airmen to go to Lille – more likely to Paris.

'Presently we heard the call for papers. German police and Gestapo eventually reached us. They were satisfied with Costello-Bowen and the guide's identity cards but they were not satisfied with the papers and answers of the Belgian and he was taken away. Then it was my turn. I gave them my identity card. They asked me something else (not knowing the language I didn't have a clue what they were saying), so I gave up my rail ticket. Another question and I didn't have anything more to give them I just answered, "Hmm". It didn't mean yes and it didn't mean no but it satisfied them and they gave me back my identity card and ticket and passed on. A close shave! Later the guide told me that they had asked where I was going (the ticket answered that) and then was I going to Lille to work in the mines? My "hmm" satisfied them.

'The next stop was at the Belgian–French frontier where everyone had to get off the train and walk to the checkpoint, where all they checked was the contents of the attaché case, then on to Lille. At Lille we went to a restaurant near the station and had a meal, a little walk around and then to the station to board a train for Paris. There were no checks on this journey. At the Gare du Nord there was no trouble and we three walked to a safe house and there our guide left us. The owner of the flat was a very good man, and he looked after us very well. The food was excellent and he told us (there were four of us at the flat) that after we had gone, he would have a spell with no evaders or escapers and he entertained some Germans, from whom he got the excellent food we were having. What a man! He turned over one of the pictures on the wall and there was a portrait of Hitler! No wonder they didn't suspect him of any dealings with escapers.

'Besides being careful when out, it was very important not to smoke English cigarettes or tobacco. (Very early on one chap was picked up because a German had smelled the English cigarette), so me being a pipe man, I had to smoke French tobacco – not very nice, although I didn't smoke outside because not many Frenchmen smoke pipes and I didn't want to arouse any suspicion.)

'We were taken on the Saturday to another flat where a man (I know now to be Dédée's father, Frédéric de Jongh) was writing and stamping our passes for the forbidden zone along the Atlantic coast. The next day, Sunday, we were to leave the Gare d'Austerlitz at 2200 hours. It had been decided to leave Costello-Bowen in Paris. With his injured ankle he would not be fit enough for the journey over the Pyrénées. (He enjoyed a week in Paris to get fit, and he even went to the cinema.) We handed over our money pack (containing French, Belgian and Dutch notes, which all aircrew carried). I left the house about 2030 hours and was told to turn left outside the front door and about 100 yards along I would see a jeweller's shop and a girl with a red hat would be looking in the window. This was my guide to the railway station. She was there and we duly went to the nearest Metro to board a train for the Gare d'Austerlitz. There were plenty of Germans in uniform around and two of them sat opposite us. After about five minutes one of them leaned over to me and asked me a question. (I later learned he wanted to know where to change to get to a certain station.) Quick as a flash my guide answered, then nudged me and we got out at the next station (in case he wondered why I hadn't answered). We made our way on foot to Gare d'Austerlitz (much safer).

'We met the others there – Frédéric de Jongh and another guide – so our party was seven; three and four evaders. We had quite a time

19

to wait at the platform barrier but there was no trouble and then as we passed through, we had to show our tickets, identity cards and Atlantic coast pass. Now came the cheekiest bit. We had a reserved compartment and when we reached it there were some people occupying it. They wouldn't vacate the compartment so Freddy de Jongh fetched the German commander of the train and other officials, who made them get out and let us get in. (That took some guts.) We had a pleasant journey. They came around and checked all the papers again and we had no trouble. The German commander even looked in later to see if we were all right and wished us a pleasant night.

'Ste Jean de Luz was the destination at about 7 am and here was a tricky situation. All passengers had to queue on disembarking and only a single exit door was open to go through. On the other side, on each side of the queue there was a German and French official checking papers. It meant about one in four was checked. (We were told that if one of our evaders was stopped and caught, the others should break out of the queue.) There was a low wall about 50 yards to the right. We would have to jump over and hide in the town if possible.) However, all went well. They checked the Frenchman in front of me so I quickly passed through. In fact, we all got through. My guide was waiting and we all made our way deviously to our safe house. This was Monday and we were due to set course for Spain on Tuesday. We were given a Basque beret and a pair of espadrilles (shoes for the mountains). Now we looked the part with our Basque beret and shoes. We four evaders left Saint-Jean-de-Luz on the Tuesday afternoon, separately, with our guides to make our way to the farmhouse at Urrugne, which was in the foothills of the Pyrénées. It was about two hours walking and about two miles inland from the coast. I went with Albert Johnson. We passed over the railway bridge just past Ciboure, exchanged greetings with the German sentry guarding the bridge, cut across country and reached Urrugne without any trouble. We all met up, had a meal and later met our Basque smuggler guide Florentino, a very tall and rugged man who spoke only Basque. He checked we were all kitted out correctly and that we all had a stout stick.

'At nightfall at about 8 pm Florentino, Johnson and us four evaders set off in single file, Florentino leading and Johnson checking all was well at the rear. Luckily the weather was fine. There was no moon so the darkness suited us. We moved silently up the mountain paths. No one talked, as German patrols in the area were constantly on the lookout for evaders. At last, we reached the highest point on the French side and could see the lights over the border. We could see the lighthouse at Fuenterrubia sweeping around at the coast where the River Bedasson flowed into the Atlantic. We paused for quite a while, sitting around very close to each other. Florentino had found the bottle of brandy, which he had hidden, and we all had a swig.

'As the next part of the journey was dangerous (down to the valley where the river flowed, then across the river and into Spain) we waited for quite a while. Florentino was waiting to hear the sound of a bird (his lucky bird). At last, we heard the bird call and were on our way. We reached the riverbank and Florentino went up and down checking both banks. On the right-hand side some way up, we could see the frontier post with all the lights on. We knew that the Spanish police would be patrolling the other bank. We were told that after crossing the river there was a grassy bank about 20 yards wide, then a road (down which now and again passed a car), a railway track and after this a steep bank, which led up the mountain. (With quite a few small trees and bushes at the beginning of the climb.) The river was fordable at this place, the water up to our waists. We were lucky as after heavy rain and during the winter the river flowed quite fast and was often up to the shoulders. One of the chiefs of the line drowned there in December 1943.

'Away we went across the river, Florentino leading and Johnson at the rear. We held hands and crossed in a chain in case anyone lost their footing. No trouble and we all climbed the other bank and waited a little. There appeared to be no one around. All was quiet. Florentino led and we ran across the road, railway track and had started climbing into the bushes when suddenly we were ambushed. A voice called "Halt!" Then shots rang out. We had been told if anything happened to go back across the river and wait; the others would do the same and we would all eventually meet up. I ran back and caught my leg on some barbed wire near the river. I had to untangle myself and got a deep gash in the calf of my left leg. (The only injury I suffered during the whole war!) I was lucky as when I reached the riverbank I found Florentino there. We could communicate only by sign language but I understood what he wanted to do. We hadn't heard anyone cross the river so we waited about five minutes and then went forward again to see if we could find any of the others. Again, the same thing happened. Ambush. We both ran back and this time re-crossed into France, went upstream for about a mile and crossed back into Spain, no trouble at all and we steadily climbed up and up. We got to the top and then went steadily downwards and eventually reached gentle slopes and green fields. It was still dark and we had to keep a sharp lookout for the Spanish police for we had stirred up a "hornet's nest". No doubt they were searching the entire frontier.

'We at last reached our destination, a friendly farmhouse. Florentino threw some small stones gently up to the bedroom window and out came the farmer and his wife. We were very tired as we had been marching for about ten hours. A quick hot drink and we went to the barn. Cattle were there but on the first floor there was plenty of hay stacked up to about 5ft. We climbed up and were soon fast asleep. About 1000 we were woken up with big plates of hot soup. We each had two helpings. Just afterwards the farmer returned and talked to Florentino. Police were approaching the farm. Florentino beckoned me and we looked out of the window stealthily. Two armed police were there, chatting with the farmer and his wife, and having a glass of wine. We went back and covered ourselves with hay. About an hour later the farmer reappeared and must have given the all clear. About midday Florentino returned and, pointing at his watch, made me understand that he was going away, but he would be back at about 7 pm. I dozed and when I looked over the side there was a family of rats playing just below me. However, they didn't worry me. Time passed very slowly but eventually Florentino returned. We bade farewell to the farmer and his wife and started on our way downhill. Eventually, we reached a main road where a car was waiting. We boarded and the next stop was the consulate in San Sebastian, where we found out that Johnson had arrived on his own. One Polish evader had also made it by himself. We told the consul the names of the other two who were still missing. No doubt the police had captured them. I was told later that this meant a week or more in a disgusting frontier prison, whilst the systems of release started rolling from the officials in Madrid. The Spanish were in no hurry to admit they were in custody. From there they would be moved to the concentration camp at Miranda del Ebro, where it would be about three weeks before the embassy could secure their release.

'A nice hot bath and a good meal made me feel a different man and also now that I had no need to look over my shoulder, the outlook looked much brighter. After breakfast the next day, we met the attaché from Madrid who always collected the evaders, and boarded his diplomatic car for the journey to Madrid. We stopped at a very nice roadhouse on the way and had a slap-up lunch. At each village and town armed police saluted the car as we passed. If they only knew! Eventually we drove into the British Embassy in Madrid. There was a large Army-type hut in the grounds and we found there were about a dozen servicemen there. We were interviewed by the attaché and told that we would remain at the Embassy until clearance could be obtained for us – perhaps a week to ten days. Then we would go by train to La Linea and across no-man's-land to Gibraltar. It was quite pleasant in the Embassy, although we were confined to the Embassy police HQ to prove our identity. None of us would be using our own names (I was "Sergeant Major Cook") but we were to give them our proper home addresses. It was the name that mattered. We went in front of a senior policeman and filled in a form. All was well and we returned to the Embassy. The next day four of us, escorted by the attaché, were delivered to the railway station, where we boarded the train for La Linea. We were locked in the carriage with an armed guard outside. We had sandwiches and were given coffee. An uneventful journey and when we reached La Linea we were escorted by guards to the frontier post police station. (We had been told by the Embassy to expect just an identity check.) I was asked my name. "Sergeant Major Cook," I replied. All was well and we were taken to the frontier gate, released, and we walked to the gate and on to Gibraltar soil; a great moment. It was 21 September, four weeks less a day since I was missing. We were given a medical, a billet and a night's sleep. Next day, identity, interrogation, kitted out with battledress. We were given £5 spending money and taken to the post office to send a cable home.

'A week later, as we waited for transport to the UK, Costello-Bowen arrived in Gibraltar, fit and well. We had a reunion drink. One went back to UK on the first available transport and eventually I boarded the battleship HMS *Malaya*, and escorted by three destroyers left Gibraltar. A few days later (6 October) we anchored in the Clyde off Greenock after a very pleasant trip, often with a Sunderland escort. We were first off the ship and taken to a barracks under guard, and next day to catch the night train to Euston. We were locked in a carriage under guard and on arrival in London, escorted to the transit camp at the Grand Central Hotel in Marylebone. We were interrogated by MI9 and eventually issued with a certificate to take to RAF Uxbridge. Then we were free to send a telegram home and were taken to the Air Ministry. We were given a written note stating our identity, had a couple of interviews, and asked where we wanted to be posted. I was told 105 Squadron had now moved to RAF Marham and 1655 Mosquito Training Unit was being formed and I agreed to be posted there. At Uxbridge I was completely kitted out, given three weeks leave and a railway warrant to Portishead, and one to King's Lynn on completion of my leave. So I returned to my family at Portishead. My two brothers (both of whom were in the Army) obtained leave and my sister, who was drafted to the Bristol Aeroplane Company, was there also. I enjoyed my leave! My father and mother had never given up hope and naturally were delighted to see me. (My second brother Bob was killed in action whilst with the Royal Armoured Corps at Medjez el Bab, North Africa, in 1943.)'

Edgar Costello-Bowen AFC was killed on 9 August 1943 while Chief Flying Instructor at 1655 MTU when he was a passenger on a Ventura flown by Flying Officer Abbot, pilot of an Oxford. He was 30 years old. After a rest as Chief Ground Instructor 1655 MTU, 'Tommy' Broom resumed operations with Flight Lieutenant Ivor Broom (no relation) with 571 Squadron, 128 Squadron, and then 163 Squadron; Ivor as wing commander and 'Tommy' as a squadron leader. 'The Flying Brooms', as they were known, did another 58 operations (21 to Berlin) in 8 Group Pathfinder Force. Ivor later became Air Marshal Sir Ivor Broom KCB CBE DSO DFC** AFC.' He passed away on 24 January 2003. 'Tommy' left the RAF in September 1945. He worked for the Control Commission in Germany. Unable to speak German, he was allocated an interpreter, a young German war widow. In July 1948 they married and returned to Portishead in 1949. He later worked in the accounts department of Esso Petroleum. He passed away on 18 May 2010.

# Chapter 3

# Journey to Toulouse

*On 12/13 May 1943 over Duisburg, three Halifaxes on 138 Special Duties Squadron at Tempsford were at large over France on Operations 'Roach 10', 'Lime 16' and 'Donkeyman 1' engaged on supply-dropping trips to the Resistance. One of the Halifaxes was 'M-Mother' (BB313), which Squadron Leader C. G. 'Robbie' Robinson DFC had taken off in at 2235 hours.*

'M-Mother' was home-bound at low level after completing the first drop on Operation 'Donkeyman 1' but they were unable to complete 'Roach 10' and then the aircraft was hit by light flak from an airfield and fire took hold. 'Robbie' Robinson gave the order to bail out. Having completed a five-month tour of duty as CO of 4 Group's 158 Squadron in March, he had dropped a rank and volunteered for Special Operations. Thirty-three-year-old Sergeant William H. 'Pop' Marshall DFM, the flight engineer, and 22-year-old Pilot Officer John T. Hutchinson DFC, one of the gunners, managed to abandon the aircraft at about 700ft before the Halifax crash-landed in open country south west of Troyes (Aube). Marshall had pulled the rip cord on his chest chute so quickly upon leaving the aircraft that it hit him right in the face and dazed him. He described the landing as 'very hard'. Hutchinson had, because of the low altitude of their escape, landed on the other side of the large field in which the Halifax crashed and the two men pretty much remained together throughout their time with the Resistance and escape lines.

Sergeant John C. Tweed, the 2nd pilot, who had just celebrated his 21st birthday when they had taken off, had sprained his ankles, injured a hand and had a deep gash in his leg. Fire continued to burn through the aircraft and Tweed managed to help free the injured from the wreckage. No one had been killed. Robinson, with injuries to head and legs, was hospitalised in Fresnes until 1 August before internment in Stalag Luft I, Barth, where he joined Flight Sergeant Luther Martin DFM and Flying Officer R. R. Piddington. Flying Officer F. C. Jeffery, navigator, and Pilot Officer R. G. Johnson, air bomber, were confined in hospital due to injuries until they were repatriated on 6 February 1945.

Tweed, meanwhile, limped slowly across the countryside. Every step was agony and progress desperately slow. A nearby field of corn would keep him out of view for the night, but he knew the burning aircraft was still too close. The choices had been made for him. He was in no fit state to go any further. Searches would begin at first light, so his best chance was to rest up and make a decision then.

The dawn came. All remained quiet through the morning. Passing foot and occasional motor traffic looked routine. There was no sign of military vehicles arriving, enemy soldiers with dogs or discovery by the locals. Tweed decided to gamble on remaining undiscovered if he stayed put. His injuries must have been the deciding factor in arriving at this decision. His ankles and leg were not up to walking and an injured man limping painfully about in daylight was a sure way to attract attention.

One thing did occur to him. Although it was not a welcome thought, it might inadvertently help him. His Halifax carried a crew of eight instead of the usual seven. If the remaining men had been captured, the Germans would be likely to cease search operations in the crash area. Tweed resolved to hide in the field until after dark, then attempt to stand up and find help. Once night fell, it became clear that walking even short distances would remain a problem. He would almost certainly be picked up if he wasn't sheltered quickly. He knew some key choices had to be made, as becoming a PoW without doing everything possible to evade was simply not an option.

Tweed chewed a caffeine tablet from his escape kit to give himself a lift and struggled off towards the nearest village, which was just visible. Pommereau merged into the blackout, but there was one house showing a light, so he stayed in the shadows and hobbled towards it. He edged along a wall to a window where the light was showing and heard the call of an *Ici Londres* radio broadcast. Listening to this station was strictly forbidden, as it came from the Free French in London and the news contained coded messages.

A house not properly observing blackout might be a good starting point to seek help, although in the countryside of southern France, there were isolated lapses that did not automatically signify anti-German attitudes. Tweed knocked on the door. Hurried activity followed and the radio went silent. A woman holding a small boy answered and looked straight at the pilot's wings on his battledress. Tweed had not removed any insignia from his uniform as advised in his evasion training and he was hurried into the room that contained the radio. A group of men sat in silence looking at him.

Monsieur Charton was the husband of the woman answering the door. The couple ran a farm and set about attending to Tweed's injuries as best they could. The other men left and he was fed before being hidden in a partly derelict farm building used by some of the workers. Madame Charton brought him food twice a day and she altered his RAF battledress to resemble the clothing of a local labourer.

The routine remained unchanged until a week had passed, when a villager arrived to ask a series of detailed questions. The next day his injuries were treated by the local doctor and Tweed was left to rest up. During this time, the information he had given was thoroughly examined to ensure that he was not a German 'plant'. Unknown to Tweed, he was right in the middle of the local 'Goélette' Resistance Group,[1] who were controlling each move of his shelter, right down to the doctor visiting. Primary or secondary radio contact with London would be a virtual certainty and when Tweed's identity details were

---

1  Schooner, a fore-and-aft rigged ship having two masts.

verified via radio, the Resistance would decide on the validity of the rest of the information.

Three further weeks passed before Tweed began his journey. He was moved to a safe house in the town of Troyes, where a photograph was taken for his false identity card. That evening further questioning took place. An Englishman arrived (unknown to Tweed, a member of SOE supporting the local Resistance movement) and he drilled down to find out more about Tweed before letting him move on to another safe house for the night. The next afternoon Pierre Malsant, the leader of the 'Goélette' Resistance Group, took him to a café in a small village west of Troyes to await the next part of the plan. He stayed in an upstairs room for three weeks apart from being allowed downstairs for a time in the evenings to exercise, courtesy of the café's owners Monsieur and Madame Bourgeois.

Whilst in hiding, Tweed was visited by a young Frenchman attempting to escape to England. The pair decided they could reach the Pyrénées via Biarritz and the Frenchman would reconnoitre the route. Unfortunately, he was arrested by the Geheime Feldpolizei (GFP Secret Field Police), ruling out any further attempts that way.

The Resistance decided to route Tweed via Paris. Although Malsant fronted the operation, it is likely SOE had a hand in the new strategy. French guide Sam Chevalier escorted the airman to the capital and gave Tweed shelter for two days before taking him to the home of Monsieur Henri Boucher and his wife, where the airman hid for eight weeks.

For the evader placed in this situation, it paid to remain vigilant, although as per their training, they were expected to follow instructions given to them by the Resistance. It is unlikely that Tweed knew the full extent of who he was involved with or details of what would happen until the last moment. It made sense to work on a 'need to know' basis in exactly the same way as the escape lines and other Resistance organisations.

It may have come as no surprise that 'the Englishman' Tweed had met in Troyes turned up at the safe house address. What may have surprised him was the hour deadline to prepare for the next move in his evasion. 'The Englishman' took Tweed to a café, where the handover to Pierre Piot took place. Piot worked for the Swiss Red Cross, which provided an ideal blind for carrying out work helping evaders. He was able to shelter Tweed in his flat in Rue Montmartre for a week before a sudden move instigated by 'the Englishman' came early in the morning of 17 September. The pair travelled out of Paris by train and arrived at a country station near Angers and met their contact, who advised that 'the reception' would be that evening. The two men were escorted to a farm where four other travellers were waiting.

'The Englishman' revealed his identity as Captain Benjamin Hodkinson Cowburn MC, leader of the SOE 'Tinker Circuit' supporting the Resistance in the Troyes area of France. Cowburn was born on 3 March 1909. He had arrived in Paris, aged eight, with his parents and studied at a British school in Boulogne-sur-Seine and then at a lycée. He later studied electrical engineering and worked for the American firm Foster Wheeler, building distillation plants for oil refineries throughout France. He was a fluent French speaker and was married to a Frenchwoman. Due to his knowledge of the oil industry in France, he was seen as an excellent acquisition for the Special Operations Executive. Recruited in 1941 into SOE's 'F' (French) Section, Cowburn was trained at Wanborough Manor in the spring of 1941.[2]

---

2 Cowburn first parachuted into occupied France from a Whitley bomber on 6 September 1941 with Pierre de Vomecourt (aka 'Lucas'). His mission was to obtain information on the best targets for the sabotage of oil and fuel stocks. He returned to Britain in March 1942 via Spain. On the night of 1/2 June 1942, Cowburn parachuted from a Halifax bomber and provide direction for the French Resistance 'Tinker' circuit in the Indre area. With the help of Augustus Chanteraine, Cowburn organised the reception of two airdrops of weapons and explosives that equipped the first resistance group in that area. He also conducted several sabotage missions, including the power lines from the power plant to Éguzon, and disrupted production at the Bloch aircraft factory at Chateauroux by tampering with the machine tools. He returned to Britain in a Lysander in late October 1943. Cowburn parachuted into France again from a Halifax bomber and took control of the 'Tinker' circuit from Troyes. Cowburn's final mission was to set up a new Resistance cell near Amiens. Arriving by parachute on 30 July 1944, he was also looking to see if he could intercept two fellow SOE agents arrested by the Germans. He was unable to locate the agents and shortly after the British liberated the area. He was never detected by the Germans and holds the record for the longest period as an active SOE agent operating in an occupied country.

Cowburn described his meeting with Tweed in his book *No cloak No dagger*: 'Like all my fellow agents, I had occasionally to cope with escaping airmen. In fact, we had been meeting with them since early 1942, and, as our bombing increased, the number of aircraft shot down over Belgium, Holland and France grew. Many of those who reached the ground uninjured escaped the German patrols and were hidden by French country-people.

'Among the several secret organizations at work in France was the Royal Air Force escape network. This section, like our own, must have suffered many ups and downs, for on several occasions, when I had escaping airmen on my hands and radioed London for a contact to send them off, the reply was that, at the moment, the escape routes were blown and I would either have to keep them or find a way myself.

'Nevertheless, airmen were trickling down to the Spanish frontier and getting across it.

'A bomber would be hit by flak, the survivors among the crew would bale out, several would be caught by German patrols but one or two would get away to a farmhouse. The farmer might happen to know somebody who was working for the Resistance, and who would come and take them away. In other cases, he would enquire from people he could trust and after a while make a connection.

'The escapers would be provided with civilian clothing and passed from town to town, generally with guides for each part of the journey. At one of the stages, they would be given false identity cards. And so, whether they happened to fall in with a "regular" escape organization, with a special agent like myself, or merely friendly French people who spontaneously arranged for acquaintances and relatives to help them all along the route, they could, with luck, hope to reach the Spanish frontier zone, where a smuggler would get them across.

'Once in Spain most of them were caught by the Carabineros and taken to a jail or concentration camp such as Miranda. The British Consul would be advised and sooner or later, their bona fide as RAF personnel having been established, they would be released for transfer to Gibraltar.

'The RAF men whom I saw after they had happened to be "recuperated" by some of my own people were generally not quite unprepared for escaping. Before leaving England, they had been given a little French money, a map in the form of a silk handkerchief, a cunning trouser-button which could serve as a tiny compass and a few other "aids to navigation". Some even had names and addresses of French people to whom they could apply if they crashed in a particular area.

'I have never asked whether such names and addresses were supplied by the RAF or privately by brother-airmen who had already been through the process.

'Not all the escapers had to go through Spain. Some were exfiltrated by boat. Once I arranged for an airman to be flown back home by a Lysander "pick-up" operation. This was against the rules, as we were not supposed to use our own devices for other purposes than our work.

'In fact, the official attitude was that we should never risk the security of our circuits by handling escapers. However, no special agent would turn one away. Some of my brother-agents even handled so many that they built up quite a large "side-line" in this respect. After all, the RAF was our particular friend, our transport and our RASC. When some of the boys in light-blue were in trouble, we felt we were in honour bound to help them if we could.

'For instance, "Johnny", the young sergeant who went home by Lysander, was a special case ... He had hidden in a cornfield and not been found when the German patrols reached the wreckage. He later crawled to a farmhouse but the farmers were unable to shelter him for long. One of them knew of me and passed him on to one of my boys. London could give me no contact with an escape route just then, so I considered that as this man was engaged on dropping operations, he was a kind of "distant cousin" and at least knew that there was some funny business going on, it would do no harm if he saw a bit more. Therefore, I finally got him a seat in a Lysander.'

A rendezvous with the aircraft would take place that night. The group set off just after twelve and waited in a field under cover of darkness. At the sound of an aircraft engine, the recognition signal was flashed by torch and a Lysander piloted by Flying Officer Jimmy Bathgate on 161 Squadron that had taken off from Tangmere was guided in by two lines of torches. In typical style for this kind of operation, the engine on the aircraft remained running while three passengers got out, messages and parcels were exchanged and three members of the party who had bicycled to the location somehow jammed themselves into the rear cockpit, which was designed to take one person. The Lysander was soon on its way back to RAF Tangmere. It had taken Tweed four months and five days to get home.[3]

'Pop' Marshall and John Hutchinson, meanwhile, had been recovered from a barn in the forest of Lancy on the night of Friday/Saturday, 11/12 June by Alfred Prieur, a garage mechanic who had created a Resistance movement in Sens in 1940. Alfred drove his car from the village of Thorigny-sur-Oreuse to Sens in the Yonne department, where he hid the two airmen in his house above his garage at 1 rue de la République. (He was arrested on 13 October and deported in January 1944. He survived incarceration at both Buchenwald and Dora Mittelbau-Dora concentration camps and was released by Russian troops near Parchim in 1945. He died in 1985 aged 82).

Hutchinson and Marshall went into hiding in Paris and had many adventures, including a ride on the Paris Metro during which 'Pop' Marshall dropped a penny coin in the pocket of the German soldier seated next to him. Georges Broussine, the chief of the 'Burgundy' (Bourgogne) escape line, introduced them to a French teenager named Peter (probably 19-year-old Pierre Maroger),[4] who spoke perfect English. Georges Broussine was born in Paris on 19 February 1918.

---

3 *See Agents by Moonlight: The Secret History of RAF Tempsford During World War II* by Freddie Clark (Tempus Publishing Ltd, 1999) and *Shot Down and on the Run: True Stories of RAF and Commonwealth aircrews of WWII* by Air Commodore Graham Pitchfork (The National Archives, 2003).

4 *They Came from Burgundy: A study of the Bourgogne escape line* by Keith Janes (Matador, 2017).

Before the war he had studied medicine. Called to arms in 1940, he escaped to Britain after the armistice. He was selected to train as a wireless agent and set up the Burgundy escape line. Broussine was parachuted into France in February 1943 to establish the Bourgogne (or Burgundy) escape line. The organisation was based in Paris but had connections with other groups throughout France. The first routes that Bourgogne used to take men across the Pyrénées to Spain were via Andorra but the extreme bad weather in the winter of 1943–44 forced a change to the lower mountains south of Perpignan. When that more obvious route became too dangerous in December 1943, men were sent out through Pau. Broussine was also involved in other ventures, including sea evacuations from Brittany by fishing vessels.[5]

On 2 July the two RAF evaders were taken to the Gare d'Austerlitz to catch the 8 o'clock overnight train to Toulouse by Peter and another Frenchman called simply 'Chief', but who had been in the French navy at Dakar. 'Pop' Marshall later described part of his journey thus: 'There were Germans in their hundreds on the platform, many of them no more than boys in their teens, with – incongruously – a sprinkling of elderly veterans among them, probably of some Pioneer Corps. I noticed the loose-fitting, untidy uniforms and thanked the gods that I was not in the German Army. The train came snorting in; a big, black, ugly locomotive, greatly ornamented with pipes and pistons, enveloped us in smoke. This was the express to Toulouse. I got in and was lucky enough to get a seat near the window. A large, stout woman with a basket and a red, greasy face settled herself next to me, her ungainly body overlapping one of my shoulders.

'The train gathered speed. The stout woman rustled in her basket and took out some magazines. I remembered my journey to Paris and the embarrassment a girl hiker had caused me. I hoped that this old dame would occupy herself with the magazines and not try to hold conversation with me. I looked out of the window. Soon we would be out into open country. I would close my eyes and doze.

---

5 www.conscript-heroes.com/escapelines/EscapeLines.htm.

'When my neighbour had looked through one magazine, she turned her big head and eyed me for a moment. I was leaning with my elbow on the window ledge, my cheek resting in the palm of my hand. My eyes were almost closed in sham sleep, and all would have been well had I not sensed that the woman was scrutinising my face. My eyelids gave an almost imperceptible flicker. She nudged my shoulder with her great sturdy arm and proffered me the magazine.

'My heart sank. Again, I was cornered! Again, I was to be pestered by another traveller. If this woman found I was a foreigner she might scream her information to the guard, or to the Germans at the line of demarcation!

'There came ten minutes of peace during which I browsed slowly through the unintelligible journal. I prayed that the woman would not trouble me again. It was possible, I thought, she might fall asleep with the rocking of the train.

'No. She began rustling in the paper bags in her basket and brought out two hard-boiled eggs.

I considered the other occupants of the compartment. All, except one, were looking at the stout woman as she shelled the eggs. The one, an old man with a beard, sat in the far corner, slobbering over a meerschaum pipe. His shrewd old eyes looked straight at me!

*'Voulez-vous un oeuf, monsieur*? said the woman, giving me another dig with her elbow.

'I took the egg because I was afraid to offend the woman. She held out a paper with some salt in it. I dipped the egg and started to eat, taking my time. This would have been an embarrassing situation for me in England; here it was ten times more so, with all the people opposite watching me with cow-like eyes, thinking about me, wondering who I was, and guessing much of the truth.

'When the first egg was eaten the woman offered me another.

'"*Merci madame*," I said, smiling a grim smile. I wondered why she didn't go to hell with those wretched eggs! When I had finished that egg, I decided, I would go to the lavatory and have a smoke. While I was away the woman might go to sleep. I swallowed the last large lump of egg and got up. I staggered past the people in the corridor and reached the lavatory.

'There was an obnoxious smell! The place had no water. I lit one of the American cigarettes the Resistance had given me and stood puffing for a few minutes. The little place was hot. Flies crawled thickly across the floor. This was far worse than the woman with the eggs! When I got back the woman was dozing. I wriggled myself carefully into position beside her, rested my head on my hand and tried to sleep. For half an hour the compartment was silent.

'I felt certain that all the occupants of the compartment knew I was a fugitive, but there was no escaping the consequences of that: I was surrounded. I went to sleep and dreamt I was going on leave and changing at Crewe, with people jostling and pushing. There were so many foreigners in my dream.

'I sat up suddenly, my heart throbbing.

'The woman had nudged me again.

'"*C'est un voyage fatigant celui-ci,*" she yawned. She took out some sandwiches and I ate two of them. In the gloom of the compartment, I could see the eyes watching me. When the woman talked, I answered "*Oui, madame*" quietly. She grinned. She knew me. She knew I was English.

'It was a weary night of futile conversation, smoking, yawning, dozing, eating, muttering.

'The train began to slow down. At last, we had reached the danger spot. It must have been 1 o'clock in the morning. The train crawled into the station. Suddenly the Resistance guide appeared in the doorway. He nodded. The woman nudged me. It was an urgent nudge, yet, I felt, friendly. "*C'est ici qu'on devra passer le contrôle* she told me."'

The train was halted at the Demarcation Line. Peter and Chief learned that the Germans were making their way through the train and rounding up young Frenchmen for their labour service in Germany. Seeing six young men being marched off under guard, Hutchinson slipped unseen from the train and hid underneath another one on an adjacent track. But then he was faced with a problem, for heading his way was a 'wheel-tapper', accompanied by a German guard, checking the carriages and peering underneath them. Drawing himself up Hutchinson managed to remain unseen.

Marshall meanwhile had got up quickly.

'Get out, monsieur, quick – under train,' the guide whispered.

'Without thinking of the stir I was making, I opened the door of the compartment and looked out. Another train came panting into the station from the opposite direction!

'Could I get out in time before the other train came alongside? I would have to wait until the engine passed the compartment. The driver would not see me then. Thank God it was fairly dark! Perhaps the train would shield me from curious eyes on the far platform.

'When the engine had snorted past, I jumped down. There was steam, heat, dust and grit. I banged the door and sped a little way along the track between the two trains. Underneath it was dark, dirty and stinking. I could smell the wagon-grease. I got on to an axle and found an iron bar with my groping feet. My knees quivered with the excitement. My back soon began to ache. I clung on grimly.

'There was a great deal of shouting from the platform, with noise and lights being switched on. Then footsteps. There came a sound underneath the train as of gravel being shifted. I guessed it was Hutchinson who had been travelling in another part of the train for security's sake. I wondered how long we would have to wait.

'I thought of my predicament. Supposing the train began to move? I could not hold on to this precarious position. I would fall to the ground on to the gravel. My body might be mangled. Was the floor of the train high enough to allow me to lie flat? I could not tell in the blackness. Even if it were, when the train had gone the policemen on the platform would see me. It was death or arrest: a mangled body or Stalag Luft. The thought that six weeks of hard freedom were to be thrown away was agony.

'There was a crunching of gravel from behind me. Someone was coming, murmuring to someone else. The feet stopped. There was a tapping sound. The feet again, the tapping sound. Nearer and nearer – the wheel-tapper and some others!

'A light came dodging between the trains, over the sleepers. Feet, heavy, lumbering feet. Jack-boots came tramping past, reflecting in a yellow streak the light of the lamps.

'My mouth was full of spit. I trembled and almost fell. The wheel-tapper was actually tapping the wheel of the axle I was on. I could feel the vibration through my backbone!

'Then the men had gone past. I wondered about my companion. (Hutchinson had rapidly re-joined his companions just as the Toulouse train started to move off.) Then I realised how unbearably my back ached. My legs were stiff, knees cramped, arms hard with muscular strain. How long now? I can feel the horror of it to this day – waiting for the train to go, to tear me to pieces! To be harried into this danger after all our wanderings! I felt the sweat and tears of despair on my face.

'The long minutes dragged on. Before much longer, I knew, I would collapse and fall unconscious on the ground.

'And then someone hissed. Someone whispered: "*Com, monsieur.*"

'It was the stout woman with the red face!

'I crawled out, staggered back, following the woman. How she found the compartment in the dark I don't know. I climbed in and closed the door. I mopped my brow and sat down, trembling.

'They were all excited and very anxious. Someone gave me a flask of coffee. I drank it gratefully.

'The guide was in the doorway again, like a genie of the lamp.

'"That was very dangerous, monsieur," he said. "They have caught forty young men. You have been most fortunate, eh?" He smiled and went away. I sank back and felt myself against the soft arm of the stout woman. She murmured something and moved her weight in order to give my shoulder more support. She seemed a motherly, kindly old soul at that moment. When the train started everybody sat back, deeply relieved. The old fellow with the beard and the meerschaum wiped his mouth with a red handkerchief.

'"Train late," he said softly, looking across at me. *"No more, big contrôle monsieur."*

'I could only look at him and smile my incredulity.'

As it happened, Marshall's departure was unnecessary, for the Germans never got as far as their carriage to test the false papers. He might even have got through the control.

'Thenceforth the journey was pleasant I had to admit,' Marshall recalled. 'I was surrounded by so many friends who kept looking at me and smiling in sympathy. They whispered together and conjectured who I was. No matter, they were on my side, whoever I was.'

The train rolled into Toulouse, some hours later, puffing great clouds of smoke to the high, curved rafters. From Toulouse the two airmen and Peter took an electric train to Foix, arriving at 3 o'clock that afternoon. They were taken to the outskirts of Foix, where they were picked up by a car and driven to some woods to join two more Frenchmen and two Spanish guides. At 10 o'clock that evening, Hutchinson and Marshall set out to cross the Pyrénées with their guides. It was a gruelling journey and Hutchinson complained about his rope sandals he was given to wear. Finally, in mid-morning on 6 July they arrived at Ordino in Andorra, where they stayed for two days before being driven through the capital, Andorra la Vieja, to Sant Julia de Loria, where they rested for another three days in a hotel. Finally, on the 11th they set off across the Spanish border with two guides and a local tobacco smuggler. Avoiding Spanish patrols, they walked to Manresa. It took them a week and then on the 18th they caught the 7 o'clock morning train to Barcelona and the British Consulate. They were provided with clothes and accommodation. Surprisingly, told to report to the Spanish police, Hutchinson was advised to say that he was 19 and Marshall that he was 42. They were also told to say that they had escaped from a civil internment camp in France. Whether or not the police believed their stories, the two airmen were issued with ID cards and taken to a hotel, before leaving for Madrid on 22 July. Marshall had retained his forged identity card given him by his helpers. He had also kept and secreted about his person a pencil notebook with the names of all the places he had passed through during his evasion. It was only when he got back to England that he realised that if the Resistance had found this he would likely have been shot.

They flew back to England from Gibraltar on the night of 5/6 August. A year later, on 15 August 1944, 'Pop' Marshall was awarded the DFC and was promoted flying officer.[6]

---

6 See *RAF Evaders: The Comprehensive Story of Thousands of Escapers and Their Escape Lines; Western Europe 1940–1945* by Oliver Clutton-Brock (Grub Street, 2009).

# Chapter 4

# Passport to the Pyrénées

*Countless Allied airmen who were brought down in the skies over Friesland owe their lives to people like Tiny Mulder. She and her other brave members in the underground movements were responsible for the escape lines out of Holland and into Belgium and France. But it was not always possible for downed crews to escape from Holland with the help of Resistance workers. Up until late 1942 RAF aircrews were told that if they were shot down over Holland, they were not to involve the population but to make the best of their own devices or wait for the Germans to make them prisoners of war. After 1942 this policy changed. Air crews were told to try to return to England with the assistance of the Dutch population and preferably with the help of the underground. By that time London knew that in Holland escape lines to neutral countries had been organised. It was very dangerous work. Sometimes German agents succeeded in penetrating the escape organization and claimed quite a few victims.*

*The first escape line from Friesland started at Drachten. It had been organised by three men in charge of all underground work. From the outset they were only too aware of the risks downed airmen entailed. They endangered other Resistance work, like sabotage. Therefore, escape work was not only kept secret from the rest of the population but even from other members. Mr R. C. Vermeulen was placed in overall charge of the escape line. He later went into hiding in Leeuwarden but Drachten remained a major centre in the escape network.*

*Mr Vermeulen continued organising the escape line to England through Belgium, France and Spain. But until airmen could begin their journey along the line they had to be hidden in 'safe houses' and provided with false identification papers, clothes and food. This part of the organisation required a lot of time and energy. Tiny Mulder had been working for the Dutch underground since the spring of 1942. She spoke English and had been freed from the task of hiding Jews and other people in danger and placed in charge of helping downed airmen.*

The day 10 May 1940 was one Tiny Mulder, a 19-year-old Dutch girl living in Drachten, would never forget. When she awoke, she wondered what that noise was up in the air. The radio confirmed that the Germans were invading. There was no declaration of war. They just came. Just like that. Holland was a small country then, of eight million, overrun by a large army. Overrun, but not defeated. Like many Dutch citizens, Tiny decided to work in the underground Resistance organisation. The Germans treated the Dutch very well at first, to gain their trust and then they began to see what was coming. Tiny worked in a local government office, regulating the distribution of clothing, food and oil. There never was a military government in the Netherlands; Dutch collaborators were appointed to higher offices in The Hague by Reichscommissar Artur von Seyss-Inquart, an Austrian Nazi who had been appointed by Adolf Hitler to govern Holland. Tiny's boss, Pieter Wybenga, never had any Nazi sympathisers working for him. Wybenga was one of the earliest members of the underground and he recruited Tiny. Her first job was to work as a courier, travelling by train to Rotterdam or Amsterdam to deliver maps with information for the Allies. During her missions she wore a green hat to identify herself. 'You never gave your name to anyone. What you don't know, you can't reveal,' she said.

In 1943 Tiny gained additional duties with the Resistance, taking on the job of rescuing Allied airmen shot down in the northern

Netherlands. She was particularly happy to be helping the airmen. Not only were they destroying German war industries, but they also lifted the morale of the Dutch. 'When we saw the beautiful vapour trails of the B-17s and B-24s in the beautiful formations we felt that we were not alone, that someone was helping us.'

She believed she was chosen for the difficult assignment because of her command of English. 'It was dangerous work,' she admitted. Two of her girlfriends had been captured doing the same job and were moved from one prison camp to another until they were finally liberated by the Russians at the end of the war. There was danger at every step of the way. During the initial contact with the fliers, Tiny had to find out if they were real Americans or fake Americans. When they saw them coming out of an American plane, that was all right, but if they just turned up early one morning, then she would become suspicious. Once their nationality had been determined, the next step was to find clothing for the men and a place to stay. Her own parents took in some of the airmen.

Second Lieutenant Edwin ('Ed') F. Pollock, from Grove City, Pennsylvania, pilot of B-17 *Weidner's Wildcat* in the 385th Bomb Group, that crashed yards from Lake Sneekermeer, Offingawier in Holland, on 11 December 1943 on the raid on Emden, remembered the Mulder family very well. 'Our plane, hit by flak near the German border was on fire and two of my men were killed. Of the remaining eight, five were wounded. Tiny came along and took me to her house, where I stayed for three months. I played chess with Mr. Mulder every night. They were wonderful people and they risked their lives for us.'[1]

After placing the airmen in a safe house, the next step was to advise the national Resistance organisation of the new arrivals and send a message to London over the wireless, giving their name, rank

---

1 At the end of May 1944, Pollock and the surviving members of his crew attempted an escape route via Antwerp but were betrayed by some locals and were eventually sent to Stalag Luft III at Sagan.

and serial number. When it was time for the airmen to make their escape, Tiny and her fellow workers provided them with false Dutch identity cards, kept under lock and key in the town hall. Members of the underground had various methods of obtaining the papers from helpful officials. A photographer who could be trusted took the airmen's photos for the cards. The whole process had to be repeated for Belgium and France, the countries through which the men would pass on their route to Spain and on to London via Gibraltar.

'Many did not make it,' Tiny admitted. 'The chain of guides between the Netherlands and Spain broke all the time.' The weak link was in Antwerp, where a Canadian of German origin offered to help the Nazis by infiltrating the underground. 'He didn't disturb the underground movement, but picked off the Allied soldiers and sent them to prison,' Tiny recalled. 'He was executed in Belgium after the war as a traitor, but that was too late. Communication with London did not always work well, either. The London office was sloppy about letting us know if the men made it but they always sent us messages, urging us to return the men. They said they could build aircraft faster than they could replace crews. This was war. They didn't count lives.'

At Thorpe Abbotts in Norfolk, home to the 100th Bomb Group, escape and evasion lectures were probably more pertinent because the group sustained such heavy losses at intervals in the European Theatre of Operations that it was referred to as the 'Bloody Hundredth'. It had all started early in the war, or so the story went, when a pilot of a badly shot up B-17 in the 100th Bomb Group knew he could not make it home. He had indicated surrender to incoming German fighters by lowering his wheels. However, as the German fighters closed in to escort the ailing bomber to a Luftwaffe airfield, his gunners had opened up and destroyed some of the German fighters. In revenge the other German fighters shot the B-17 down and from then on, the 100th became known as a 'marked' group, to be singled out by the Luftwaffe at every available opportunity. This story passed into legend and was told to every new crew who joined the 'Bloody Hundredth'. The story was so widespread that crews passing through replacement depots even got to hear about it before being assigned to combat duty. They prayed fervently that they would not be posted to the 'unlucky' 100th Bomb Group. Those that were sent to Thorpe Abbotts were usually greeted with the sardonic retort of 'You'll be sorry' or 'Fresh meat on the table'.

But, after surviving their first few missions, First Lieutenant William ('Bill') H. McDonald's crew in the 350th Bomb Squadron felt confident enough to name their B-17 *Salvo Sal*. McDonald hailed from Union County, Arkansas. The 24-year-old co-pilot, 2nd Lieutenant John L. James Jr, was from Delaware County, Pennsylvania. Navigator, 2nd Lieutenant Carl L. Spicer, aged 25, came from Mercer County, Ohio. Tech Sergeant Charles S. Ashbaugh, the 23-year-old engineer/top turret gunner who came from Westmoreland County, Pennsylvania, had been born in Leechburg. The 22-year-old radio operator, Tech Sergeant Fred Pribish, was from Will County, Illinois. The ball turret gunner, 25-year-old Staff Sergeant Ross W. Detillion, was from Spokane, Washington. Left waist gunner, Staff Sergeant Douglas H. Agee, a 23-year-old Texan, born in Saltillo, hailed from Hopkins in Texas. The tail turret gunner, Staff Sergeant Paul G. Sears of Pulaski, Kentucky, was the youngest at 19. The right waist gunner, Staff Sergeant Victor P. Intoccia, who was 21 years old, came from Kings, New York.

Second Lieutenant Frank McGlinchey, the 23-year-old bombardier, who also hailed from Kings, recalls. 'All the crew felt good. After finishing nine missions we felt we had a good chance of finishing our tour and being home for Christmas.' But it was not to be. 'On 8 October we were called out at 0230 hours. It had never seemed so dark. With briefing in an hour, we didn't have too much time to get dressed. Everyone was quite anxious as we sat down in the briefing room waiting for the white curtain to be drawn and reveal the target for the day. One could hear a few groans as we saw the line which marked our course heading straight to Bremen. Take-off was not for several hours but waiting around always seemed to make us very nervous. However, they made it tougher today as take-off was changed twice. We didn't actually leave the ground until 1130 hours. In the meantime, I sneaked down to the mess hall and had what proved to be my last meal in England. It was roast pork and it wasn't bad either.

'The raid was to be a major effort. Our group had little trouble forming up and it wasn't long before we were out over the Channel. P-47s had given us good support and things seemed rather quiet as we winged our way toward the target. Minutes passed and soon we were over the IP. With bomb bay doors open, we turned on the target. The groups in front of us were enveloped in a huge black cloud as they passed over the target and dropped their payloads. It was the most intensive flak I had ever seen. We had a good run on the target and our bombs went away very well. Just after the bomb bay doors closed the ship jumped as we received a very bad hit just to the rear of number two engine. All three ships in the lead element were also hit. The two wingmen went down in flames. The leader, apparently partially out of control, fell out of formation. I looked for our two wingmen but saw no one. Our whole squadron of nine ships had been knocked out. (I learned much later that only one ship made it back to England.)[2]

'Although out of formation and heading back to England by ourselves, we seemed to be doing all right until a flight of German fighters bounced us. Suddenly, the intercom was alive with the actions of fighters bearing in from all directions. All our guns, with the exception of the two nose guns, were knocked out in fifteen minutes. Our waist gunner, Douglas Agee, was shot in both lungs and bled to death after taking a direct hit from a fighter about two minutes after the fighting started. All our left controls were shattered and we had to put out several fires. Our radio too was gone. One engine was "running away" and two more were about to go. We were

---

2 *Salvo Sal* was one of seven 100th Bomb Group B-17s lost on 8 October 1943 and one of 88 American bombers lost on three successive days from 8 to 10 October. In that same period the 100th Bomb Group alone had lost a staggering 20 Fortresses, including 12 on the 10 October mission to Münster.

losing altitude rapidly and it was apparent we would not make it back to England. Suddenly, fire shot out from the rear of number three engine. With the Zuider Zee directly in front of us, Bill McDonald gave the order to bail out.

'But things had got so bad in the ship he wasn't sure that everyone had got the message so he asked Carl Spicer, the navigator and I to jump from the rear of the ship so that we could check that everyone had got out. We went back along the catwalk along past the bomb bay section and into the radio shack. By now *Salvo Sal* was a rattling old airplane. Fire was coming out of the undercarriage and beneath the wing.

'Everybody except Agee, who lay slumped beneath his machine gun, had gone, so I motioned to Carl Spicer to jump first. He jumped and I looked out to see if his 'chute had opened. It had. Then I went back to Bill McDonald and informed him that everyone had gone. The enlisted men had been the first to go. All six were captured by German patrols shortly after landing. John James, the co-pilot, had jumped with a parachute that had been holed by a cannon shell and he broke his leg in a bumpy landing. He was taken prisoner by German soldiers and hospitalised.

'McDonald said to me, "Now it's your turn and my turn right behind you so let's get out!" I went back to the bomb bay. I took one last look around and stepped onto a couple of brackets, saying goodbye to *Salvo Sal*, I took a long deep breath and jumped. Suddenly, everything went quiet. It was fantastic after such a hectic experience. This was my first jump and I couldn't get over the feeling of falling in space. I guess I fell about a thousand feet before pulling the ripcord. My 'chute opened at about 5,000ft. Off to the right I could see Bill McDonald's and Carl Spicer's 'chutes and our B-17 suddenly starting to circle around. It began to glide and eventually crashed on the Dutch countryside some miles away.

'It took me about five minutes to come down. Beneath me I could see a canal, which I was drifting towards. I suddenly realized I must activate something to avoid falling in it. I shifted pulls of the 'chute and managed to drift away from the canal but the ground was coming up pretty fast. As I was about to hit, I suddenly realized that telephone wires were immediately beneath me. I fell past them but in doing so my 'chute got hung up in the wires and prevented me from hitting the ground. I stepped out of my 'chute harness and was met by a group of Dutch farmers. They welcomed me to occupied Europe. No one spoke English but they seemed to understand it was important I should get out of the area. A motorcycle roared into the area and I thought all was lost. But it was a local Dutch policeman. He realized my problem and held back the crowd. In the meantime, they had pulled my 'chute down from the wires and had hidden it. The policeman guided me across the field and waved me on. Using sign language, he indicated good luck and goodbye.

'It was a very strange feeling to find oneself in a foreign land. We had not been briefed to any extent in England about evading or escaping. Things came naturally and I started to walk. I spotted Spicer, perhaps a mile away, running across the fields. I took after him and had quite a time catching the tall, gangling Midwesterner. He had seen me minutes after I started running and had mistaken me for a German. Eventually, I caught up with him and we hugged each other. Exhausted, we lay in the field deciding in a general way where we were and which way we should travel. (We had actually landed about ten miles due south of Drachten in Friesland near the town of Jubbega-Schwuega.)

'We decided to travel in a southern direction as we were quite sure that we were still east of the Zuider Zee. We had come down about 4 o'clock so we still had a number of hours of daylight left. We stayed off the roads because the traffic was most likely German vehicles carrying troops scouring the area for us. It was not until sunset that we stopped walking. We lay on a small hill in the Dutch countryside looking through our escape kits not really sure where to go.

'Suddenly, out of the farmland area came an old Dutch farmer carrying a brace of buckets on his shoulders. He had obviously been milking his cows. He smiled and offered us a drink of milk.

Shortly thereafter out of the trees on a nearby road came a nurse on a bicycle. We assumed she was a nurse because she was all in white. She asked us in English if we were fallen fliers. We told her we were and she said she would try to get us some civilian clothes if we would wait for an hour or so. Several hours passed and she did not return. We grew uneasy. We did not want to lose an opportunity of securing help but to wait any longer might be dangerous so we started walking again. It was pretty damp and chilly. When we had stopped to rest the cold would shake us and make us walk again. We kept near to secondary roads and walked all night, about ten miles.

'As dawn approached Carl and I, pretty much exhausted by this time, realized we must decide on the next move. We were confronted with the problem of where to hide during the day. Finally, we decided to head for a nearby farmhouse and await the outcome when the farmers went out into the fields. It was not long before an elderly farmer ventured into the fields with his dog following closely behind. The dog picked up our scent and took off after us. As the farmer approached, we stood up and raised our hands.

'Using sign language, we indicated we had been shot down and needed help. He grasped the situation pretty quickly and took us to his farmhouse, where his wife gave us breakfast. Using sign language, again we indicated we would like to sleep. We were taken upstairs to a bedroom and we just fell onto the bed after taking off our shoes and a few other garments. We slept the entire day. Just as the sun was going down, we were awakened by footsteps. There was a knock at the door and in walked a Dutchman who turned out to be a teacher. In English he asked us who we were and how we had got to the farm. He seemed satisfied with our answers and he listened patiently to our hopes of reaching either Switzerland or Spain. He told us he could not be of much help himself but he did know of an organization in Wolvega, Friesland, where he could get help.

'We slept and relaxed for two days at the farm and the couple looked after us very well. On the evening of the second day our teacher friend returned, bringing two young men with him. After talking with

49

us for some time in English they were satisfied we were bona-fide fliers. They explained that they were going to take us to a hiding place under the control of the underground. We said our goodbyes and cycled along the lane from the farm. I, having been warned and having forgotten, rode along the wrong side of the road and almost ran down some pedestrians!

'Our two young Dutch friends put us straight and we headed for the town of Meppel. We arrived that evening and were taken to a church. It was empty but we went in by the back door and were taken up to the loft and told to wait until someone arrived from the underground. We were told it would probably take one or two days to make contact and determine what help could be afforded us.

'The rector of the church visited us during the evening hours and brought us some food. He talked to us briefly and said we should make ourselves at home, such as it was, beneath the belfry tower. We could see out into the town but we were very nervous. We could not be certain that somewhere along the line we would fall into the wrong hands and be turned over to the Germans. On the third day the rector appeared with a girl aged about 23. She introduced herself and chatted with us in quite good English and seemed friendly. She took some papers out of an envelope and told us it was very important to her and to the Dutch underground that from this point on we must be certified as legitimate fallen fliers otherwise we would endanger their whole underground set-up in the area. It took us quite a while to realize that if we did not co-operate, we would not be vindicated.'

McGlinchey and Spicer were to discover later that the young woman's name was Tiny Mulder. She recalls, 'Screening new arrivals was a dangerous and complicated task. I gave Frank McGlinchey's and Carl Spicer's addresses and serial numbers to the central organization of the escape line and this information was then sent to London for reference. The central organization then arranged when they could be put on the escape line. All this was very necessary because sometimes German spies infiltrated the escape line by presenting themselves in American uniforms and speaking in a Texas drawl.

'It was sometimes hard to identify an airman. There was not always a crashed plane to account for the presence of one or more flyers as often they had walked for days. The underground asked airmen who were already in hiding for questions we could throw at the newcomers that could only be answered by an airman who had come from England, America or Canada recently. The awkward result was that sometimes the airmen suspected that I might be a German spy, which led to unhappy situations for us both. This happened later when Carl Spicer moved further along the underground with Fred Boulter, a Canadian radio operator. For a time, I did not trust Boulter. One of my friends was behind the door with a pistol while I interrogated him. Fortunately, after a long time I found out he was alright but he remained suspicious until he realized he was not being turned in by Germans but was being given everything he needed to appear a normal Dutch citizen.'

McGlinchey continued, 'Tiny Mulder explained that the underground had radioed London, who had informed them that the two Americans were genuine airmen. She added that the Dutch underground would do what it could for us. Tiny and a companion ushered us out of the church and into a large van. We were amazed but assured that there would be no problem in transporting us this way. After about three quarters of an hour, we arrived in Drachten, where we were to hide out at the Mulders' house. The family welcomed us and Tiny introduced Carl and I to a young Jewish girl the Mulders had adopted. The Germans frequently checked out families very methodically but she was safe with the Mulders. Her parents had disappeared from the area many months before.'

McGlinchey was full of admiration for the risks the Dutch underground was taking. 'Though a delicate operation this group of Dutch patriots had dedicated themselves to help fallen fliers evade and escape. We talked of several schemes during the next two days. We were told that there was an opportunity, if the proper signal could be made, for the Royal Navy to pick us up. But this could not be done and so we were to remain in hiding for a time. Later, a route would be developed to move us out of Holland by train, car and bus, through Belgium and France through to the Spanish border area.'

Carl Spicer was later taken to Sieberen van Velden's little farm near Drachten. Tiny Mulder told McGlinchey, to his surprise and happiness, that Bill McDonald had also evaded capture and was being hidden in the house of M. J. Peper, a sports teacher in Drachten.

McGlinchey waited patiently at the Mulders' house until an escape route could be arranged. During the day he kept out of sight and tried to stay quiet in the rear of the small and unpretentious house. It was located just outside Drachten on a canal road. Tiny's 13-year-old brother was also in hiding in the outlying farmlands during the day. Occasionally, he would venture into the house at night but McGlinchey saw little of him because of the danger it presented.

Tiny and Mrs Mulder arranged for some paperback books to be given to McGlinchey and many an hour was passed in thoughtful solitude. Mrs Mulder could not speak English so communication had to be made using sign language. Mr Mulder, a car mechanic and salesman, was usually at work in town. However, on his return home he would often teach McGlinchey the very difficult Frisian dialect. McGlinchey reciprocated by teaching Mr Mulder American slang. He also helped Mrs Mulder with some of the household chores and even turned his hand to churning butter. In the evening he slept in a small alcove off the front parlour. In the dark shadows he watched German soldiers patrol the town. The proximity of these patrols and their frightening implication if the house was searched served to increase the admiration the American flyer felt for his Dutch hosts.

During the darker evenings Tiny and her younger sister, Alle, walked with Frank McGlinchey across the farmland. Equally gratifying were the occasional visits of Bill McDonald and Carl Spicer. These visits were very dangerous and could only be attempted under the very best conditions. One overconfident move could have brought certain death to the Dutch organisers, the Mulder family and possibly to the American airmen themselves. Outwardly, the Dutch Resistance did not seem to consider the outcome of the risks they were taking. It was even suggested that the airmen stay in the Drachten area and fight with the Dutch Resistance movement. But they understood that the Americans' mission at that time was to try and get back to England.

The underground activity continued unabated while the American and other Allied aircrews were sheltered by Dutch families. One dark night several young Dutchmen entered the Mulder household by the back entrance. They sat down at the table looking nervous and depressed. Mrs. Mulder offered them coffee while Tiny tried to console them. They had been on a very difficult assignment against a Dutch 'Quisling' farmer and his family.[3] It was very evident that the incident had left them drained. No Dutchman or woman liked fighting against their own country folk but it was a question of survival. The young men of the underground movement were fearless and daring and carried out hit-and-run missions against the Germans at all times.

During the second week of November 1943 Tiny Mulder informed Frank McGlinchey that plans for moving the American airmen from Drachten on the first stage of the escape route were nearing completion. The airmen were to move in pairs with guides in the daylight hours. Each pair plus a guide would move several days apart. McGlinchey asked to pair off with his pilot, Bill McDonald.

It had always been intended that the Americans would dress in suitable civilian clothing to avoid suspicion. Throughout their concealment the underground had meticulously collected enough clothing for them. However, the clothes were only part of the operation. The Dutch underground had prepared cards that identified the escapees as Dutch students travelling on the Continent. On 19 November McGlinchey and McDonald boarded a train at Drachten

---

3 Quisling, which is used in Scandinavian languages and in English for a person who collaborates with an enemy occupying force is named after Vidkun Quisling, who in the 1930s, founded a pro-Nazi party in Norway. When Germany invaded Norway in 1940, Quisling attempted a pro-German coup against the government. From 1942 to 1945 he headed a pro-German administration. After the Second World War Quisling was tried and convicted on charges of treason, and he was executed by firing squad on 24 October 1945.

with Tiny as their guide. She had instructed the two Americans not to talk if questioned. It would not arouse suspicion because Dutch people always refused to talk to the Germans or answer their questions unless it was absolutely necessary.

The train journey lasted several hours. Nearing their station, Tiny gave a predetermined signal to indicate that they must leave the train. The two men followed her down the platform, handed in their tickets and went out into the street. Without any parting formalities, Tiny gave the two Americans farewell glances, turned, and headed back into the station for the return train to Drachten. McDonald and McGlinchey were sad to see her leave but Nel Estes, a young woman who was to be their next guide, was waiting to meet them. She had bicycles waiting further down the street. McGlinchey and McDonald mounted their machines and followed Nel along the road for 7 miles to a large house in the country, which turned out to be the home of Nel and her husband, Dick. Both were doctors, having graduated from Amsterdam University during the German invasion of their country. They had immediately gone into hiding and were taken in by the underground. They had married and had two children.

The Estes' home was small and cramped but the two airmen were made to feel very welcome. Dick was away most of the day and evenings, working for the Dutch underground radio network. Nel, meanwhile, scoured the area for food for themselves, their two children and now two extra mouths. She was also actively engaged in Resistance activities during the two weeks the two Americans were in her care. Despite the dangerous risks they were taking, the Estes were delighted to shelter two downed airmen of the 8th Air Force. It was unusual how peace-loving Dutchmen and women could suddenly become involved in Resistance work and help Allied airmen avoid capture. Sadly, Dick was shot by retreating German forces on the very day their area was liberated by Allied forces.

Early in December McGlinchey and McDonald were turned over to 'Uncle Joe', a Dutch surgeon, whose real name was Doctor J. P. Kummel. 'Uncle Joe' escorted them to Amersfoort, a stopover en route to the Dutch–Belgian border to the south. But the news that the underground movement in the area had been discovered by the Gestapo effectively closed that part of the escape route. 'Uncle Joe' was very distressed but the Resistance members were never downhearted for long. It was decided that they would head east to Stavoren instead. 'Uncle Joe' escorted McGlinchey and McDonald to a pig farm and introduced them to the farm owner, part of 'Uncle Joe's' big, happy family. All through Christmas 1943 and New Year 1944, the two airmen remained at the farm. Occasionally they were housed in safe homes in the area to help minimize the risk the local people were taking.

'Uncle Joe' was always in evidence behind the scenes and was the perfect host. 'He was quite a daredevil,' recalls McGlinchey, 'and delighted in taking us for rides on bicycles through the countryside. He knew the area very well and even at night he had us out. One evening we had a narrow escape. We were almost killed by a crashing bomber, which ploughed in only a few hundred yards from our cycle path. Fortunately, we were able to leave the area quickly and were not discovered. But it was this kind of escapade that really frightened Bill and I.'

Early in January 1944 'Uncle Joe' advised the two airmen that a new underground route had been established for their escape. Bill McDonald and Frank McGlinchey travelled by cycle and train to Utrecht. They bade farewell to 'Uncle Joe' and continued through several small villages to what appeared to McGlinchey 'the smallest village of all', at Erp. Their new hosts were the Otten family and the two airmen stayed at their lovely home for five days. Although retired, both the Ottens were very active in the underground movement. Special hiding places were built into the walls of the Ottens' home for any eventuality such as a search by the Gestapo. McGlinchey recalls, 'This was a wonderful family. They were very gracious towards us and they took us upstairs to a beautiful old-fashioned bedroom and put us to bed. Bill got into bed and disappeared into the soft mattress. We laughed at each other!'

The two men waited in their room. It looked out to the rear of the house across a typical lovely Dutch farmland scene. For a few days arrangements were made for the safe transfer to the next stage of their journey. It was still a constant source of amazement to McGlinchey and McDonald that their Dutch hosts throughout the 'line' and especially the Ottens, continually put their lives in jeopardy by caring for downed airmen. Like all the other people in the escape line, the Ottens became the 'finest people' McGlinchey has known in his lifetime.

Orders came for the two Americans to move on quickly. A car collected them and took them to the station. where they boarded a train for Maastricht at the very tip of Holland. They walked from the station and stayed several days with another Dutch family in a big town house. McDonald and McGlinchey were quartered on the third floor while plans were made for their successful escape across the Dutch border into Belgium. New identity cards were forged. This time they showed that two students were travelling between colleges in Holland and Belgium. No difficulties were anticipated because this was a common practice among students in Holland at that time.

During the night of 21 January, a guide collected the two Americans. They walked through the town to the border area and waited nervously in the shadows. A young woman in the distance brought refreshment to the German border guards. After a short time, the two airmen were led quietly along a dark path around the control house and through a gate into Belgium. It was difficult to believe that after so many weeks of waiting patiently, it had all been so easy.

Now the Belgian guides took over. They kept McGlinchey and McDonald quietly hidden in an area near a railway station until early morning, when they boarded a train for Brussels. By now both men were highly excited. It was heightened by the sudden arrival of truckloads of German soldiers. They disembarked, boarded the train and searched it, asking for identification as they did so. In a heart-stopping moment a German soldier asked for McGlinchey's pass but the fake identity card stood the test. He glanced at it and walked on.

The train quickly became very crowded and continued to Brussels without further incident. It steamed into Brussels station around late morning. McGlinchey and McDonald were met by another link in the underground chain and were whisked away to a house in the middle of the city. The excitement they had felt at the border overwhelmed them in the beautiful but occupied capital. The impact was so great that McGlinchey had only a fleeting recollection of his visit. He and McDonald were quickly taken to an upstairs room, where they remained for 24 hours. Fake identity cards were produced and the two men were told they would travel the next night on the International Express to Paris. McGlinchey and McDonald were unable to contain their delight. Their nervousness and anxiety showed and their Belgian hosts had to continually reassure them that all would be well.

'Their enthusiasm must have been infectious,' recalls McGlinchey, because I was carrying a letter from the Dutch underground to Queen Wilhelmina in London and it no longer seemed to bother me. It had been given to me by some Dutch patriots on the understanding that I was to present it to her Majesty personally. I was also told that if I was captured en route I was to destroy it.'

When night fell on 23 January McGlinchey and McDonald left with their guide for the railway station. It seemed unusually dark. Both men carried bits of clothing and a few toilet articles in small bags. The station was crowded and so too was the train. Undeterred, their Belgian guide showed them to their seats and sat down beside them. There were a number of German soldiers travelling on the train: a fact that seemed to delight their guide.

The train arrived at the Franco–Belgian border and everyone had to leave their seats and queue at the border control checkpoint. It was a very anxious moment for the two escapers. Their bags were inspected, their train tickets checked and their identity cards scrutinised. But all went smoothly and they were quickly through the control onto French soil. A little bewildered, McDonald and McGlinchey looked at each other while the train was shunted along the tracks. It had taken the two men only two days to reach France; a marvellous achievement that, without the help of the Resistance movements, would have been impossible.

The train soon filled to capacity again. It pulled out of the station and headed for Paris. On the afternoon of 24 January, it steamed into one of the capital's stations. Once again, the two airmen were met by Resistance members, this time French. They took them by metro to another part of the city and to a large housing complex. Once more, McGlinchey was too overwhelmed to notice much of the beautiful city he now found himself in. Only four months earlier he and McDonald had dropped bombs on this very city from their Flying Fortress; now they were hiding in it.

The two men were led downstairs to the basement, where several other men were clustered in dimly lit rooms. Altogether, there were about two dozen would-be escapers, who, their guide explained, were being assembled for movement to southern France and the Spanish border. But the movement did not begin at once and time passed slowly. Despite the Resistance members' forebodings about unnecessary talking, the escapees bided their time comparing stories. An eerie atmosphere pervaded the basement.

It seemed days before events began to gain momentum. French identity cards were issued and food rations were distributed for the journey. Food was scarce and McGlinchey's rations included only sugar and cheese. Train tickets were issued for the first part of the journey through France. The first stop was to be Toulouse, a large industrial city about 60 miles from the Pyrénées.

Twenty-four escapees and four French guides left during the night. Twelve of the escapees were Allied servicemen, mostly fallen fliers. The other twelve were civilians fleeing from the Germans. The party split into groups of four and departed to the metro station. McGlinchey descended the stairs to the platform and was singled out by a French policeman and asked to produce his papers. McGlinchey nervously showed him his card. The policeman read it but did not seem to be entirely satisfied. He glanced at McGlinchey's bag, prodded it and asked to see its contents.

The cheese and sugar seemed to interest him and then he turned his attention to the owner. He studied McGlinchey for a moment and then placed his arm on his shoulder. With a wink of his eye, he told McGlinchey to go on.

Utterly relieved, McGlinchey carried on down to the train but his companions had gone. Fortunately, he had been told how many stops it would take to reach the train terminal. He counted them off on the short ride and reached the terminal without further incident. But once there, doubt began to set in and he realised he was lost. In despair he walked down a street and into a bicycle shop. Using his train ticket and some sign language he asked the woman proprietor the way to the terminal. She shied him away but an elderly man, who sensed his predicament, took him by the arm and escorted the lost American several blocks to the terminal. An incredible sense of relief and elation pulsated through McGlinchey's body.

McGlinchey was spotted by the French guide as he made his way to the terminal. The Frenchman ran over and hugged and patted him as only Frenchmen can. McGlinchey was equally overjoyed to see him. The two men walked through the doors into the heart of the terminal building. It seemed to McGlinchey one of the nicest he had ever seen; at least that is how it appeared to him at that moment. Bill McDonald greeted his long-lost crew member and shook his head in disbelief as McGlinchey poured out his story.

Without further ado the group boarded the train. It seemed that trains were always crowded and this one was no exception. McGlinchey did not want any more setbacks but there were no more incidents on the long journey. On the afternoon of 30 January, the train pulled into Toulouse. It was a very tired group of evadees and their guide who boarded the bus for the foothills of the Pyrénées. They drove for several hours before the beautiful mountains loomed before them. All the evadees were excited and noisy. Although weary, they were happy to have come so far without being detected. All knew that freedom lay on the other side of the mountains in neutral Spain but despite their impatience, the crossing could not be attempted immediately. Instead, the group were taken to a large hotel that was more acquainted with hosting tourists in the summer. It was now closed and had probably not seen tourists since before the war.

The evadees were like excited schoolchildren on a winter's holiday. Their French guide supervised and tended to their needs but showed concern for the older members who arrived to join the group, worried they would not be able to make it across the mountainous slopes.

Several days passed and finally on Saturday, 15 February the bus reappeared. It picked up as many of the evadees as it could and the driver headed for a mountain pass. The Pyrénées were silhouetted against a starlit evening sky and it was difficult to imagine that war was raging in Europe. The bus driver drove the party as far up the mountain sides as he could. The escapees and guides alighted and walked single file through the mountain pass. They walked for hours, stopping periodically for short rests. After midnight a sudden storm enveloped the area and it began snowing. It quickly turned into a blizzard and although walking became very treacherous, the guides urged everyone to keep going.

Finally, in the early hours of the morning the column came to a halt near some huts close to the Spanish border. The men took shelter and rested in the huts before moving on down the sides of the mountain led by their guides. Suddenly, shots rang out! Dogs chased the evadees and some bullets found their mark and men fell dying. It had all happened so quickly there was no escape, although McGlinchey had the presence of mind to destroy the letter he was carrying to Queen Wilhelmina and dispose of it. Although the guides knew the mountain terrain very well, they had overlooked the possibility of German border guards being in the area on Sunday mornings at a different hour to those during the rest of the week. It was their undoing.

In despair the cold and bitterly disappointed survivors were herded onto an army truck and transported to the German outpost at Saint-Girons. They were held in the small village for a day before being taken to Saint-Michel prison in Toulouse. McGlinchey and the others were questioned but only name, rank and serial numbers were given freely. The Germans confiscated McGlinchey's dog tags and reminded him he was a political prisoner, captured in civilian clothes. McGlinchey, McDonald and the other survivors were turned over to the Gestapo and taken to Fresnes prison in Paris. All the captured men were separated and put into cells with civilian prisoners. McGlinchey was questioned repeatedly, threatened but never mistreated.

On 24 March the prisoners were transported to Frankfurt, arriving in the city during a daylight bombing raid. Fires were raging and the city was in chaos. The prisoners were marched through a part of it and only came through unharmed through divine providence. Their captors were furious. McGlinchey was sent to a prison in Mainz and placed in solitary confinement but it was not long before the warden called him forward to answer for the 'many crimes committed by the "terror-fliegers" of the American Air Force'.

He threatened McGlinchey with all kinds of punishment but finally sent him back to his cell for ten days' solitary. The civilian prisoners gave him their rations and constantly reassured him that all would be well. They were right. Unexpectedly, the Gestapo collected all the airmen prisoners and took them on a tour of Wiesbaden to sing the praises of their pretty town. 'Indeed, it was despite the bombing,' thought McGlinchey.

However, the end of the ride was even more unexpected. It culminated at Dulag Luft Interrogation Centre at Oberursel, where Luftwaffe interrogators put the prisoners through very intense and frightening periods of questioning. 'It was name, rank and serial number all over again,' says McGlinchey, 'they accused me of everything and threw all kinds of data at me. Surprisingly, some of it was quite accurate.'

In between the interrogations McGlinchey was declared a PoW and subsequently transferred to Stalag Luft I at Barth in Pomerania with Bill McDonald. They arrived at the camp on 14 April 1944. Two weeks later they located John James, their co-pilot, who had a damaged chute, went down rapidly and broke his leg when landing – going through the roof of a house. Early in May they learned from an airman in a new intake that Carl Spicer had made it home to England via France and Spain. Spicer and Fred Boulter had left Drachten a little later than McDonald and McGlinchey. They went through many adventures (a pub where they were staying in Brussels burned down) and arrived in Spain, where they spent some days in prison before being set free by a British officer. They arrived home on Christmas Eve 1943.

After D-Day and the Allied breakthrough at Avranches no more downed airmen were sent along the escape lines out of Friesland. One hundred men had nothing more they could do but sit it out and wait for liberation. Tiny Mulder next served as a translator for Allied forces when they arrived in 1945. After VE Day she went to work as a journalist for a Frisian newspaper. She also began travelling to England, Canada and the United States, where she renewed her friendship with many of the seventy American, Canadian and British airmen she had helped rescue. In recognition for her service, Tiny received the American Medal of Freedom with the Silver Palm from the United States. A short time later, the British government awarded her the King's Medal for Courage in the Cause of Freedom. Her citations state that she helped and assisted almost one hundred downed airmen in the war.

# Chapter 5

# 'See you at Breakfast'[1]

'See you at breakfast!' With this remark eighteen Lancaster crews on 550 Squadron at Killingholme were leaving the mess after the 'ops meal' and were about to attend briefing regarding the 'target for tonight', 3/4 May 1944. The idea never occurred to Sergeant John Goffin 'Jack' Pearce, the 30-year-old mid-upper gunner on Warrant Officer T. A. 'Lofty' Lloyd's crew, that it would be some time before he would sit down once more to a good English breakfast. Why, the crew was now, in official terms, an experienced one, having taken part in a number of operations on the squadron. It was Jack Pearce's 13th operational sortie. He had grown up in Thorpe St Andrew, Norwich, and had been a printer by trade working for Her Majesty's Stationery Office. He was an altar boy at the churches in Norwich including St John's Maddermarket and St Peter Mancroft; he studied Greek and Latin and considered the priesthood as a vocation; a devotion to the church that would continue into later life. On 4 June 1940, Jack joined the RAF Volunteer Reserve. The family history suggests he was in India, and was near Singapore before it fell in February 1942. He holds The Burma Star, so any service in that theatre must have been after 11 December 1941. Jack would then find himself back in England and from late summer 1943 would train to become an air gunner on Lancasters. His logbook places him at 2 AGS at Dalcross (Inverness). He then passed through 83 Operational Training Unit

---

1 The author is most grateful to Dave Cole for his kind permission to quote freely from his article, https://farmboysandpioneers wordpress.com/2021/03/04/see-you-at-breakfast

at RAF Peplow in Shropshire – a Wellington training unit, and also RAF Faldingworth in Lincolnshire, 1667 Heavy Conversion Unit for the Halifax and Lancaster. After that he appears at RAF Hemswell, near Gainsborough, which was home to No. 1 Lancaster Finishing School for training aircrew on the Lancaster.

The Panzer depot and training centre at Mailly-le-Camp almost halfway between Troyes and Châlons-sur-Marne, about 50 miles south of Reims, was target for over 346 Lancasters and 16 Mosquitoes on Wednesday/Thursday, 3/4 May 1944. It was not what crews considered difficult. 'A piece of cake,' Sergeant 'Jumbo' Moore, Lofty' Lloyd's wireless operator, remarked. 'Well, target was reached with little opposition as far as we were concerned,' wrote Jack Pearce 'and Pathfinders were already busy with their marking. This method with which all were now familiar consisted of dropping red flares, or target indicators (TIs), around the area to be "flattened out". The assembly point was reached at 0200 hours at 8,000 ft. "J-Jig" orbited for nine minutes until ordered to bomb by the "Master Bomber" [Wing Commander Leonard Cheshire], who was going to give us the OK to bomb by wireless telephone. If the markings were not, in his opinion, accurate enough, the Pathfinder would mark again, and so on until he was satisfied. Meanwhile, 15 miles east of target we were to circle around until the order was given. This point was marked by "chandeliers", flares which burned in the air. We circled these for 15 minutes, passing remarks to one another not at all complimentary to the controller: "We don't mind waiting"; "After a gong, chum" and the like, until the calm voice reached us over the radio with, "Hello, main force, you may bomb now!" Down we went and unloaded an assortment of ironmongery for Adolf's Wehrmacht to share among themselves and with a lighter aircraft and lighter hearts we turned for home. But "Jerry" had taken advantage of our delay in bombing and his fighters were lurking around.'

On the run in to the target from the Assembly Point a Lancaster 600 yards west of 'J-Jig' was shot down in flames. No parachutes were seen to open and the crew skippered by Flight Lieutenant Arthur

James Grain DFM accompanied by the Station Defence Officer, Major Sidney Whipp of the Duke of Wellington's Regiment on 'H-Harry', all died.

'After bombing at 0033 "Jig" proceeded on the way home,' wrote Jack Pearce. 'A nasty little 410 sneaked underneath us and ripped our belly with a burst of cannon fire, but no vital hit was registered, and we continued on our course. Five minutes later our adversary returned and gave us another burst. I caught a glimpse of him as he "broke away" beneath the starboard wing and was able to give him a short burst from the mid-upper turret, in which I was flying that night for a change. Whether I hit him at all I never knew.'

At 12,000 ft 'J-Jig' was hit by light flak – ground-fired red tracer, which damaged the port wing, tail and rear turret. Lloyd called on the intercom for details of damage and possible injuries to the crew. No reply was received from Sergeant Anthony Constantine Crilley, the rear gunner. 'Jumbo' Moore was sent to investigate. He met Crilley halfway along the fuselage, bleeding profusely from the face and dazed and suffering from shock. Moore put him in the wireless operator's seat to apply a field dressing but Crilley refused all assistance and, the rear turret being unmanned, the W/Op took over the rear gunner's duties and left Flight Sergeant 'Steve' Stephen, the navigator, to deal with Crilley. On reaching the rear turret 'Jumbo' Moore found the intercom plug torn away so he returned up the fuselage to get the 10ft lead and was about to enter the turret when a long burst from a fighter shot away the H2S, which was thrown against him. The burst continued up the fuselage and 'Lofty' Lloyd saw the tracer appearing in front of the nose of the aircraft. The burst damaged the hydraulics and the port inner engine refused to feather. The aircraft went into an uncontrollable dive with flames and smoke filling the fuselage. The bomb doors remained open, flaps down and elevator tabs u/s. 'Jumbo' Moore was able to pass a message as to the damage and casualties and also get fixes. The dive put out most of the fire and Sergeant 'Terry' Burke, the flight engineer, who had been assisting the pilot to put on his parachute, and 'Jumbo' Moore put out the remaining flames by using extinguishers, coffee flasks and their hands and stamping their feet. 'Steve' Stephen, who had been badly burned on the face and hands, was unable to lend assistance and was so shocked that he refused all aid.

As there was no response to the controls, Lloyd gave orders for the crew to bail out. It struck Jack Pearce how perfectly his skipper gave the exact, laid-down instructions, but 'Lofty' never panicked. 'OK Skip, going out!' came the voices of the crew in the correct rotation. 'Jumbo' Moore assisted Jack Pearce and Crilly to open the entrance door to the nose escape hatch, which seemed to be jammed and took a few seconds to open. Flying Officer 'Eddie' Yaternick, the 27-year-old air bomber born in Gimli, Manitoba, in 1917, escaped in the normal way and Jack Pearce and Crilly left the aircraft between 12,000 and 9,000ft. 'Jumbo' Moore was just about to do so when 'Lofty' Lloyd, who had been wrestling with the controls, suddenly regained control and stopped the furious descent. The enemy coast was crossed; control of the aircraft being most difficult; Lloyd having to wrap his arms around the stick and also grip it hard with his knees, Terry Burke assisting at intervals to take the strain while Lloyd rested his muscles. The lights of Ford airfield on the Sussex coast were 'a glimpse of heaven', to quote the skipper, and at the second run the aircraft belly landed at 0300 hours. All emergency facilities were laid on and the crew could not praise too highly the work and reception by all concerned. 'Lofty' would receive an immediate DFM for getting the Lancaster back.[2] Over 1,500 tons of bombs hit their target, destroying over 150 barrack buildings and transport sheds together with over 100 vehicles, including many tanks but 42 Lancasters of the main force were shot down, as were a Mosquito and a Halifax of

---

2 After the lucky escape of May 1944, ND733 was back on operations by October with 463 Squadron RAAF at RAF Waddington, Lincolnshire, bearing the identifier JO-L. It flew on until 16 April 1945, when it was shot down over Juvincourt, France, during its return from a raid to Pilzen, Czechoslovakia, just two weeks before the end of hostilities in Europe. The crew bailed out and all survived.

100 Group. Just 58 of the 315 men lost in these 44 aircraft survived, 24 were taken prisoner of war and 34 evaded.

So, what became of the three men on 'J-Jig' who bailed out? Crilley and Yaternick became prisoners of war but for Jack Pearce the spring morning of 4 May was thankfully going to end better than it had started.

'I scrambled from the turret. Nasty red flames and black smoke filled the fuselage. It was hot and choking. I paused for a second, and the thought came to me, "Well, this is the end", but at once I forgot it and scrambled to get my 'chute, which was stowed slightly forward of the turret. I decided to make my way to the rear door, as it looked pretty hopeless to attempt to leave by the escape hatch, which is situated in the bomb aimer's position. On reaching the rear door I found "Jumbo" already there, and between us we managed to open it. Apparently, it had been jammed by wreckage. A rush of cool fresh air came in and I stood back for "Jumbo" to go out, but he motioned me forward, so I gingerly slipped off the step into space. Our height at the time of the attack was approximately 8,000ft and, therefore, there was no difficulty regarding oxygen. My first sensation was like that of the steeplejack, who called his mate to the top of the tall chimney on which they were working and remarked, "Ain't it quiet up here?" Yes, after the roar of the aircraft's engines the stillness was almost painful, and I merely seemed to sway this way and the other, as the wind caught up the 'chute, and no pulling sensation was apparent.

'Another thing I noticed was that I had no recollection of pulling the rip cord. The handle to which it was attached was still in my hand. It seemed a long time before I caught a glimpse of the ground, which I no sooner saw than it rose to meet me with remarkable swiftness. I came in contact with it with a gentle bump. Sitting up and looking round, I observed I had landed right by the side of the road and my 'chute was entangled in the telegraph wires. There was no time to be lost; I was in enemy territory and a most unwelcome reception committee might arrive any moment.

'By the side of the road was a ditch and into this I dumped my helmet, gloves and outer flying suit; then, disentangling my chute from the wires, I added it to the collection; over one hundred pounds' worth of good flying kit and, as I found later to my great dismay, twenty Players cigarettes which were in my flying suit pocket. I took a quick look round for other members of my crew, nobody. There was nothing for it now but to put the greatest distance between that spot and myself in the shortest time, so away I went as fast as my flying boots, very unsuitable for hiking, would allow. After walking a short distance, I arrived at a small village and decided to go straight through rather than attempt to make a detour. I was endeavouring to travel roughly south-west, checking my bearings by a small compass which I had removed from my escape kit.

'The time was now around 2 am and everything in the village was quiet, except for the occasional barking of a dog. I paused at the village fountain – an ornate affair with water continually gushing from a lion's mouth – to wash the blood from a nasty cut on my face and fill my rubber water bottle. Then I hurried on towards open country. Later, I disposed of my inner electrical flying suit in a disused well. It was almost dawn when I came on a wayside railway station and a goods train apparently waiting for the "all-clear" signal. On the spur of the moment, I decided to attempt to board it, and so try to get well clear of the district. I started to run, but when I had almost reached the train the whistle blew with that curious note peculiar to continental trains, and it moved slowly away. Perhaps it was just as well, I reflected, for it might be going the wrong way! As I crossed the track I heard a shout from the station, but didn't stop to argue. It was now almost dawn and the birds were twittering and the cuckoo could be clearly heard. I wondered if I was not more the cuckoo, alone in an enemy country but with high hopes of getting home.

'For the past hour I had been looking for a haystack in which to hide and rest myself until nightfall, but I saw never a sign of one, so, deciding it was unsafe to travel farther, I betook myself to a small wood and prepared for rest. First, I checked over my escape kit: compass, Horlicks tablets, chewing gum, adhesive plaster, glucose, chloride tablets, and needle and thread. Why a needle and thread, I wondered?

As if to give me the answer, my braces, for some unknown reason, suddenly parted, so before turning in I made the necessary repairs, blessing him or her whose forethought had caused their inclusion in the kit. Then, after checking my position on my map and deciding on my future course, I covered myself with dry bracken, and slept.

'Thus, my first and subsequent days passed, and things became rather desperate. I had blisters on my feet of uncomfortable size, and I was badly in need of a shave, not to mention being decidedly hungry.

'Early one morning I came across a stretch of countryside freshly covered with British propaganda leaflets and saw an old labourer pick one up and, after a quick look round, put it in his pocket. "It's likely," I thought, "he is on our side", so, emerging from cover, I spoke in my best schoolboy French to him.

'To my great relief, he was on our side, and after leading me to cover he asked me various questions to try to prove my true identity. These I answered as best as I could without disclosing "official secrets", but not the least convincing to him were the tattoo marks on my arms, souvenirs of my previous service in the Far East. At this point a young lad, probably the old man's son, arrived, bringing his breakfast, which the old man gave to me; needless to say, I gratefully accepted it. Meanwhile, the old man was excitedly talking to the boy, who went away and returned later with a young man, who said that although he was not an active member of the underground movement [which Jack Pearce came to know was Georges Broussine's 'Burgundy' ('Bourgogne') escape line, which would assist no fewer than 327 men to evade capture by the end of the war[3]] he was

---

3 See *They Came from Burgundy* by Keith Janes (Troubador, 2017). Georges Broussine was returned to France in February 1943 to establish the 'Bourgogne' (or 'Burgundy') escape line. The organisation was based in Paris but had connections with other groups throughout the country. The first routes that 'Bourgogne' used to take men across the Pyrénées to Spain were via Andorra but the extreme bad weather in the winter of 1943–44 forced a change to the lower mountains south of Perpignan. When that more obvious route became too dangerous in December 1943, men were sent out through Pau. Broussine was also involved in other ventures, including sea evacuations from Brittany by fishing vessels.

in sympathy with it and that he would contact them for me. The boy had brought some dungaree overalls, which he gave me to put on over my uniform. I was told to remain in hiding and left alone once more. My next visitor was a lady, astonishingly, an English lady, who told me she had been born in London and had married a Frenchman during the last war. It was grand to talk in my mother tongue once more. She told me some interesting things, chiefly that in the nearby village where she lived was stationed a detachment of SS guards, and that six of them were billeted at her house. Also, a nearby farm, which we could see across the fields, was used as the officers' mess. I had thought of going there a few hours before!

'The young man returned and spoke to her, and she translated to me, saying that I was to remain hidden until the evening, when a man would pass my hiding place who would be carrying a cross-cut saw on his shoulder. I was to follow him. A long day passed and evening came at last, and with it the man with the cross-cut saw. I followed at a respectable distance, and round a bend came on the English lady, standing almost hidden by the trees. She waved, and disappeared. Following my leader, we came out in a lane, where waiting for us was another man with a horse and cart loaded with empty boxes. I climbed in and was hidden beneath the boxes and then we rumbled away down the uneven road, passing through the village in which the SS guards were billeted, and on to the next village.

'Before we entered in I was invited to emerge from my hiding place and sit up in the cart, and to my surprise I received quite a welcome from the villagers, who evidently knew that I was coming.

'I was taken to a farmhouse and given more food, surrounded by a crowd of eager French people all asking questions: "When were we going to invade?" and so on.

'Soon, my host cleared the house and gave me a drink tasting something like whisky. Then he suggested I should get some sleep, which was easy! At about 2330 hours I was awakened and told that I was to be taken to the next village, but before I left, I was to have supper with the oldest inhabitant, a dear old lady. This meal too was eaten to the accompaniment of endless questions.

'At last, we set off – myself and two young Frenchmen. The next village was about three miles distant and upon arriving there I was taken to a house where, after the seemingly inevitable wine, I went to sleep in a real bed. I slept until around ten in the morning, when the lady of the house awakened me with breakfast – bread and milk.

'Neighbours began to drift in and soon my bed was surrounded by yet another questioning throng. Some of them had brought me articles of clothing. My visitors withdrew at last, and I dressed myself in my "civvies", which consisted of trousers, real "drain-pipe" type, exposing about six inches of ankle, a white shirt, a pair of white socks and a well-worn pair of patent shoes several sizes too large. Later in my travels I acquired a beret. A young Frenchman who spoke some English then arrived and gave me to understand he was taking me to Paris immediately, so with the good wishes of my new friends we set off together after many warm handclasps, good wishes and urgent requests for me to tell the British "to come soon", and to send them arms.

'The railway station was about four miles away and, of course, we had to walk (no buses available!). My friend produced a packet of cigarettes and a box of matches, which he gave me; a very welcome present, I assure you.

'We had almost arrived at our destination when we overtook a gentleman carrying under his arm one of those long loaves of bread peculiar to France. He apparently was well known to my friend, and at his invitation we adjourned to his house for lunch. It was not a sumptuous meal – eggs, fried in oil, and vegetables, with large portions of the aforementioned loaf, and wine, of which my tumbler never seemed empty, a kind of whisky, followed by champagne! Our genial host, suddenly remembering that the staple British beverage was tea, insisted on making me some, in spite of my assurance that I had surely drunk enough for one day. We chatted for a short time, then, after a drop of his special wine (one for the road!), he clamped a small black beret on my head and bade us adieu.

'The station was only a short distance away, so my guide gave me my instructions: after obtaining my ticket and passing it on to me, we would split up, and I was to follow him at a distance and do as he did. I had a French newspaper to get behind and prevent my being too closely scrutinised by fellow travellers; also, it would by my appearing deeply interested in it, prevent me being drawn into conversation.

'The train duly arrived, an hour or so late, I understood, but that was usual; and I installed myself in the compartment next to my guide's. After a seemingly endless journey, although lasting only about two hours, the train steamed into Paris. As casually as I could, I followed in the wake of my guide. By the time we reached the barrier most of the passengers had passed through, and my friend presented his ticket to the collector. I followed suit. Then came a dreadful moment. My friend was sharply called back by the collector. I learned later it was something to do with the date of his ticket.

'Thus, I was left alone, and rather bewildered. It seemed that the whole German Army, Navy and Air Force were stationed together on the station. Squads of them in full kit were being marched on and off different platforms. I took up a position near the platform I had left, and after lighting up one of my precious cigarettes, with, I admit, a trembling hand, I waited for my friend to reappear.

'Suddenly I observed a huge German officer marching straight towards me. I really did sweat then. When, however, about only three paces away from me, he smartly "about-turned" and marched off in the opposite direction. I breathed again!

'But then, after about thirty paces, came another smart "about turn", and again he came straight towards me, eyes fixed on me. But again, three paces away came the "about turn"; and so, it continued – a kind of sentry-go drill. It occurred to me later that he was awaiting the arrival of a train and this was his way of passing the time.

'At last, my friend reappeared and, allowing him to pass me without any sign of recognition, I, as casually as possible, sauntered after him. He made his way to the station buffet, and sat down at one of the small tables near the door. Seeing me enter, he sprang from his seat and, clasping my hard, addressed me rapidly in French. I didn't understand a word, but got the idea that I was supposed to be an old friend, whom he had thus unexpectedly met. He ordered wine and bread rolls, faintly smeared with something like jam, for which he had to surrender coupons. Later, he told me these were printed in England. We had now, he said, to take the underground railway to another main-line station and proceed from there to a small village 20 miles the other side of Paris. Most of us are familiar with the rush hours on the London underground. In Paris it was infinitely worse. Civilians and German service men and women were all in one seething, writhing mass. I saw one German soldier in full kit neatly tripped by two Frenchmen, his equipment flying in all directions, and cheerfully tramped on by the crowd. Such little incidents I found to be fairly common.

'We reached our destination at last and just had time to scramble aboard the local train. Since we were now old friends, my guide and myself sat side by side, he making most of the conversation in French, with an occasional remark to me in English in an undertone.

'The journey lasted about an hour and a half, and upon alighting from the train we found a gentleman awaiting us who, ignoring me, chattered away to my friend. Imagine my surprise when, after leaving the station, he addressed me in English and told me that he was British, but had resided in France for many years! In the main streets of the small town, we spoke little, but once in the suburbs he asked me about my adventures. I replied as evasively as I could, for the strict training I had been given made me naturally a little suspicious. But Monsieur [Henri] Boutellier was all right. I found out later that he had been imprisoned three times on suspicion of being a member of the Resistance movement. He was an insignificant-looking little chap, but as brave as a lion.

'In due time we came to the outskirts of the town and to a large, old-fashioned house. We walked past twice before going up the steps, and after Monsieur Boutellier[4] had knocked, giving, I thought, a signal, we entered, and passed into a brightly lighted room. Here about a dozen people, both men and women, were gathered. I received quite a hearty welcome, with much of the hand-shaking the French seem so fond of.

'Then followed a very stiff interrogation, for it appeared that more than one German had tried to pass himself off as an English aviator and so discover the leaders of the movement. This business I suppose lasted about two hours, after which I went home with Boutellier. His house was not far away and was a very large old rambling place. He introduced me to the other members of his family and after meal took me to my room and gave me instructions as to how I should make my escape and where to remain in hiding should we have a surprise visit from "Jerry". I remained with him some days, and was very surprised to see the documents and maps relating to German troop movements, petrol and ammunition dumps that were daily being sent to England. It was also arranged for a doctor to visit me to examine me for any injuries I might have received while on my travels. My heels, which were very blistered, had been receiving attention from the ladies of the house and I was now feeling much better.

'Arrangements, meanwhile, were being made for me to move to a safer area, and one evening after dinner I was introduced to a fine old gentleman who, I understood, had at one time been an officer in the French Army. I was told that he would take me to his house and that I would remain there until further arrangements were made for me to start the journey back to England.

'This gentleman, whom I will refer to now as "Monsieur P", lived only a few miles away. He spoke a little English, and I by now could make myself fairly well understood, so we soon became good friends. At dusk we set off for his home and on arrival I was introduced to his wife and son, SS, who was a fine, hefty lad about my own age, and

---

4  According to National Archive intelligence files, one of the MI-9 'helpers' of 23 Rue du Colonel Durand at Lagny.

we had many good times together. I soon settled in my new home and the daily routine: breakfast about eight, consisting of a large bowl of coffee, of a decidedly acorn flavour, and bread; lunch around midday, of vegetables, and dinner at eight in the evening, the main meal of the day, which consisted of soup, vegetables and anything they could get from the black market, and, of course, the inevitable wine! The meat ration was drawn every month in one lot, so as to make something like a decent joint. Even then it was far less than the normal British ration. I was thankful for it, all the same.

'After a few days "close confinement", I ventured out into the garden with Squadron Leader Sparks[5] and helped him to chop wood for the fires. Coal was unobtainable and the gas was only on at a low pressure for a short time each day. Electricity did not come on until eight in the evening, when we would listen to the BBC news, with the set well turned down! As the days passed, I got bolder and we would go to the café in the village, which was well patronised by the German Air Force personnel who were stationed in the district. Many of the villagers had been introduced to me and would greet me with sly nods and winks, raising their glasses in my direction. One night a German airman in rather an intoxicated condition was attempting to converse with me in French.

'I tried to talk to him in German, which he thought a huge joke, though I saw nothing funny in the situation. I felt awfully hot round the collar!

'Thus, the time passed and while boating on the river one day with Squadron Leader Sparks I was suddenly recalled to the house, where a lady was awaiting me. She informed me that all was settled

---

5 On 7 May Pearce was moved across the river to Dampmart and sheltered by Michel Place in his bakery at 7 rue du Chateau, where he was joined by Squadron Leader Ernest Neville Monkhouse 'Ned' Sparks pilot of Lancaster JB402 on 83 Squadron, two of whose crew were taken prisoner and six escaped about a week later – and the rest of his journey was with him. Sparks returned to England and was shot down on Königsberg on 26/27 August 1944 and taken prisoner.

and that in the morning I must return to Paris to start my long journey homeward. I left early in the morning, after much hand-shaking, and with gratitude in my heart for all that had been done for me and the risks that they had taken on my behalf. Squadron Leader Sparks accompanied me back to Monsieur Boutellier's house and, after wishing me luck, he returned home.

'I set off to the station, riding on the pillion of a very diminutive motorcycle, skilfully piloted by a young man whom I knew to be a very active member of the "Organisation". Squadron Leader Sparks, who had left earlier, was awaiting us there and had got the tickets. He told me that he was to accompany me on the first part of the journey in order to introduce me to the person who was to take me to "The Chief" for final instructions as to my homeward route. [National Archive intelligence files describe 'The Chief' as a man called Octave Boutellier.][6]

'We broke our journey at a small wayside station and went to a café in the village, where we were apparently expected. Squadron Leader Sparks ordered coffee and while waiting to be served, a lady entered whom I vaguely remembered having seen her before. It transpired that she was the wife of the local Resistance leader. It was she who was to be my guide. We returned to the station and here I took leave of Sparks, who, I am sure, felt the parting as keenly as I did, for we had become very attached to each other.

'On our arrival at Paris we made our way to a small public garden, and sat down among the office workers who had come there for the

---

6 Pearce landed near Dampierre-en-Yvelines (south-west of Paris) and was heading towards Rambouillet when he approached a man and his journey was arranged. Pearce was taken by horse and cart to Monfort-l'Amaury, where he was given a meal at the home of the cart driver before being sheltered overnight with a neighbour. Next day, a young man came to take Pearce to Rambouillet, where they had lunch with the (unnamed) owner of an artificial manure manufacturing business, before taking a train to Paris. They went on through Paris to Lagny, where Pearce was taken to a man called 'the Chief'. After an interrogation, Pearce was taken to stay with Henri Herbert Cane at 13 rue de la Paix, Lagny. *They Came from Burgundy* by Keith Janes (Troubador, 2017).

lunch-hour break. Soon, a young fellow sat down beside us and entered into conversation with my companion, who then, after wishing me luck, left us together. With my new friend I left the gardens in rather a bewildered state: things changed so rapidly!

'Together, we strolled through the streets, chatting in broken English. Suddenly he stopped, shook hands with me, and strode off in the opposite direction. As he left another young man stepped from a shop doorway and fell into step with me.

'It was he who took me to the home of the Resistance leader, where we had lunch, and I received my French identity card, complete with new name and supposed occupation. After all these formalities were completed, I went sight-seeing with my host, visiting, among other famous places, Notre-Dame, joining in with a group of young German airmen in a conducted tour of the building. We returned home, and I was advised to rest awhile before dinner.

'Immediately after our meal we were on the move again, this time to what appeared to me to be a school room of some kind. There to my amazement were gathered seven American and five British airmen!

'We briefly introduced ourselves and then listened attentively to the orders given us. We were presented with tickets to Toulouse and a most welcome gift – a small packet of tobacco and cigarette papers. We were told to leave the building in ones and twos and to make our own way to the railway station. We had two guides who we were told to follow, keeping a respectable distance behind them. No difficulty was encountered in reaching the station but the train was more crowded than the August Bank holiday trains returning from Yarmouth!

'Somehow, we managed to scramble in and wedge ourselves in among the mass of humanity in the corridors. Two hours later the train set off and twenty-two hours of travelling lay ahead of us, during which we had the doubtful pleasure of meeting the RAF and seeing for ourselves the efficacy of their bombing!

'On arrival at Toulouse we were to continue by local train to a small town some thirty miles south-west, but because we arrived very late, we missed the last train. However, we decided that it would be unwise to remain in Toulouse, and so we boarded a local train going our way, so travelling as far as we could and finishing the night on a small wayside station. Never did thirteen men seem such a crowd! No matter how we tried to split up, we all seemed to come together in a huddle again.

'After what seemed an endless night, we caught the early morning train and arrived at our destination after a short journey. We left the station and entered a nearby park that had been previously described to us. There we were supposed to make contact again with the Organisation.

'"Just walk around", we had been told, "and someone will be looking out for you." We did walk around – from 7 am until 5 pm – feeling more conspicuous every hour, with our unshaven faces and oddly fitting clothes: and, of course, we were extremely hungry. The guide who had accompanied us then left us to try to find out what had gone wrong. After about two hours he returned, and told us to follow him, keeping our distance and in ones and twos. We left the park at intervals and trudged wearily along the road leading from the town for a mile or so, just keeping in sight of one another. A message passed down to us told that we were to leave the road and enter a gateway. We did so and found ourselves in a farmyard, through which we hurried, into the wooded slopes beyond, until we reached a farmhouse almost in ruins. These were to be, for the next ten days, our quarters.

'A nearby spring gave us water and our food was sent from the farm below. It consisted of one meal per day, mainly composed of haricot beans, an occasional bottle of wine, but very little bread. Usually, we received this late in the evening. We made a communal bed of hay in the only habitable room and passed our time in swapping tales of the adventures we had met with.

'Some of them made my tale seem very tame indeed. One American had been almost a year in enemy territory! Occasionally, we were visited by an American lady living in the town, who brought us cigarettes.

'It was she who gave us our moving orders. We were to leave the farm, some in the evening and others at intervals during the next day, and meet at the local bus station. She would be in the crowd to point out the bus we were to take. I was one of the last to leave the farm, and, after a careful survey to make sure that no traces of our occupation remained, left with a young navigator with whom I had become rather friendly.

'A large crowd was gathered at the bus station, and we could pick out here and there the members of our party. Tickets for our journey were given us, as well as the name of our destination. Our American friend stood near the bus to indicate it was the one to take. Entering the already crowded vehicle, we set off on the next stage of our journey home.

'Apart from the rather uncomfortable heat, the ride was fairly uneventful, except that, temporarily losing my balance when the bus swerved, I missed the strap and grabbed the hair net of a lady sitting in front of me. She was understandably annoyed and I was very embarrassed, but I dared not apologise because of my limited French.

'When we arrived at our destination the bus conductor, who was in on the secret, opened the emergency exit at the rear of the bus and motioned us to get out that way. "Round the corner," he whispered as we passed, so round the corner we went, and there found an elderly man awaiting us who hurried us off down a lane and pushed us behind a hedge. A few minutes later two cars drew up and we were bundled into them and were away in a flash. We travelled at high speed for some twenty miles; we had no time to ask questions, but could only hope for the best.

'A stop was made close to a small wood. There we left the cars and took cover to await the guides, who, we were told, would come for us when darkness fell. The cars drove off and we were again alone.

'In the distance could be seen the peaks of the Pyrénées outlined against the evening sky. It proved to be a long wait, and our impatience to be on the move did not make the time go any faster. We were, also, hungry again, and we dared not smoke in case it should attract unwelcome attention.

'At last, the guide arrived. He was a lad aged about sixteen. We followed him in single file across the fields for some miles, then, telling us to stop and rest, he left us, warning us to remain silent.

'We had only been settled a few moments, however, when the next guide arrived to take over. He was an older man, Spanish, I thought. He never spoke, but just motioned us to follow him. The path was now growing steeper and our guide set a fast pace. At times we had almost to trot to keep up with him. No further halt was made throughout the night, and at dawn we arrived at a rough stone building high on the mountainside.

'These stone huts, I learned, were used by the shepherds who grazed their flocks on the mountainside. The guide left us to rest, and although by now we were exceedingly hungry we soon slept.

'Late in the afternoon he returned with another guide, who told us we were to join with a party of French refugees. Later, they arrived, a party of thirteen, including three women and two elderly men. The refugees had an assortment of baggage with them, and we decided to share these out among us to relieve them and keep the pace up, although, owing to the elderly men, it was bound to be slow. I was allotted a large Gladstone bag. What was in it I never knew, but it soon came to be known as the "Crown Jewels". My navigator friend shared this burden with me, each of us carrying it for roughly half an hour. One of the refugees, a tall Frenchman, who was accompanied by his wife and daughter, carried nothing. We understood he was in poor health, but he did have a bottle of cognac, a few drops of which he gave each of us on lumps of sugar. He was promptly nicknamed "Coneyack" by one of the Americans.

'We travelled on through the night, along steep mountain paths, and in the darkness we could sometimes hear the roar of a mountain stream. Towards dawn it came on to rain, and our guide hurried us on until we reached another of those stone mountain huts, where he again left us.

'We were now soaked to the skin and my socks were worn completely out. Before attempting to rest we made such repairs to our clothing as was possible. Sleep in our condition was impossible. We just sat waiting to move on again. During the afternoon, however, we were visited by a gentleman who lived in the vicinity. He had been sent by the guide. He offered for sale a few thin biscuits, which were eagerly exchanged by the refugees for a pair of shoes. We had no shoes to spare; in fact, I had scarcely any shoes at all. However, we managed to purchase one hard-boiled egg for two hundred francs. One hard-boiled egg among thirteen hungry men! It was divided by a young pilot officer, watched by thirteen pairs of eager eyes.

'Early in the evening we left our hideout. It was still raining heavily. We had a new guide, a short, rather fat little man almost enveloped in a large black cape, an excellent camouflage against the dark rocks. We struggled along the steep path, slipping and sliding, grabbing hold of anything that would help to pull us along. It was now definitely colder and a keen wind added to the discomfort. At times the track appeared almost vertical. The women and old men of the refugee party were feeling the strain, and we had almost to carry the old men along. The oldest man asked us to leave him behind, but, of course, we could not do that, and we struggled on as best we could.

'"Coneyack's" bottle was now empty, and the "Crown Jewels" seemed to weigh a ton, but we had reshuffled the baggage, and I now had two to share my burden with. The new help was "Thunderbolt", an American pilot whom we had nicknamed after the aircraft he flew.

'Only a short stop was made during the next day, as we were now in a dangerous area, and it was thought best to push on and get clear. About midnight we almost ran into a German patrol. Some of our party said they heard them talking. We hid among the rocks until they had passed. Then on again. Early in the morning our guide informed us we were now in Spanish territory. We all cheered, and with renewed effort pushed on to the limit of our endurance. Unfortunately, the "Crown Jewels" had been lost during the night. Thunderbolt had dropped them over a precipice, whether by accident or design we shall never know; but none of the carriers was sorry. I am sure, however, that the bag did contain something valuable, for the owner offered a large sum of money to the guide to go back and recover it. He refused. Possibly he may have thought to recover the bag at his leisure, but for all we know it is still somewhere in the mountains.

'Snowdrops were now frequently met with and an icy wind tore through our tattered, sodden clothing, but we were winning through. Early the next morning one of the Spanish frontier guard mountain patrols caught up with us and arrested us for illegal entry into Spain. After rounding us up, they marched us off to a small village on the mountainside. The gaol was not large enough to hold us all, so we were ordered into the courtyard and then each called up to be searched.

'Towards evening we were sent to another village and were lodged for the night in the loft of a large stable. It was very cold and our clothing was still damp and rather uncomfortable, but we huddled together for warmth and tried to sleep. At about 10 o'clock two of the guards entered bearing a large saucepan of boiled potatoes, our first meal on Spanish soil. The women members of the party had been lodged in a small hotel, as well as one of the old men. We remained in the loft until the next afternoon, when we were sent to the nearest town, and lodged in the gaol. Here we remained until released through the intervention of the British consul.

'While further proof of our identity was being sought, we were interned at a hotel in a nearby village: "Hotel Continental" we called it, for there were French, German, Dutch, American, and British all there together. We were allowed out of the hotel only for a distance of 200 yards, either up or down the main street.

'As a change from boiled potatoes, our diet was now wholly of beans – boiled, fried, and pickled. Having, however, been supplied with a little money by the Consul, we were able to supplement our food by frequent visits to a café just within bounds.

'It was during our stay here that we heard of the D-Day invasion, which we celebrated to the best of our ability. After a few days we left our French friends, and went as guests of the Spanish Air Force to another hotel some distance away. We had, by the way, now been fitted out with respectable clothing, and we were all feeling much better in health and spirits. Our stay there was rather short, however, and before very long we were sent to the British Embassy at Madrid.

'I was very pleased to see the Union Jack flying from the building and to know that I was almost on British soil again. We got a great welcome from the Ambassador and his staff, and we received new clothing and toilet necessities. A short interrogation took place, we were given money and cigarettes (the money was placed to our accounts: I was £26 in debt when I got home!), and then we were sent to a very nice hotel. We really had quite a good time for the next few days, attending, among other things, a bullfight, which was most exciting. We concluded our short holiday by having dinner, followed by a dance at the Embassy. All the staff turned out to see us leave for Gibraltar by the night mail, and they gave us a great send-off.

'It was late in the afternoon of the following day when we arrived at Gibraltar and we received a cordial welcome from the commanding officer and the intelligence officer. The latter relieved us of all souvenirs, identity cards, and the like that we had collected on our travels (incidentally, I had all mine returned to me after the end of the war), and, after a short address on "careless talk", etc., left us to amuse ourselves.

'The next evening, we flew home to England once more, this time in a York. We had a most comfortable journey, and landed just after dawn in the west of England at a Transport Command RAF station, in good time for a very belated English breakfast!'[7]

---

7  Jack may have had a second lucky escape, as there are accounts of a following group a day or so later being betrayed by their mountain guides, and a group of Jewish refugees being murdered by a German patrol. After 550 Squadron said cheerio to him, Jack went on to his next adventure with 228 Squadron Coastal Command crewing Sunderlands at RAF Pembroke Dock in Wales, chasing U-boats and E-boats in the Atlantic. He would see out the war there, being released in January 1946.

# Chapter 6

# With the Maquis

*'I spent my early years beneath the shadows of the cranes in the East End of London. I was born on 26 August 1922 in Poplar and went to school on the Isle of Dogs before going to Clarks College, Walthamstow. When the war started, I was about sixteen or seventeen and had just started work in a stockbroker's office in the City. During the Blitz we were bombed out of our house, so we moved up the road to East Ham and exactly a month later, what the first bomb hadn't done to our family's possessions, the second one did. My parents more or less lost everything. Being from a fairly tough area, we were brought up to fight back. I naturally wanted to go into Bomber Command and joined the RAF at the outset of 1941 and was sent to Canada for training as a navigator. By September 1943, having already completed a tour of 30 operations in Stirling heavy bombers and been awarded the DFC, I was posted with my crew for another type of 'bash' with 138 Squadron dropping supplies and SOE agents from converted Halifax bombers to ground parties in occupied Europe.*

Flying Officer Reginald 'Reg' William Lewis spent most of 1942 on bombing operations on XV Squadron flying the Stirling. He and his crew completed 30 operations at a time when only about 25 per cent of crews survived so many missions. Due for a rest tour, he and the others on the crew had formed such a strong team that when their captain, 23-year-old Squadron Leader Tom C. Cooke DFC AFC DFM, offered the possibility of flying the Halifax on 138 Special Duties Squadron all of them volunteered. He and Cooke (who was on his third tour) and the others arrived at Tempsford on 10 September 1943 and had completed fifteen operations when, on 7 February 1944, on Operation 'Jockey 5', the seven-man crew were told that they must drop an agent and a quantity of supplies 'at all costs' to the Resistance network organised by Lieutenant Colonel Francis Cammaerts. Born in London and raised in Radlett in Hertfordshire, the 6ft tall son of Professor Emile Cammaerts, a Belgian poet and Tita Brand, a successful actress, began extensive training with SOE in October 1942. He was given the rank of captain and the code name 'Roger' and flown into occupied northern France in March 1943. Cammaerts was assigned to the 'Donkeyman' circuit, then operating in the upper Rhône Valley. After discovering that 'Donkeyman' had been penetrated, he moved to Saint-Jorioz in the mountains of Savoy and set up his own circuit ('Jockey'). In the later part of 1943, he established several small semi-autonomous groups, all part of his 'Jockey' circuit.[1]

'Tempsford was a very hush-hush place – the only airfield in the country from which the two special duties squadrons operated – 138 Squadron and 161 Squadron. Churchill was responsible for the formation of the Special Operations Executive (SOE), after the fall

---

1   Thomas Charles Seymour Cooke was born in Southsea, Portsmouth, on 23 July 1921. He joined the RAF as war began in 1939, aged 18, and trained to be a bomber pilot. Rising to the rank of squadron leader and decorated three times, Cooke bombed Berlin on 7 October 1940 in a Whitley Mk. V, nearly ditching in the North Sea. Throughout this tour he faced the usual dangers of wartime aircrew, his aircraft being hit by AA fire on several occasions, once almost having to order his aircrew to bail out but landed safely at the last minute. They were also attacked by night fighters, encountered icing and even shot up a train and bomber station at tree-top level. Flying Wellingtons and Stirlings, Cooke took part in the famous 1,000-bomber raids on Cologne and Essen. See *Flying Among Heroes: The Story of Squadron Leader T. C. S. Cooke DFC AFC DFM Ae*: by Norman Franks and Simon Muggleton. (The History Press Ltd, 2012).

of France. Basically, his instruction was to set Europe ablaze and that really meant encouraging fighters throughout the enemy-occupied countries. The only way to do that was to infiltrate skilfully trained agents, saboteurs and suchlike into the Continent; to instruct the local people in the use of arms and supply them with everything they'd need to inflict damage on the enemy and eventually to train them to form some sort of fighting force. Of course, we did also drop the odd spy. On 5 November that same year we went into Germany, which was very unusual, to drop someone, God only knows who he was, but he was wearing a Luftwaffe uniform. I never found out what happened to him. You had to be careful taking these people around. You couldn't just drop them anywhere, but into a precise corner of a field if required.

'Unbeknown to us, of course, the "D-Day" landings weren't far away and it was important that we got a number of agents into France to organise the Resistance and cause as much havoc as possible for the Germans. Our squadron had been trying to drop one agent in particular – I think they'd had about two or three goes. Eventually on 7 February 1944 we were called together by the Station Commander, Group Captain Edward "Mouse" Fielden,[2] Captain of the King's Flight, who said, "You're taking this man" - his code name was "Roger" – "You're going tonight. He's got to be dropped to on the outskirts of Marseilles."

'We took off in our Halifax at 1930 hours, in absolutely bloody awful weather. It was foul, dreadful rain. We went straight into cloud

---

2 Fielden's discretion and self-effacement earned him the nickname 'Mouse'. His association with the Royal Family began in 1929, when the then Prince of Wales, who had acquired a Gipsy Moth, appointed Fielden as his personal pilot. In October 1933, the Prince appointed Fielden as his Chief Air Pilot and Extra Equerry. On 21 July 1936 Fielden was appointed Captain of the King's Flight. He was charged with the carriage not only of members of the Royal Family, but also members of the Air Council and other important state personages. He was promoted to wing commander in 1936. In early 1942 he took command of 161 Squadron at Tempsford. In October 1942 he was promoted to group captain and assumed command of Tempsford.

and had to resort to dead reckoning, hoping the cloud would break later on. We got down into central France, where the ground gets rather high and flying in cloud, in winter, we iced up. Eventually the starboard outer overheated and caught fire so we feathered the starboard outer, starving the fire of fuel. This meant we were on three engines, still battling against the ice. It wasn't very long before the port inner went. We were losing height and tossing overboard things to try and lighten the load, but it was obvious that we weren't going to deliver the agent we were carrying to the appointed dropping point; we didn't know who he was, but we knew he was important. He bailed out but it wasn't long before our pilot, "Cookie", said, "we'll have to abandon aircraft." It was about 11.30. I'd thought it would never happen to me – we thought we were fireproof!

'I was the first one out and the flight engineer [Flying Officer Leonard John (Len) Gornall] was soon after me. I can still remember that awful crack as you tumble over and the parachute opens. Then I was dangling in eerie silence. I heard my wireless operator calling out, "Rocky" – that was my nickname. Anyway, I got down a bit further and all I could see was this great expanse of water. I thought, "Christ! Just our luck – we're all going to perish in some bloody frozen lake!" But as it was, it was an illusion – vapour or fog, or something. In fact, I landed in deep snow.

'It was a mountainous area, out in the sticks and very cold. I buried my parachute and then I tramped off across the snowbound fields. It wasn't long before I came to a house, all shuttered up in true French style. I thought it was a bit silly to knock at the first place I came to, so I walked on, but there was nothing else in sight. It was desolate. I was somewhere in the hills above the Rhône Valley, very wild, rugged country. I went back to the house and banged on the door and a little old lady's face appeared. I was standing there in flying kit. They hadn't taught me much French back in Poplar, but I had a smattering and I tried to explain that I was English, in the RAF – which frightened the daylights out of her. You see, it wasn't unknown for the Germans to dress up, to try to crack these underground groups in the Resistance areas. And the French knew that if they were caught sheltering airmen, it was all up for them – concentration camp at least. They were taking great risks. But to her lasting credit, she took me in. She had a daughter who was probably twenty. There were no men in the house, they'd been sent off to do war work for the Germans. I was knackered, worn out. Just before I fell asleep, I thought about my mother whom I had kidded I had a job flying VIPs around England. I thought, "Now, tomorrow morning she's going to get that nasty telegram, saying that her darling, darling boy is missing." And that upset me greatly.

'In the morning when I woke there was another young lady there and she did speak a bit of English, so I was able to find out where I was – actually a few miles north-east of Valence. Meanwhile, the old girl had disappeared. They said she'd gone for help, but I wondered if she'd gone to turn me in. I was very worried; she was away for such a long time. She came back, though, with a man, both riding bicycles and we had lunch. People were starving in France, but somehow, they rushed up this food. I made them all laugh because I asked if it was horse meat. My mother had told me that was all the Froggies ate! After lunch they produced a brown serge suit and a pair of shoes. The old lady's husband must have been a big man because his suit went over the top of my battledress. Then I was told to go with the man on the bicycle. We cycled for what seemed an eternity. We went down this bloody mountain through the snow, on and on and eventually came to a village called Saint-Donat. We went into the pharmacy – the name on the outside, "Jean Chancel", stuck in my mind.

'The next day I was taken to a greengrocer's shop nearby and within two days I was together with three other members of my crew – the rear gunner [Flying Officer R. L. Beattie RCAF], the bomb aimer [Pilot Officer E. Bell] and the wireless operator [Flying Officer J. S. Reed].

'We were then taken to a barn. We were there with some tough-looking guys, with guns – members of the Resistance. And after a while, in walks a captain in the full uniform battledress of the American

*Right*: Flight Sergeant Frank Ellison Gatland DFM MiD, on 214 Squadron.

*Below*: A Short Stirling I on 214 Squadron, the type flown by Frank Gatland's crew at Stradishall, Suffolk, in July 1942.

*Left*: Countess Andrée Eugénie Adrienne de Jongh (aka Dédée ('little mother' and also known as 'Postman') and her father, Frédéric de Jongh (aka 'Kiki') of the Belgian Resistance, who organised and led the 'Comete' line, assisting Allied soldiers and airmen to escape from Nazi-occupied Belgium. Frédéric de Jongh was executed on 28 March 1944 by a German firing squad.

*Below*: Flight Lieutenant Edgar Alfred Costello-Bowen and his navigator, Sergeant 'Tommy' Broom.

*Above*: Squadron Leader 'Tommy' Broom with Wing Commander Ivor Broom (no relation), aka 'The Flying Brooms' – who later in the war completed 58 operations (21 to Berlin) in 8 Group Pathfinder Force.

*Right*: Captain Benjamin Hodkinson Cowburn MC, leader of the SOE 'Tinker Circuit' supporting the Resistance in the Troyes area of France.

*Left*: Sergeant John C. Tweed, the 2nd pilot on Halifax 'M-Mother' on 138 Special Duties Squadron at Tempsford, which Squadron Leader C. G. 'Robbie' Robinson DFC was flying on 12/13 May 1943 on a supply-dropping trip to the Resistance when it was shot down.

*Below*: HM King George VI and HM Queen Elizabeth speaking to American Carpetbagger personnel during a visit to RAF Tempsford.

Westland Lysander army co-operation and liaison aircraft, which in August 1941 began use with a new squadron (138, Special Duties) to undertake flights into occupied France for the Special Operations Executive (SOE) to pick up Allied airmen who had been sent down the escape and evasion lines.

Second Lieutenant 'Ed' F. Pollock (kneeling left) and his crew of B-17 *Weidner's Wildcat* in the 385th Bomb Group, which crashed yards from Lake Sneekermeer, Offingawier in Holland, on 11 December 1943 on a raid on Emden.

Tiny Mulder, one of the many brave members of the underground movements responsible for the escape lines out of Holland and into Belgium and France.

Crew of the *Salvo Sal* in the 350th Bomb Squadron, 100th Bomb Group, who were shot down on 8 October 1943. Kneeling from left; William McDonald, pilot; John James, co-pilot; Carl Spicer, navigator; and Frank McGlinchey, bombardier: Standing from left: Charles Ashbaugh, engineer/top turret gunner; Victor Intoccia, waist gunner; Fred Pribish, radio operator; Douglas Agee, waist gunner; Ross Detillion, ball turret gunner, and Paul Sears, tail gunner. James and Pribish were hospitalised and became PoWs. Ashbaugh, Intoccia, Detillion and Sears were also taken prisoner. McDonald and McGlinchey were captured much later at a border post in the Pyrenees. Spicer arrived safely in Gibraltar.

*Right*: Sergeant John Goffin 'Jack' Pearce, the 30-year-old mid-upper gunner on Warrant Officer T. A. 'Lofty' Lloyd's crew on 550 Squadron at Killingholme, who were shot down on the Mailly-le-Camp raid on 3/4 May 1944. (Chris Cole)

*Below*: Lancaster silhouetted over Mailly-le-Camp during the raid on the night of 3/4 May 1944.

Post-raid reconnaissance of Mailly-le-Camp.

Warrant Officer T. A. 'Lofty' Lloyd's crew on 550 Squadron at Killingholme, who flew the 3/4 May 1944 operation on Mailly-le-Camp. Back row L-R: Sergeant T. P. (Terry) Burke, Warrant Officer T. A. 'Lofty' Lloyd, Flying Officer Eddie Yaternick, Flight Sergeant D. M. 'Steve' Stephen. Front row, L-R: Sergeant R. L. G. 'Jumbo' Moore, Sergeant Jack Pearce, Sergeant Tony Constantine Crilley.

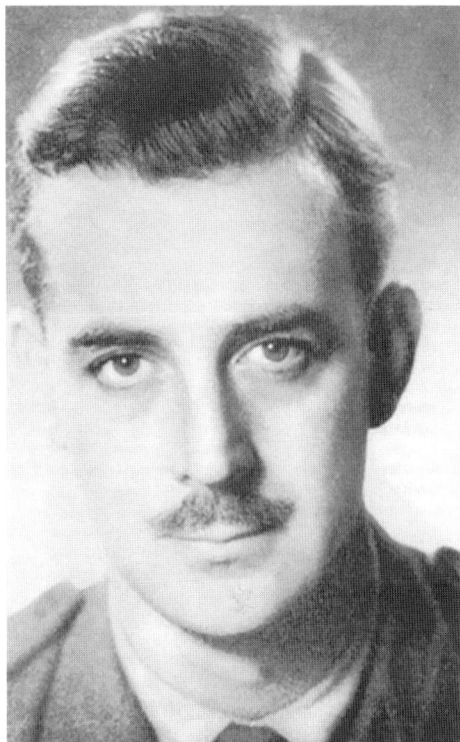

*Right*: Colonel Francis Cammaerts, who was assigned to the 'Donkeyman' circuit but it had been penetrated and he moved to Saint-Jorioz in the mountains of Savoy and set up his own circuit ('Jockey').

*Below*: Captain Pierre Ortiz of the American OSS.

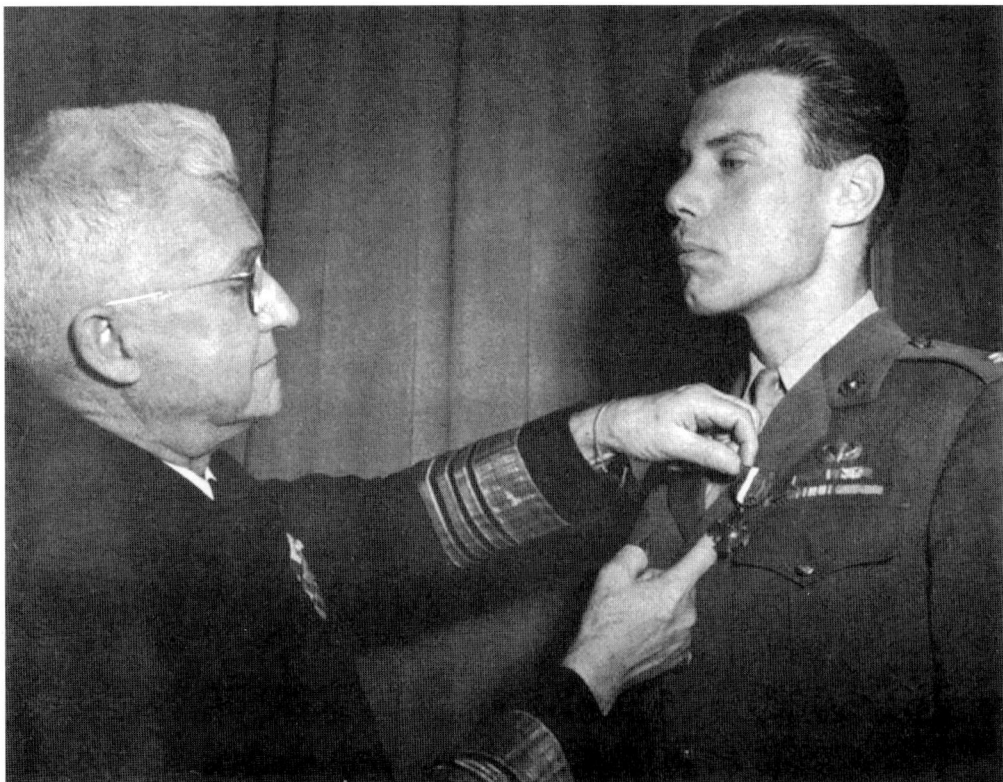

*Above left*: Flying Officer Reginald 'Reg' William Lewis.

*Above right*: Sergeant Harry Simister, flight engineer on Halifax II 'R-Roger' on 158 Squadron at Lissett, who had completed 20 operations when on 31 August 1943 he and the crew were one of four squadron aircraft shot down by night fighters on the Berlin raid.

Sergeant John Donald Brinkhurst, air gunner on Flight Lieutenant William Ian Adamson DFC's Lancaster crew on 101 Squadron, at Ludford Magna.

Crew of the *Squat n' Droppit* in the 448th Bomb Group, 8th Air Force.

B-24 Liberator *Squat n' Droppit.*

*Above left*: Ben Isgrig (left) and George Cooksey photographed in their French clothes at Little Rock, Arkansas, on their return to the USA. The rifles are German. (Isgrig)

*Above right*: Staff Sergeant Robert Starzynski, 367th Bomb Squadron, 306th Bomb Group, Thurleigh, England, in January 1944.

A Stirling on a SOE operation.

Five Lancasters on 115 Squadron at Witchford were lost on the night of 7/8 June 1944 (D-Day+1) when the target was a major road bridge between Chevreuse and Massy-Palaiseau. Pilot Officer John Todd and five of his crew (pictured) were killed in HK552.

Cinema poster advertising the British feature film *Frieda*, the storyline of which featured an RAF pilot who returns home from the war with his new bride, Frieda, a German girl who helps him escape from a prisoner-of-war camp. It is based on the true story of Donald Meese on 622 Squadron and 19-year-old Fräulein Ursula Hosier, who helped him escape from a prisoner-of-war camp and whom he later married.

Paratroops of 3rd Platoon, 21st Independent Parachute Company, assemble on the perimeter track at RAF Fairford, Gloucestershire, in front of Short Stirlings of 620 Squadron on the morning of 17 September at the start of Market Garden.

*Above left*: Flight Lieutenant 'Jimmy' Edwards, a Dakota pilot on 271 Squadron at Down Ampney, who towed a glider on the 17 September 1944 Market Garden operation and flew on successive days from the 18th to the 21st.

*Above right*: Dakotas heading for their drop zone.

Flight Lieutenant Geoff C. Liggins and air gunner Sergeant Walter T. Simpson, who evaded after they were shot down on Stirling LJ868/R during Market Garden on 19 September 1944.

Stirling LK545 *The Saint* on 299 Squadron, having dropped supplies during Market Garden on 21 September 1944, was hit by flak and was forced to belly-land near Beuningen, west of Nijmegen. With the help of the Dutch, six crew evaded capture and managed to reach their own lines, while two were taken prisoner. Today this fuselage part is kept safe in the Museum of the Dutch Aircraft Examination Group at Deelen airfield just north of Arnhem.

*Above*: de Havilland Mosquito B.IV ML963 of 692 Squadron based at Graveley, Huntingdonshire. B.IV MM184 on the same squadron was being flown on 14 October 1944 by Flying Officer Francis Humphrey Dell and his navigator, Flying Officer Ronald Arthur Naiff when they failed to return.

*Left*: Flying Officer Francis Humphrey Dell.

Marines. He had hand grenades strapped to him, knife, guns; every bloody thing! A real tough guy. He was Pierre Ortiz of the American OSS, who had been walking around France in his uniform.[3] He was highly suspicious of us and most unfriendly. He took our details and said, "Look, you're going to be kept under control by these men." And by golly they went everywhere with us.

'One false move and I'm quite sure we would have been dispatched. The next day Ortiz came in again and he said, "Well, I've been in touch with London. I'm reasonably satisfied that you're who you say you are, but there's nothing I can do for you for the moment." The next night we were taken up into the hills to a sort of logging camp; we were in with the Maquis. We could sit outside and look down at a German airfield in the valley. Their Storches used to hover around during the day – I suppose they were trying to see what the Maquis were up to. Now and again Ortiz would come up – always in his bloody uniform – he'd take us down to the village, for schnapps and back up again. Very disciplined. He told us the sort of things he'd been doing – such as tying this rope between two trees across the road to pull a German motorcyclist off his bike before they shot him. He really was a soldier of fortune. He brought us some money, shaving tackle, all that sort of thing. He looked after us very well.

'Not all the Maquis we were with were reliable. Apparently one of them had had a few drinks too many in the village and shot his mouth off about the RAF chaps up in the camp. Fortunately, somebody fed the information back to us. The Maquis held a court martial for this chap and they shot him. We felt quite bad about it, because we knew it was through us being there that all this had happened.

'They were only youngsters, really, these boys. At the end of an evening, we used to have sing-songs – all Communist songs, mind you. One night, we were woken up by flashing torches. Ortiz was

---

3 Major (later Colonel) Pierre Julien Ortiz served in both North Africa and Europe throughout the war, as a member of the Office of Strategic Services, operating behind enemy lines several times.

there, in his uniform, saying, "The Germans are coming. They're on their way!" He drove us about thirty miles south, to the home of a village doctor, Doctor Sambuc in La Paillette just outside Dieulefit, east of Montélimar, further down the Rhône Valley. By then, we'd noticed that Ortiz was no longer wearing a captain's three pips, but a major's crown. He'd been promoted. One of our own squadron aircraft had dropped the crown with some supply packages for the Maquis. Incredible!

'Doctor Sambuc had been an army medical officer in French Indo-China, but he'd retired and settled down in this village. Well, we stayed there for three weeks, never went out. I hadn't changed my clothes since baling out. We were lousy. We slept two to a bed – and we were always hungry. But somehow the doctor's wife found food for us; her stockpot was constantly on the go. They had two nieces, girls of about eighteen, who used to practise their English on us. We had to behave ourselves, with the old girl hopping around. The doctor's surgery was downstairs and people were in and out all day, including the local kids who came here for Sunday school. It all went on with four RAF airmen upstairs; the family was understandably terrified and very brave. There was no sign of Ortiz. We thought we were there for the duration and it was embarrassing because, apart from the danger, Mademoiselle Sambuc had to feed us. We did have our escape maps, of course, folded silk maps, and were studying the area, so we could break out and take a chance. We knew the only way back home was to get down to the Spanish border and into Gibraltar.

'After about three weeks, when we'd given him up, Ortiz arrived one Saturday evening. "You're off tomorrow," he said. He duly came and we motored all the way to Valence, right through this damned great town – with him still in his khaki uniform, with his crowns and guns and everything else. He took us to a little terraced house and said, "I'll come for you this evening and I'll take you to Valence station. You'll only have tickets, no travel passes or anything, but I'll explain what you've got to do." When it was dark, he took us to the station, put us in the waiting room and said, "Separate. Scatter yourselves about. At 10 o'clock a train will come in. Get into the same carriage, but sit in separate corners. It's a full night's train ride and the Germans sometimes check the train for passes. If they do, I'm afraid you've had it unless you can bluff your way out. I'll be on the train too, keeping an eye on you."

'So, off we went and as the hours ticked by the waiting room filled up with people. It was a babbling mass of humanity by the time the train came in. Ortiz had told us not to board until the last minute so we made our rush along this blacked-out platform – straight into a couple of German officers – knocked them arse over tit! We didn't wait. Thank God we didn't say "sorry" or something like that! We found an empty carriage, sat down, went right through the night without any interruption at all. As daylight came, we pulled into a station. To our horror on the platform were about 200 German troops. As they boarded our carriage, we thought, "Christ, what's going to happen now?" But thank God, they couldn't speak French. They even offered us cigarettes. We just bluffed our way, quite frightened. Fortunately, they got off again after another station or two.

'We reached Carcassonne at about 9 o'clock in the morning. Ortiz came in and said, "You'll make contact with a priest on the platform." And sure enough, there was a priest on the platform. He took us on a two-track, two-carriage electric train and after an hour or so we got out at a village up in the foothills of the Pyrénées and we stayed in a house there until nightfall. Then we walked all night, through disused railway tunnels, past waterfalls. We walked for hours. It was very tiring. We weren't fit; we'd been doing nothing for six weeks.

'At about 6 o'clock in the morning we passed a field where there was a bonfire. We walked towards it and as we got nearer, we could see a crowd of people. Suddenly we heard an American voice. There were a lot of Americans there, airmen who'd been shot down doing daylight raids on Bordeaux and had somehow been filtered into this area. There were people on the run from every corner of Europe: Czechs, Poles, Greeks, a right unholy mixture. We spent the day round the bonfire and in the evening, we started walking. We'd been given a couple of loaves of bread in a brown carrier bag and a great hunk of roast meat, so we guessed, correctly as it turned out, that some serious walking lay ahead for us.

'We walked for the next week with only one night's rest. We walked and we walked and we walked. I was the only one of the crew who'd kept his escape pack with him when we bailed out. It was a plastic container, with a bit of chocolate, condensed milk, that sort of thing … but it also had this wonderful drug, Benzedrine. And I was taking these tablets – to keep me awake. But, suddenly, after three days I ran out of them. I took a nosedive and collapsed. The guides more or less decided to leave me on the mountainside, because they were in a hurry. But, and I learned this afterwards, my Canadian rear gunner persuaded them to give me another chance. I had a rest and was able to carry on. You kept climbing ridges and each time you got to the top you'd see another bloody great ridge in front of you, but eventually, right in the middle of one climb – it was about midnight – this Spaniard said, "Now, rush for it!" And we rushed and staggered up this ridge and he said, "You're in Spain." And that was a wonderful feeling. We'd made it.

'Of course, we didn't know that it was another two days' walking the other side before we'd reach civilisation. Still, we found an old farm where we slept in with the sheep. We were absolutely knack-ered, but delighted. On the Sunday afternoon a lorry arrived, an open-backed truck, and we all clambered in. They threw a tarpaulin over us and after about three hours that was brutal to our backsides, it stopped. Somebody said the English must get off and we got off. There in front of us was a door with a brass plate on it, which said: British Consulate, Barcelona. Marvellous! We had lovely showers and they gave us new shirts and vests, shoes and socks. They put us up in a flat with a Spanish family who had a beautiful daughter. We had to draw lots for the one who'd go out with her that evening. The bloody Canadian went off with her – as he would – Beattie was the best-looking one anyway! We spent two nights in comfort. Then, one morning, a huge car drove up with Union Jack flag on the wing and we were driven to the Embassy in Madrid. Sir Samuel Hoare, the ambassador, and Lady Hoare gave us a marvellous welcome. We stayed there a week or two, while they got false papers for us. We couldn't go out, but we had haircuts and a bath every day.

'Eventually we were given our passes and put on the train one evening in Madrid. At 8 o'clock we arrived at La Linea. They'd told us that we'd see the Spanish workers, all waiting for the gates to open so that they could get into Gibraltar to do their day's work. We went through the gates with these Spaniards and reported to the Air Force station. Marvellous moment! They got us into bloody uniforms straightaway – battledress, no insignia of ranks, they hadn't got any hats. Our nice Spanish clothes disappeared. They said, 'Right, you can go into town.' Well, we had a few beers and were immediately arrested by the military police for not having hats and carted straight back to camp! We spent a couple of days there and then eventually, at 0030 on 12 April 1944, we flew back to RAF Lyneham, squashed into a Liberator, while German generals – prisoners of war of course – occupied the posh seats upstairs.'

A few days after Lewis had bailed out over France, it was announced that he had been awarded a DFC. He was no doubt gratified to learn that all seven crew members – including Flying Officer A. B. Withecombe, the mid-upper gunner – had successfully evaded and were safe too.

Reg Lewis never forgot those in France who had helped him, and for several years he tried to trace them. Eventually, with the aid of the RAF Escaping Society, he managed to identify one of his key helpers and locate his relatives. In 1970 he set off to seek out his French friends, but tragedy struck when he was involved in a car crash that killed his wife, Joyce, and left him with severe injuries.

Determined to succeed in his quest, however, two years later he joined a party of fellow escapers travelling to France and eventually he located Madame Giraudin, the lady who had first given him shelter. After meeting others, he remarked, 'So many people had risked their lives to help me, it meant everything that I could finally thank them in person.'

# Chapter 7

# Bail out over Berlin

*Sergeant Harry Simister, the flight engineer on Pilot Officer Kenneth Ward's crew on Halifax II 'R-Roger' on 158 Squadron at Lissett, was just short of his 20th birthday when he joined the RAF in April 1940. He had completed 20 operations with 158 Squadron when his tour suddenly came to an abrupt halt on 31 August 1943, when about two thirds of the 47 aircraft that were lost were shot down over Berlin by night fighters. No. 158 Squadron was particularly badly hit, losing four Halifaxes.*

'The briefing had not been unusual and take-off was at 2100 hours,' wrote Simister. His thoughts then were more with his mother. She had just received a telegram from the Air Ministry telling her that his brother, a navigator on Beaufighters, serving in the Mediterranean area, was missing.

'The trip out was uneventful and we arrived over Berlin at 2330 hours, right on time. The old "Hallybag" lurched upwards as our bombs fell away. Then all of a sudden, we came under attack from a German night fighter. The port engines were set on fire and the controls were shot away. "Ken" Ward cried: "Bail out, bail out." We'd gone through practices like this, with the hangar floor only feet below. This time it was for real. The sky outside was lit up by the searchlights, the fires and the tracer bullets. We were all calm as we lined up to jump out into the dark void. My parachute billowed out and pulled me roughly out of my free fall. Below me the bombs burst with deep "crumphs" and the fires seemed to cover the earth. As I glided down, I noticed the smoke from the fires was drifting away from the fires. At least I wouldn't be roasted alive.' Simister landed in a field about 5 miles south of Berlin. It was just before midnight.

Ward and Pilot Officer Alfred Percy Arnott, the air bomber, and Sergeant Thomas Lockerbie Craven, the mid-upper gunner, died on the aircraft. 'Seconds earlier and the whole crew would have perished – instead of only three,' wrote Sergeant Ronald Arthur Thurston, the wireless operator. 'Bailing out of a blazing bomber over Berlin could possibly be described as "bailing out of Hell, into Hell". No evasive action can possibly be carried out on a bombing run. To bail out of a blazing bomber, still under attack, with two engines on fire and completely out of control, coned by the searchlights amongst over 600 bombers dropping bombs from various heights, night fighters, flares and bursting shells from anti-aircraft guns gave more thoughts of the extreme danger when the parachute opened and gently drifted away from the nightmare of the target.

'Thoughts in the dark and dangerous sky of the fate of the rest of the crew. How many had been killed in this Hell? You look around in the darkness for parachutes – you see nothing. The searchlights sweep the sky as if looking for you – assisting the night fighters in their attack. You watch with fascination the blazing target, the explosions of the bombs and the retaliation of the anti-aircraft guns, with little thought of the danger of the thousands of tons of flak in the air. You wonder if the tracer bullets you see are coming from an air gunner's turret or from an enemy fighter attacking another bomber. You watch with dismay a blazing bomber plunging to earth and wonder if anyone got out. Your parachute now seems to be going up instead of coming down and you feel slightly sick with the swaying. You begin to wonder what height you are when you see a night fighter only a little way above you and how long and where will you hit the ground? Will you be shot when you are in the hands of the enemy or shown mercy as a PoW? All these thoughts as you slowly, alone and completely helpless descend into the unknown. Your face feels wet with perspiration – or is it raining? You feel a little numb in this dark unreal world and wonder if you are dreaming. The crunch of an anti-aircraft shell nearby reminds you that you are not, as the bombing continues. You listen to the humming engines of the bombers. Some will be shot down on the way home – perhaps over the sea. All the way back to the English coast – and sometimes inland – they will be pursued by determined enemy night fighters with their excellent radar and equally brave pilots eager to be credited with the destruction of another bomber. The bomber crews are alert to all this and do not relax for one moment. As you are mesmerised by the red glow in the sky from the fires, observing the flashes from the anti-aircraft guns and the shell bursts in the sky, you begin to think of your loved ones at home. In a few hours they will receive that dreaded telegram, which they have been expecting ever since you started operational flying – Regret to inform you that your ..." and you begin to wonder when and if you will ever see them again.'[1]

'Ron' Thurston, William Nicholas Avery, the rear gunner, and Norman John Stubbings, the navigator, were taken prisoner.

Simister quickly hid his parachute and remained in a wood for the night, and at dawn he removed his badges of rank and flying badge and also cut the tops off his flying boots, making them into shoes. Then for some three days it was a case of walking at night and hiding in woods during the day. On 3 September, Harry saw a bike leaning against the wall of an old farmhouse, so he stole it and then cycled towards Brandenburg, but turned off before reaching there and set off in a north-westerly direction. Once again spending the night in the woods, he set off the next day, passing through Schwerin, and then took the main road for the port of Lübeck, which he reached that night.

When morning came he made for the docks and began looking for neutral ships and found a Swedish vessel guarded by a sentry. He walked straight past him, up the gangplank, without pausing.

---

1 *Into the Silk* by Ian Mackersey (Robert Hale, 1956).

He went into the galley, where he met six Swedes; showing them his cigarette case with RAF embossed on it, he was able to make them understand who he was. He was given a meal and, discovering that one of the sailors could speak English, asked him if he could hide. Harry was told that the ship was not sailing until the next day and to come back then and take his chance. However, when he returned the next day, the ship had gone! Harry wandered about for the rest of the day looking for a likely ship but with none available he left the docks and that night slept in the wood.

On 7 September Simister decided to make for Rostock but there were no neutral ships there either so on the 9th he returned to Lübeck. He tried to buy some cigarettes but was told he needed coupons so he went into a public house and asked for a beer, handing over a 100 Franc note to cover the cost, and telling them he was Swedish. After some hesitation he got his beer! Seeing the proprietress sitting in a corner, Harry approached her and asked for food – up to this time he had been living on food tablets from his escape kit and stolen apples. She gave him some black bread to eat.

Returning to the docks, he saw a Swedish schooner. Once again, he walked past the guard without any problems and boarded the ship. However, finding all the doors locked, as the crew were ashore, he made his way to the wheelhouse and promptly fell asleep. He was later awakened by one of the returning crew; again, he showed the cigarette case and was given a meal. He found out from one of the crew who spoke English that they were not sailing for eight days, and that there was nowhere to hide on the ship. That night he slept in a bus shelter, and the following day, 10 September, decided to make for Holland on his bike. His route took him through Hamburg, Bremen and Osnabrück to Rheine, where he reached the river.

'On the way I had a puncture,' read his report, 'so I exchanged it with another one which was leaning against a wall of a cafe in a small village. On arrival at Rheine, I went to the railway station hoping to find a wagon bound for Holland. There were many people about and I had to be most careful not to be seen loitering around. As I was unable to find a wagon labelled for Holland, I went to the outskirts and spent the night there.'

On the 13th he cycled towards the Dutch–German border, where he saw passes etc being checked so he had to make a detour through a wood. By going over two fields, he finally got over the border into Holland. On the 16th, just before reaching the Belgian border, he stopped at a cafe in the village of Borkel Schaft, asked for something to drink and told them who he was. Louise, the girl in the cafe, went and told her mother, Madame Steenbergen, who supplied him with a civilian suit and put him in touch with the Resistance movement.

The next day a Dutchman named Frank Spee came and accompanied him on a bicycle across the border, where his brother, who was a guard, ensured that they wouldn't be stopped, to Exel. Here he stayed for three days, and then went on to Neerfelt, where he stayed with the Spooren family for about a week. It was here that he met Sergeant 'Reg' V. Wallace and was given a false ID card.

Wallace had bailed out over Holland the same night and had evaded from near Münster, on their way to Belgium. He was the flight engineer on 21-year-old Sergeant Edward Thomas Samuel Rowbottom's crew on Halifax II 'B-Bertie' on 102 Squadron at Pocklington. He and Sergeant John Kenneth Keele, his 19-year-old navigator, and three others on the crew were killed. Flight Sergeant 'Russ' Lloyd Collins RCAF, one of the air gunners, was taken prisoner.

Towards the end of September, Harry, together with Wallace, travelled by train with a female guide to Brussels via Antwerp and then to Virton, where they stayed for two weeks. On 13 October they entered France with a guide, walking over the border to Écouviez. From there they travelled by train to Nancy via Montmédy, where they stayed the night, then journeyed on the next day to Belfort and on to Montbéliard. The next day they walked to Audincourt and stayed the night; the next morning they went into the woods with a party of woodcutters and waited until evening. The two flyers were then taken to a guide who was waiting to take them over the border into Switzerland. Reaching Fahy, they were immediately arrested by

Swiss guards and spent two days in prison before being sent to Bern and the British Embassy.

Harry Simister recalls, 'We spent the time there living in a hotel. Then we were taken to a ski resort at Arosa, where the embassy had two chalets for escapers and evaders; almost all RAF aircrew. Here we spent most of the time skiing. In the summer season we went to Montreux in the Vevey region. Finally, in August 1944, we left Switzerland by climbing over the mountains to France. Once in France we stayed and fought with the Free French Forces and with their help we made contact with the Americans at Sisteron and hitch-hiked a lift to Saint-Raphaël on the Riviera. From there we had a "busman's holiday", flying to Naples, where we met the British Army, then to Tunis, Algiers, Oran and Casablanca. From here Coastal Command flew us to St Eval in Cornwall, landing one year and ten days after baling out over Berlin. (10 September 1944).'

In November 1944 Harry Simister was recommended for the Military Medal and this was gazetted on 19 February 1945. Simister's remarkable achievement was the one of the few morale boosts that Lissett was to receive, for 158 Squadron lost four crews on the raid, which brought their total to nine crews missing from two major attacks flown against the 'Big City' during August 1943.[2]

---

2 See *RAF Bomber Command Losses of the Second World War: 1943* by W. R. Chorley.

# Chapter 8

# Nuremberg No Return

*John Donald Brinkhurst was born in June 1921 at Wandsworth. He and his brother, John Derrick Brinkhurst, shared the same parents, Howard Marchant Brinkhurst and Cicely Cox, who married in June 1919 and lived in Slough. John Derrick Brinkhurst became a sergeant pilot on 106 Squadron at Syerston. He was killed in action aged 23 on the night of 21/22 December 1942 when he was the skipper on Lancaster R5914, which was attacked by a night fighter on the raid on Munich. Two others of his crew were also killed, but Flight Sergeant John Alexander Shepherd RNZAF, one of the four survivors (all of whom were taken prisoner of war), reported on the outstanding courage of his pilot. According to Shepherd, when Brinkhurst was told that the forward escape had jammed, he left the aircraft's controls and went into the Lancaster's nose, where the hatch was located, and released it. Returning to the cockpit, he held the Lancaster steady to enable those who could to escape. John Derrick Brinkhurst was awarded the DFM on 17 April 1945 with effect from 20 December 1942.*

It was February 1939 when 'Don' Brinkhurst first made up his mind to join up. On 13 June the 18-year-old was sworn into the RAF and posted to Scampton in Lincolnshire. When training finally started in full swing, he was given a rifle and did seven hours' drill each day. Pay was two shillings (10p) per day, but after deductions he ended up with only about ten bob (50p) a week. Mostly he walked to Lincoln 4½ miles away. Training lasted about three months, during which he had four days 'Grant', so when he was posted he felt 'pretty smart and thought he knew all the tricks'. After ground crew postings overseas, he re-mustered as an air gunner and finally, on 24 August 1943, a whole crew of sergeants arrived at Ludford Magna to find they had joined 101 Squadron in 1 Group, which was equipped with Lancasters. Their Scottish skipper, Flight Lieutenant William Ian Adamson DFC from Bathgate, West Lothian, did his 'second dickey' trip to Mannheim on 5/6 September and Brinkhurst and the rest of the Glaswegian's crew flew their first op the following night when the target was Munich.

'We were in the last wave and the kite would not climb too well being a very old kite, but the engineer said the engines were good and that sounded good to me. We soon found ourselves over Augsburg with too much flak for comfort and also not enough of our boys around. But we passed over and made Munich and dropped our bombs before "Jerry" paid us a visit by giving us a burst which passed under our port wing after the pilot had started a turn to starboard. He started doing a corkscrew and after about five minutes there were no more sign of the "Jerry" night fighter. Soon after some flak came up very close on our starboard and which made the old kite rock about like a leaf, so we went port and then got another lot under our starboard wing, which had us right at nerves' end.'

They finally landed at Ford and then the engines spluttered one by one, having been airborne for nine hours ten minutes on a trip that was to have taken seven and three-quarter hours and for which they had petrol for eight and a half hours!

'We were then given a new "kite" of our own – 'L-Love' DV264 – and she was the tops. There was never any trouble with her and she was always on the list for flying. The crew was a little different now from when we started ops and Sergeant Murray Cohen RCAF, a Jew and "a Yank", was the special operator.' He did two ops before we went on leave, but would not come with us, so he went with another crew and was shot down on Lancaster LM371 on the Berlin raid on the night of 29/30 December 1943. We came back from that leave and met Warrant Officer "Fred" Honey, our new special operator, who had ten more to do for his second tour. This chap was with me at Kabrit in North Africa and we got on together, so on our crew he was well liked. He flew on eight consecutive operations with us, from 14 January to 24 February 1944, and we managed to finish Fred off with 57 ops under his belt.' Flying Officer Norman Marrian (24), husband of Muriel O. Marrian of Chorlton-cum-Hardy, Manchester, took over from Honey on 25/26 February, when the target was Augsburg. Brinkhurst, who was approaching double figures, adds, 'On 15/16 March, when we had done 20 trips, he had 49 ops to his credit.'

The bomb aimer on the crew was Warrant Officer 2 Allan G. Hall RCAF of Kingston, Canada; the flight engineer was Flight Sergeant Norman Hugh Bowyer DFM, married to Dorothy Marianne Bowyer, of Shirley, Croydon, Surrey; the navigator was 23-year-old Pilot Officer Ernest McClure Kippen DFC of Edinburgh; the wireless operator was Flying Officer Leonard Ryland 'Luff' Luffman DFM of Bournemouth; and the rear gunner was 28-year-old Flight Sergeant James Alexander Goodall DFM of Banff, Scotland. All the DFM recipients had gained their awards for an operation one night in December 1943. Luffman's DFM was announced in *The London Gazette* of 25 January 1944 with the following citation: 'This airman was the wireless operator of an aircraft detailed for a sortie over enemy territory. Before the target was reached the aircraft was hit by shrapnel and the mid-upper gunner was wounded. Sergeant Luffman immediately went to his comrade's assistance, helping him to a rest position and then rendering first aid. Afterwards, he manned the wounded gunner's turret. Soon after leaving the target the aircraft was attacked by four fighters. Sergeant Luffman soon proved his skill by shooting down one of the enemy aircraft whilst his excellent evading directions enabled his pilot to out-manoeuvre the remainder of the attackers. During another sortie, some nights later, his aircraft was attacked by a Junkers 88. Once again Luffman co-operated well with his pilot, who successfully evaded the enemy aircraft. This airman has displayed great skill and his courage and resource have been of a high order.'

At about 1130 hours on Thursday, 30 March, Brinkhurst went out to 'L-Love' and did his D.I. [Daily Inspection]. 'She looked like a million with 33 bombs painted on her side and fifteen of them were Berlin trips. Also, she showed a couple of fighters shot down and at that time two DFMs, which is not a bad record for any aeroplane even as it was, she was the oldest kite on the Squadron and we were the oldest crew and so we more or less matched up very well.'

Brinkhurst was at a friend's house in Lincoln when he was told to report back to camp and also collect any of the crew that he could find. When the crew of 'L-Love' went to the Operations Room and found that the target was Nuremberg, 'Bill' Adamson, the Glaswegian skipper, who was on his last but one trip, looked worried. 'Normally he would have cracked a joke, as he hardly ever spoke without one; recalled Brinkhurst. 'That's what made him the pilot who I would have flown through hell with and known if there was one chance in a million of getting through, we would be through.

'We were due to take off first so we would have to be ready before the other crews. I rushed up to my billet as we were going to have an Air Test in the afternoon. In my hurry I only changed my shirt and slacks, in which, unfortunately, I carried my identity discs and my lucky button. So that was one thing that was off the record for us. Next was the fact that the crew's mascot had left Ludford and gone to Leeds to his father. His name was Bill and he was the funniest little boy I had ever seen and the crew thought the world of him.

'At about 2200 hours the CO came round and said take-off was put forward 15 minutes, so that meant we had to get in straight away and taxi out. Well, in this hurry we nearly all forgot the rear turret duty and so that made things look really blacker for me as I had just remembered that I had my best slacks on and nothing to show for identity if we were shot down. When we went along the runway, I felt lost and was glad when we were on our way across the Channel three quarters of an hour later and my mind was on my job and not on fate.

'Another thing, Mrs Robinson, where I had breakfast, was talking about people owing her money and how much she would be worth if she could only collect it all so I said: "Well, I owe you 55/-," and she said: "I am sure of getting yours as you get paid tomorrow." But a bird said to me: "That is a debt you will not pay off Mr Brinkhurst."'

The crew on 'L-Love' saw their first fighter just after crossing the Belgian coast and got out of its way. 'But soon after' says Don Brinkhurst. 'I saw about four of our chaps going down in flames and I knew this was going to be a bad night in the history of the RAF.[1] Soon after I saw the searchlights of the Ruhr Valley and decided we would make it to the target as we were missing fighters left and right. But I did not think long as the engineer said, "Bill, four-engined job ahead," and Bill said, 'Hold on. I'll dip my wings. Don and you can look underneath and see if there are any 'Jerry' fighters near." He dipped the port wing and all I heard was: "What the ----" from the engineer before the intercom packed up. But I could see what had happened as red tracer was passing my turret ten to the dozen and both port engines and all the cabin of our kite were on fire. I called the pilot and got no answer. So, there was only one thing to do and that was "Bail Out".'

Brinkhurst jumped out of his turret, grabbed his parachute and made for the rear, climbing up the side of the fuselage to do so and helping Norman Marrian out of his seat. He opened the door, made to jump out forward but found this impossible and so pushed himself off backwards. Before going he saw Jimmy Goodall, the rear gunner, and Marrian putting their thumbs up for OK. Brinkhurst could feel Marrian holding onto the back of his parachute harness and was sure

---

1 Seven Lancasters on 101 Squadron were lost this night. Of 795 aircraft dispatched, 95 bombers in all were lost, the heaviest Bomber Command loss of the war.

that he would follow him out. 'But after I left the kite, I don't know what happened to them,' recalled Brinkhurst. 'Jimmy was killed and Norman was still missing, believed killed. The special operator, possibly with a damaged parachute, landed in trees where he was found, dead, two days later. 'All the boys in the front were killed as far as I could make out. But somehow Ray and Allan Hall got clear.'

The poorly designed escape hatches on the Lancaster made it notoriously difficult to abandon and Norman Bowyer, the Canadian fight engineer, and the two Scots, Jim Goodall and Ernie Kippen, the wireless operator, were killed outright. They and Marrian are buried in Rheinberg War Cemetery, while Adamson, their Glaswegian skipper, is perpetuated on panel 204 of the Runnymede Memorial. Some accounts say that 'L-Love' was hit when a nervous Halifax tail gunner 300ft above them opened fire and raked the Lancaster with tracer but another claim is that 'L-Love' was shot down at 0012 by Oberleutnant Hans-Joachim Witzleb of 7./NJG1. Whatever, with wings tanks full of petrol and the bomb bay carrying incendiaries and high explosives, the burning bomber was doomed. 'L-Love' crashed near the small town of Gemünd, 5km north-north-east of Schleiden.

Brinkhurst had landed about 10 miles inside Germany. His crew had always agreed that, if shot down, the survivors would do their best to get home and contact the relatives of any crew member killed or injured. 'At 0015 I landed by my parachute at Köln in the Ruhr Valley and believe me I was frightened to death. At any moment I expected to see a German soldier come through the trees while I was getting off most of my flying clothes, because that few minutes from the time I left the kite until I had touched down on German soil was a thing that would unnerve any man and it had me at nerves' end. It was like a dream after you had left the kite because one minute the flames and the noise caused by the kite in a dive was tending to deafen you and the next minute you were in thin air without any noise in the least and you think you are dreaming, but when you hit the ground, you know it is not a dream but the horrible truth and then all that there is for you to do is to give yourself up or make for a neutral country.

'The first things I did was to hide my clothes and parachute, then get a direction and head for Belgium, which I worked out would take quite a few days as it was about 100 miles from where I was to the place where I wanted to get to. So off I went and soon found that I was going to have it hard, as there was quite a lot of snow around this part of the world. After I had walked about a mile, I heard two people in the wood by me. I lay down and tried to hear them speak, but I was unlucky and I am sure down at the bottom of my heart that it was Len Luffman and Allen Hall going down into the valley instead of away from it.

'Soon after I came to a house and a river. I walked as near to the house as I could to see if I could find a bike or something to ride, but was out of luck so I tried to find some way of crossing the river and I soon found some pipes crossing the river, so with one foot on one and the other on the other pipe I made my way across, while at any moment I expected to hear a rifle fire at me, but luck was with me and I got across safe and sound.

'It was 6 o'clock when I came to the edge of the forest and made my way slowly across a part of the country which was dotted with houses and in the distance a large village. I managed to get halfway across and about a mile from the village when I came upon a lot of people working in a field right in front of me. All I could do was to lie low and think of what to do next. I got out my rations and checked over them to see what I had and also looked over my maps and tried to make up my mind what town in Belgium I would make for, so I picked Mons and left it at that, hoping that I would soon reach some place and know where I was for certain.

'It was about 6 o'clock that night before they moved off and I was able to carry on, but I was lucky that a courting couple I passed laid in the field did not recognise me as English. Soon after I hit the forest again and it was about midnight before I hit the main road and started down it towards Belgium. I had to dive into hedges every so often when I saw a car coming along the road or when I heard somebody coming.

'Soon after I came to a large village and made up my mind to walk through it and see what I could and hoping that not too many people were on the roads at this time of night. Well, I got the impression that the Germans are "night owls" as the village was alive with people. I did not manage to get the name of the village, which was a disadvantage for me as it meant that I would have to try again to find where I was so when I came across an old lady and young girl about half a mile out of the village, I asked them where I was. I was told something in German which meant nothing to me but which I pretended I knew and just carried on down the road and then turned first left when I was out of sight, in case they sent some German soldiers after me.

'After about an hour I came to a river after just coming down a very steep hill, so when I walked downstream a little way and came across a factory, I made up my mind that all I could do is to go upstream and try to find a bridge to cross. Before I had gone a little way upstream I found that there was a power house with German guards on the bridge, so that only left me one thing to do and that was to cross the river between the factory and the power house and so, in the end, I made up my mind to cross the waterfall which was just below the power house and so over I went, but two or three times I thought that I would be swept over and into the rushing river with all the rocks just hidden under the surface of the water. But I made the other side and hid while I emptied all the water out of my flying boots and my clothes etc. I then made my way up the steep hill and then over the railway onto a lane which I started to walk along, but soon found that my clothes were freezing on me and that I was finding it harder to walk. So, when I came to a small village soon after I found an old empty house and so I went into this and climbed up into the roof and took off my wet clothes and with some old clothes in the house tried to get some sleep, but it was very hard as I had very few clothes to keep me warm.

'When daylight came, I put my clothes on the tile boards so that the sun – what little it was! – would dry them. But, although they were out there all day, they did not dry up and so when, at 8 o'clock that night, I started on my way again they were still very wet and it did not make me feel very happy while walking. I soon reached a main road after leaving the village and soon found myself going along the road for mile after mile and then, when I thought I would never reach any towns or villages, I came upon a place which looked like a large village. But after I had entered and started walking through, I found that I was in a large town [probably Eupen, 30km east of Liège] and I began to get worried as I could hear everyone speaking German and, with my flying clothes on, it did not make me feel happy. After I had gone halfway through the town, I made up my mind that this was no place for me and I started to walk faster and then had the fright of my life as two German soldiers came out of a driveway and came towards me, but I just carried on and hoped for the best. Luck was with me as all they did was to laugh at me and make a remark and I laughed back and carried on as fast as I could.'

Without being seen, Brinkhurst crossed a bend in the heavily guarded railway to Herbesthal and, with his luck still with him, headed for Henri-Chapelle, managing to cross the Berwinne River between two German patrols, again without being seen. His stomach wracked with pain from eating raw potatoes, the first help he received came from a Belgian farmer at Feneur, a short distance south-west of the village of Dalhem, a dozen kilometres north-east of Liège. He had by now been on the ground for eighty-two hours and had walked 58km. He approached 'a very fat lady at an isolated farmhouse who was putting out her washing'.

Brinkhurst got to Dalhem on 2 April after he had 'walked for four days' and stayed with a Monsieur Toussaint, Rue du Soldat Felix Delhaes, Dalhem 'while ill and waiting for the White Army' or l'Armée Blanche, the collective name for the organised Belgian Resistance. On or about 5 April he left Monsieur Toussaint, moving to the house of English-speaking Madame Zalesky, headmistress of a local school in Dalhem. On his 23rd birthday on 17 April Madame Zalesky gave him a grand party. According to Brinkhurst, she 'had invited members of the Resistance to attend, including her niece. But when the girl arrived next day and said she was going to Liège to see a film at a cinema and the time then was just after 7.30 pm I knew she was not telling the truth, as I had visited Liège with a man who was acting as my interpreter because I needed photographs for my identity card and for the questions which the Resistance people required to check on each person who passed through their Group. It took us 45 minutes by the tram-cum-train, which took us through all the small villages en route. When we arrived, it was a ten-minute walk to the centre where the cinemas were so if she was going to see a film and get back to Dalhem and pick up her cycle and ride to her village, which was 3km away, by 10 o'clock curfew, then all she could see was at the most 30 minutes, which I am sure she would not go so far for for such a short time.'

Brinkhurst spoke about his misgivings to Joseph Bovy, another member of the Resistance, who lived at Rue Henri Francotte 211, Dalhem, and said that when the niece returned to pick up her bicycle, he was going to leave the school in which he was hiding and go back to the farm at Feneur. Bovy advised him against doing this, as the farmer was not a member of the Resistance: 'So in the end he asked his parents if I could stay in his home, which they did with open arms.'

They were in for shock at 0430 one morning when the German security police raided the homes of all the people who had been at Brinkhurst's birthday party on 17 April. Among those taken away were the niece and Joe Bovy. All were taken to the Citadel prison in Liège where, according to Don, 'two of them were shot before the Americans could free them. But the niece was seen a few weeks afterwards with a German major and the Belgians then knew who had informed the Germans of my whereabouts.' As a result of these arrests Don stayed in several premises in and around Dalhem, after which he went to live with René the Burgomeister at Herstal, halfway between Dalhem and Liège. At Herstal he was taken by a member of the Resistance, Robert Oliver, who lived on the Rue Paul Janson, into his mother-in-law's kitchen, where she was frying a meal. In perfect English Robert said to Don, 'What is she frying?' Unhesitatingly Don answered 'mushrooms', whereupon Robert uncocked the gun that he had in his hand and told Don that had he hesitated with his reply he would have shot him. The Resistance could take no chances that Don might have been an imposter.

At the end of April Brinkhurst was moved to Liège nearby, where he 'slept at the White Army Headquarters for one week'. He was now in the hands of brothers Roger and Joseph 'Josse' Jamblin. He was moved yet again, to the home of Madame Jeanne Parent and her two daughters, Marie Louise and Julie. Jeanne, whom Don remembered as 'Jenny', was married to an American, who 'had helped many evaders' but he had been arrested and was now in a concentration camp. In the middle of May Don met five USAAF aircrew members from two Liberators from the 445th Bomb Group at Tibenham that had evaded capture after their aircraft were shot down on 24 April. Second Lieutenants James Goebel Jr., Robert C. Tucker and Staff Sergeant Charles Westerlund were the co-pilot, bombardier and radio operator respectively on 2nd Lieutenant Franklin Kendziora's crew in which eight men including the pilot had evaded capture. First Lieutenant Joseph Pavelka, the pilot of *Sin Ship*, and his navigator, 2nd Lieutenant Philip Solomon, had also evaded in and around Liège.[2]

On 18 May the five Americans and Don Brinkhurst, Flying Officer James Hubert Lewis DFM,[3] Flight Sergeant Kevin J. Doyle RCAF; Sergeant George E. H. Flather; and Pilot Officer Reginald Albert Weedon, RAAF, were each given a Red Cross armband and put aboard a bogus Red Cross truck.[4] The truck travelled the best part

---

2  Four men in total evaded and six were KIA.

3  Lewis was the navigator on Halifax MZ578 on 76 Squadron piloted by Pilot Officer Stanley Alan Somerscales DFC, who was KIA when the aircraft was shot down on Düsseldorf on 22/23 April 1944.

4  Doyle and Flather had evaded after their 432 Squadron Halifaxes had been shot down over Montzon on the night of 27/28 April. Weedon was one of five members of the crew skippered by Flight Lieutenant A. B. Simpson DFC RAAF on 467 Squadron who had evaded after being shot down on Nurnberg on 30/31 March.

of 150km (90 miles) to the village of Cul-des-Sarts, virtually on the French border, where the evaders 'stayed overnight in the barn of a hotel'. On the following day the airmen walked the short distance to Petite Chapelle, even closer to the border. Here, in a Capuchin monastery and in the care of a monk, they were joined on 22 May by P-38 Lightning pilot, Lieutenant Jack W. Holton.

On 23 May they stayed in a barn on a farm and the following day the group split up. Only one of the Americans and Doyle, Flather, Lewis and Weedon agreed to be taken away in the 'Red Cross' truck and return to Liège, some later going to secret, large camps in the Ardennes to sit out the war until the Allies arrived. Lewis was still in hiding in Liège when the Hosdin house was raided by the Secret Police on 22 July. Before they broke into the house Madame Hosdin enabled a Canadian airman and a Frenchman who had escaped from a PoW camp to escape by means of a rope. At the same time, they destroyed incriminating documents. Arrested, she was beaten and tortured but refused to talk. She survived and was rescued by US soldiers when they liberated Liège. Lewis, who was living and being fed in St Paul's cathedral until his departure on 11 September, had a potentially awkward meeting with a German colonel and his girlfriend one day, when he inadvertently opened the door of the cathedral to them: 'He was a visitor fortunately and I told him in French that the cathedral was closed. He saluted me and went out. The Gestapo didn't arrive so apparently he was not suspicious.'

Brinkhurst and the others remaining at Petite Chapelle, who wanted to press on for home, were given permission to do so by the White Army and were also given 1,000 francs each. Crossing into France on foot, they were stopped at the border by a French frontier guard, but he let them pass and they carried on walking to Rocroi, 3 or 4km inside France, where they caught a bus, which took them to Charleville-Mézières, 29km away. Really two towns divided by the River Meuse, Charleville is to the north and Mézières to the south, but connected by a bridge over the river. As the airmen were crossing the bridge an air-raid alert sounded, and in the confusion, they ran out of Mézières with most of the locals into the fields beyond. Splitting into twos and threes, they walked away from the town, stopping to eat after 3 or 4km. They continued in these small groups, one following well behind the other and the lead group dropping playing cards as markers at turnings. After a further half a dozen kilometres or so, as they were approaching the village of Balaives et Butz, they saw a lone house on a hill, from which a young lad ran down to meet them and invited them to stay at his house. The evaders held a conference and decided to go to his home, where they were well received by his mother, Madame Hourrier, the mother of eight children. No stranger to helping airmen, she now hid the seven airmen in a shelter in Boulzicourt Wood. Identity cards were made for them and on 30 May the airmen walked to Villers before catching the train in Charleville to begin the long journey to Nancy, 220km away, in the direction of the Swiss border – and safety.

At Nancy they spent the night in the station waiting room, where their papers were examined by the French police, closely followed by German security police. In the morning the evaders caught a train to Belfort, 170km south-eastwards, but ever closer to Switzerland. After four fruitless hours in Belfort looking for a bus, they decided to catch another train, this time to Montbéliard. They waited in a café while their guide went to look for a helper who worked at the Peugeot factory. A deal was struck by Don Brinkhurst and 'Bob' Tucker for a smuggler to guide them into Switzerland. Their guide was a former officer in an Alpine Regiment, about 28 years old, 5ft 7in, husky, ruddy complexion, light hair and slightly bald. He was in charge of a dairy on the outskirts of Montbéliard. Married, with five children, he nevertheless took the airmen back to his house for the night. It was not until 2 pm on 31 May that they set off for the Swiss border and Fahy, escorted by three smugglers. The party walked for two hours and then waited for nightfall, playing cards to pass the time before continuing their journey at 2030 and crossing the border four hours later. As the crow flies the distance between

Montbéliard and Fahy is 15km (10 miles). All told they had covered, from Liège, no more than 600km (375 miles) to reach the safety of neutral Switzerland on 1 June.

Once in Fahy the men gave themselves up and were taken to the police station. The respective military attachés were telephoned, following which the seven airmen were removed to a detention barracks in Porrentruy. They complained about their confinement, insisting on their rights as escapers, and two days later they went into quarantine at Bad Lostorf, near Olten. During this period, which lasted for three weeks, the airmen were interrogated by a Swiss intelligence officer, Captain Gottfried de Meiss. After the three weeks they were released to the US and British Legations in Bern and then sent to the Hôtel de Glion. They were, however, confined to the Glion area and were told by the military attaché staff not to try to escape and official efforts would be made for their release. Events elsewhere took a surprise turn when the Allies came ashore on the coast of Normandy on 6 June. It took three months of hard fighting for the German Army to be driven back towards the Fatherland, out of France and into Belgium and Luxemburg. Once this had been achieved, the Swiss authorities permitted the internees in their country to be sent to France. Some, though, had already left, with or without the connivance of the Swiss. Charles Westerlund had gone before 6 September, while Brinkhurst and others had left at the end of August. With the help of the manager of the Hôtel Eden, where Brinkhurst was staying in Glion, he had managed to get away and cross into France from the town of Morgins, south of Glion, on 28 August. Leaving with him were 'Bob' Cant and 'Bill' Milburn,[5] Dick Mitchell, William Hamilton and Flight Lieutenant Selwyn M. Hunt RNZAF on 47 Squadron.

---

5 Warrant Officer Robert Bramley Cant was piloting Lancaster ED751 on 103 Squadron at Elsham Wolds on 5/6 September 1943, his 17th operation, when he was shot down on the Mannheim operation. He and Sergeant William R. Milburn, his mid-upper gunner, and four others on the crew evaded successfully. The navigator was taken prisoner. See www.robertcant.org.

When Brinkhurst arrived in Grenoble, he was sent south to Sisteron and from there was flown on a US C-47 air evacuation aircraft to Rome-Ciampino airfield. From there he was flown over to North Africa and on via Algiers and Casablanca back to England. Before the end of the year, he had married Vera Lodder. Leaving behind his new wife, he re-joined his old squadron and his first sortie, on the night of 2/3 January 1945 on the crew of Flying Officer M. Collins, was another raid on Nuremberg! He squeezed in a further 19 operations before the end of the war in May 1945.

# Chapter 9

# The Saga of *Squat N' Droppit*

*In the summer of 1944, all eyes were on the inevitable invasion of 'Festung Europa'. Fortress and Liberator crews of the 8th Air Force based in England flew relentless missions across the Channel and pounded the coastal regions of France and Holland. Losses among the young American air crews rose steadily with the upsurge in missions and new crews were sent to East Anglia as replacements.*

One such crew that flew their Liberator from the USA to England via the southern ferry route in the early summer of 1944 was commanded by Second Lieutenant William Bailey Jr, born in Jacksonville, Florida. Once in Europe the crew spent two weeks' theatre indoctrination training in Northern Ireland. After that the crew headed for the 8th Air Force reception centre at Stone, England. Then it was back to Northern Ireland for some ground school and escape and evasion lectures. 'We were told if we were shot down in France,' recalled Second Lieutenant George D. Cooksey Jr, the co-pilot, born in Spartanburg, South Carolina, 'we were to approach only one person at a time. We were not to go near a house with electric lights or a house with a car or car tracks. "Be alert for collaborators," our lecturers warned. "I don't think I would jeopardize my chances by drinking anything alcoholic if I was shot down," I told Second Lieutenant Ben Isgrig, our bombardier – I didn't know the French!' Benjamin C. Isgrig Jr. was born in Little Rock, Arkansas.

Bailey's crew were posted to the 448th Bomb Group stationed at Seething, Norfolk. The crew was needed immediately and they flew their first mission together, to Merseburg, on 28 May 1944. By D-Day, 6 June, they had flown a total of five missions without incident. Two more missions followed but it was not until 10 June that they could chalk up their eighth, to an aerodrome just east of Évreux, France.

Isgrig recalls, 'There were supposed to be some Me 410s down there and we were dropping 100lb GP bombs to make the field unusable. This was by far our worst mission. We were hit by flak before we got into the target area, several bursts hitting between the fuselage and the right wing tip. The ship directly behind us caught fire in the bomb bay and fell apart just as it dropped its bombs. Seven 'chutes were seen over the target – a hell of a place to have to bail out. Our left-wing ship had its right waist window shot out and some men wounded. We dropped our bombs through clouds. The weather had been terrible since the invasion started.'

Two days later, on 12 June, Bailey's crew started on their ninth mission when the Second Bomb Division despatched its Liberators to targets in France again. The 20th Combat Wing, of which the 448th Bomb Group was a part, was assigned a railway bridge about 12 miles south of Rennes. Durwood A. Stanley, the regular ball turret gunner, was withdrawn and the crew reduced to nine members.

The mission began badly for Bailey's crew. It seemed as if their ninth mission might have to wait when, just prior to take off, their B-24 developed electrical trouble. Leslie Fischer, the engineer, got the auxiliary generator running and everything seemed fine until the crew got ready to swing onto the runway. Then the entire electrical system gave out. There was very little time to check the cause so a ground crew was called for to tow the Liberator off the runway. Bailey's crew were given a replacement ship called, *Squat N' Droppit*. Air crews are normally superstitious and the change in aircraft brought mixed reactions from the nine men. George Cooksey exclaimed, 'What a name for a B-24!' He thought it was a bad omen.

The rest of the crew laughed at him. Ben Isgrig was undeterred; he thought the mission would be another 'milk run'.

*Squat N' Droppit* finally took off from Seething but Bailey had a lot of catching up to do if they were to depart the coast of England in formation. *Squat N' Droppit* carried four 2,000lb bombs in her belly and when they finally reached altitude, it became obvious they would not make it. Bailey had to tag onto the 446th Bomb Group from nearby Bungay as number three aircraft in the low lead element.

At the IP the mission turned to a disaster, as Ben Isgrig recalls, 'We started our bomb run but instead of dropping our bombs, the lead ship closed its bomb bay doors and headed towards England. Nearing the French coast, we turned and headed towards the target again but once more we did not drop our bombs. By this time other groups in the same area had started home, leaving us on our own. We made a third run with the same results. Bailey said that we were getting low on gas and would have to leave formation and go home. He changed his mind and stayed with the 446th as it started its fourth and final bombing run. As we dropped our bombs we were flying on the right of the formation.'

George Cooksey was also horrified by the actions of the lead ship. 'I'll never know what happened to the lead crew but they really screwed it up. Four times over the target! The turns caused the formation to spread. We were low on the inside and just barely able to remain above stalling speed during the left turns. By the fourth time over the target the Germans had our altitude and must have even had the serial number of our aircraft. The flak was everywhere. How demoralizing those black puffs were – getting closer and closer.'

Isgrig continues, 'We had been briefed to make a sharp left turn after crossing the target but instead of doing this, we waited too long and the lead ship led us directly over Rennes before beginning his turn. As we were flying on the right side of the formation we were in the position to catch the most flak, which we did. It was the most accurate flak I had ever seen, or hoped to see. The Germans had our airspeed and altitude exactly. We didn't have a chance. We cut sharply to the left and began doing individual evasive action. Over the interphone I guided Bailey away from where the flak was thickest as I had a good view of it from the nose turret; a much better view than anyone else on the ship. It seemed no matter which way we turned the flak still hit us. To me it sounded like someone throwing gravel on a tin roof.

'There was an occasional shudder as a larger piece would tear into the ship. I don't think I was scared; I don't know. I just wanted to get out of it as soon as possible. I wasn't wearing my flak suit as I hadn't thought I would need it, so I crouched down as far as possible in my turret and got as much protection as possible from my gun mounts and armour plating.

'After what seemed an eternity, we were in clear air again and I breathed a sigh of relief. I relaxed and started looking for holes in my turret. Over the interphone I heard Bailey ask if everyone was alright but I don't remember hearing any replies. Our interphone was not working very well and my connection in my turret was not working at all. I had opened the turret doors and was plugged into a connection in the nose.

'After leaving the flak area we were slightly behind the formation but no further behind than we had been on several other occasions. We were gradually catching up when suddenly, I looked out and saw a stream of tracer bullets coming from the direction of the tail and crossing directly in front of me at about one hundred yards. I don't believe the tracers were more than ten yards from me as they passed my turret. For a second, I was so stunned I couldn't move, then I yelled, "Enemy Fighters!" I don't know whether anyone heard me. At the same time, I turned on my trigger switch and waited for the fighter to pass the nose but he evidently pulled off to the side because I never saw him. I heard the 20mm shells explode, four of them, and our plane shuddered as they ripped into her guts. I don't know how many planes made passes at us, or how many times, but I believe it was three planes and I know that we were out on the first pass.

'A few jumbled words came over the interphone. I couldn't make them out. Then I heard Ken Zierdt, the radio operator, repeat over and over in a steady voice, "Fire in the bomb bay, Fire in the bomb bay!". In a few more seconds someone said, "Get the hell out of here" and I saw Vic Fleishman, the navigator, take off his oxygen mask and put on his 'chute. I pulled my oxygen mask and interphone connection loose as the alarm bell rang and climbed out of the turret. Meanwhile, Vic opened the escape hatch. A thousand thoughts ran through my mind but I wasn't afraid; I didn't have time. By the time I had my parachute on, Vic was baling out and Fischer had crawled up the passageway and was waiting to jump. I don't know what Fischer was doing there; he was supposed to go out through the bomb bay.'

George Cooksey was in turmoil. He thought, 'We're hit!' Those next few seconds trying to assess the damage seemed endless. The oxygen was gone and so was the intercom. 'How were the guys in the waist and tail? Number three engine gone. Right vertical stabilizer gone. Fire in the bomb bay. We were losing altitude. Bailey sounded the bail-out alarm. Where's Fischer? He's not on the flight deck. Zierdt said Fischer had gone through the tunnel to the nose. Why didn't he open the bomb bay door? How about the guys in the nose and rear? Are they still there? Are they out? How long can we maintain control?'

Isgrig and Cooksey both wondered why Fischer had left through the nose. Fischer explains, 'A round had gone through the bomb bay and set the ship on fire and I did not want to open the bomb bay doors and fan the flames. My interphone was inoperative and I couldn't communicate with the rest of the crew. Zierdt was pulling my leg to come down out of the top turret above his radio compartment. I had a little jump seat so I pulled the release and fell out onto the flight deck. Zierdt handed me a fire extinguisher. It looked as if the hydraulic tank was on fire.

'Either the fire extinguisher was inoperative or Zierdt had already used it because it did not work. I stepped back onto the flight deck and I told Zierdt, "Come on let's go!" Vic Fleishman was squatting over the escape hatch when I got there and as soon as he bailed out, I followed him.

'I didn't follow instructions like I should have. We were supposed to delay opening our parachutes until we could make out objects on the ground but I wanted to try mine out in a hurry. I must have opened my 'chute around 15,000ft.'

Isgrig watched as the slipstream whipped Fischer past the Liberator, then jumped head first himself into the torrent of rushing air. 'In a fraction of a second, I was falling on my back toward the earth, 19,000ft below me. I began to spiral like a cartwheel. It seemed to me that I had been falling for an hour and I still could not see the ground. I thought of all the times I had been told by instructors that a person had perfect control over his body as he fell and decided they were mistaken. I couldn't stop cartwheeling or turning over and I was getting dizzy. I was scared of hitting the ground before pulling the rip cord so I pulled it at about 15,000ft and the 'chute opened. I didn't experience any shock. One second, I was falling free and the next I was floating.'

Meanwhile, Cooksey and Zierdt had opened the bomb bay doors and had bailed out. Zierdt had to be helped into a spare parachute because his had been burned in the attack. Cooksey recalls, 'We were down to about 4,000 ft. The nose was beginning to head down. Out we went. Clear the plane. Pull the ripcord. Will the 'chute open? Then that tremendous jerk. Such a quiet sensation. I looked up. The canopy had billowed. I noticed that one leg strap was unfastened. The jolt caused me to lose my left flying boot and one of the GI shoes wired to my 'chute. How peaceful; how quiet.

'Did the guys in the nose and rear get out? I looked down. What pleasant looking country. Smoke was rising from the chimneys of a few scattered farmhouses. Occupied France! Only a few hours earlier I had been with friends in a warm and friendly country. Who will get my hat? It was from Oviatts in Beverley Hills. Who will want my A-2 jacket? How about all the Gillette Blue blades I had just received from home?'

Isgrig looked around and saw three fighter planes above him. 'I immediately thought they must be German. The nearest one, a Bf 109, turned and started diving at me. I thought he was going to machine-gun me and I prayed feverishly to God to help me. I pulled the shroud lines to start my body swinging; it was all I could do to help myself.

Kenneth Zierdt was hit by machine-gun fire from the Bf 109 as he descended by parachute. The 24-year-old radio operator, who was born in Nebraska on 17 August 1920, landed in a ploughed field and was alive for some time. Two Germans stood over him and would not allow the French to attend to him. After he died, the Germans cut out his zippers and took his watch and wedding ring.

Isgrig continues, 'The other two planes were Mustangs. One of them circled lazily above me while the other followed the German down. The Bf 109 cut to the left; passing within fifty yards of me, and began to climb. The P-51 was right on his tail and I never wanted anything in my life as much as I wanted him to kill the German who had shot us down. I was hysterical by this time and I screamed and cursed the German, waving and offering all my moral support to the American as he passed. The German didn't have a chance. Within ten seconds his ship began to fall apart and burn. The German bailed out and he landed 300 yards from me.'

The P-51 climbed toward Fischer after shooting down the Bf 109, circled him and waggled his wings before roaring away. (Long after the war Isgrig and Fischer discovered that their saviour had been Major George Preddy of the 352nd Fighter Group. Preddy, who was killed on Christmas Day 1944, was the number two American air ace of the Second World War in Europe.)

A young French girl, Margaret Lecotteley, had witnessed the shooting down of the Liberator and the subsequent fighter combat above her home in Romille. During the air battle, which had taken place at a relatively low altitude, the villagers had cursed as the German fired at the helpless American airmen and then had cheered as the P-51 had finished off the German fighter.

Margaret was the first to reach the German pilot, who landed in a yard in Romille. He handed her a knife and asked the young French girl to cut away the boot on his wounded leg. As Margaret stood over him with the knife German soldiers ran to the scene and prepared to shoot her. They thought she was attacking the pilot but fortunately he stopped them from firing. The pilot was not seriously hurt and probably flew again.

As Fischer descended, he could make out two German soldiers coming out of Romille toward him on bicycles. 'For a while it seemed I was going to land right on top of them. As it turned out, I flew across the road and came down in a field. I rolled under the cover of a small tree, pulled my 'chute down and discarded my bright yellow Mae West. I had lost a boot so I decided to get rid of the other one. I started running across to a tree line nearby and climbed up one of the trees about 30ft high. It wasn't difficult to climb and I went up it like a squirrel.

'I sat down on a fork in the branches and hugged the trunk. Everything was quiet until all of a sudden, I heard dogs barking. I thought they must have bloodhounds after me. A little later I could hear talking. I peered through the foliage and saw two German soldiers. They had dismounted their bicycles and had circled around to the tree line. They were each armed with a rifle and were standing right underneath my tree. Amazingly, they walked on by. However, I wasn't taking any chances so I remained in the tree until darkness and spent the night in a haystack. I ate a candy bar but saved an orange for later.

*Squat N' Droppit* had gone down at about 1000 hours. Sergeant Vladimir Kovalchick, the right waist gunner, was wounded and captured. He was taken to Rennes prison camp and then transferred to Chartreuse Musical University. Sent to German prison camp via Paris and then on to Frankfurt, he travelled by boxcar to Stalag Luft IV near the Polish border. But before the day was out most of the rest of the crew had avoided capture and were safely in the hands of the French Resistance.

Next morning Fischer knew he had to move. 'I walked down the side of a hedgerow to a sunken road. I had a compass and knew that the Allied beachhead was about 75 miles away but I had to have clothing and food before I could even contemplate such a distance.

122

I walked several hundred yards until I saw a farmhouse. I crouched by the fence and saw a young Frenchman driving some cows from the road into a pasture just ahead of me. I stood up and made sure he saw me. He did not indicate he had seen me but walked on back into the farmhouse.

'In a short while an elderly white-haired lady (Madame Felix) walked across the road and asked me questions in French. I could only say, "*Non compri*". She used sign language and determined I was an American airman who had landed by parachute. She brought me some pancakes and told me to stay low until she returned. (I learned after the war that there was another house even closer than Madame Felix's. I had missed it because it was hidden by trees. Had I gone there, things would have been different because a girl who lived there slept with Germans.)

'Madame Felix returned in no time at all and three men drove up to the farmhouse in a car. She pointed me out to them and they came over and talked to me. Monsieur Dumay was a travelling salesman who could speak English. The other two were Diney Morel and Roje Rhode. They questioned me and asked where I came from. All I could offer as proof of identity were my dog tags. They brought some civilian clothes and I tried on some shoes. I changed my clothes on the spot and walked out with Roje. We went a little way and hid my uniform.

'Roje and I took an indirect route to Geveze and I was taken through a small alley to a granary. The door was jerked open and I jumped in among the grain sacks. About an hour later all three men returned. I was told that Diney Morel owned the granary and Roje and his wife Evonne were staying there.

'I assured them I was not hurt and finally convinced them I wanted something to drink. They went through beer, champagne and cognac before I finally got to water. It tasted real good because it was the first drink I'd had for a day and a half. Then we really had a good supper and afterwards I was shown to the hayloft, where a cot had been placed.

'Diney Morel was a baker and his wife worked with him. They had two children. Petit Diney or 'Little Diney', as they called him, was four and their daughter Leon was nine. Monsieur Morel sometimes brought little Diney to visit me but Leon was not told about me. Roje was about thirty and had served in the French Navy in submarines. He was hiding at the granary to avoid being sent to a slave labour camp. Every day Evonne rode a bicycle to their home town of Rennes, where she was a hairdresser. Evonne picked up some English books for me in Rennes and covered the fact by saying she had a very smart child who could read English. I don't believe she was afraid of the Devil himself!

'The granary was so situated that I could put my cheek against the window and look down the side of the house. I could see two German sentries on the church steeple, which was used as an observation post. When the Morels learned that I had a birthday on 9 June, Evonne baked me a cake and we all had a little birthday party. Back in England we had been told not to eat too much because food was scarce in the occupied countries. However, I was assured by my French hosts that food was plentiful. This was apple country and the French seemed to drink cider more than water. I did the same because I noticed that the water came from a well adjacent to several outhouses!

'My French hosts were very good to me and seemed to have very little outward fear of the Germans, whom they absolutely detested. Roje told me of instances when they stuck pins and needles in the Germans' bicycles. If they came across any German vehicles they would short out the batteries. They would do anything to aggravate their German occupiers. Monsieur Morel told me that about the time I arrived the Germans might use his car to get out of the area when they withdrew. He knew he could not prevent the Germans from taking it so he drained all the oil from the sump. When the Germans did confiscate his car they only got as far as the outskirts of Geveze before they burned the rods out of it. Monsieur Morel rode out on his horse and towed it back to the granary and had it repaired!'

Leslie Fischer was to stay with the Morels for 57 days. 'My days were pleasant, the food good and the hospitality marvellous.

My French hosts had everything at stake and if they had been caught the Germans would have executed the whole family. You do not run across people like them every day.'

Just as Fischer had landed in a tree after bailing out of the doomed *Squat N' Droppit*, so too did Ben Isgrig, the bombardier. Several French people looked up at him slowly descending, practically falling out of control with his back towards the way he was drifting. The airman looked around for a likely place to hide after landing but almost immediately he had to kick his way through the upper branches of a tree that rudely welcomed him to France. Isgrig finally came to rest in a smaller tree as his parachute shrouds became enmeshed in the branches of the larger tree above him. It seemed hours before he finally escaped from his parachute harness and jumped to the ground.

'I used the phrase sheet in my escape kit and with the help of the French spectators who had gathered under "my tree", I discovered the precise location of the Germans. Then I ran in the opposite direction, down a slope and through a shallow pond. (I did this to throw any dogs off my scent.) One of my boots had come off during my parachute descent and my unshod foot became quite sore. A barn nearby was burning and I could see some scattered pieces of Liberator wreckage. I assumed that it was our Liberator and that the rest of the crew must have been killed in the crash.' (The wreckage Isgrig saw was a 446th Bomb Group Liberator shot down on the same raid. *Squat N' Droppit* had been cleaved in two by the German fighter attack and had crashed on the Delacroix farm at Brieux and set it on fire.)

'After stopping to look at the burning wreckage I carried on running. I had not run very far when my foot began to hurt very badly. I was tired of running so when I spotted a house nearby, I decided to try and rest there a while. A woman came to the door but when I told her I was American, she became very frightened and waved me away. For a short time I walked along the road until I heard men's voices. I stepped back into a field of barley and waited. Two young Frenchmen came into view, talking excitedly. I assumed they were talking about the air battle.

'I stepped out in front of them and said, "American!" They became very excited and one of them led me back into the field, taking great care not to leave a trail of bent barley behind us. He sat me down and motioned me to stay there until he returned. I stayed, not knowing whether the next face would be friend or foe. After a while I heard people approaching. I held my breath and said a prayer. A middle-aged man and a beautiful girl appeared. The girl spoke English and asked if I was American. I said, "Yeah". The man thought I had answered, "Ja" and pulled out a pistol. I figured that this was it but the girl caught his hand and said, "No, No!" (From then on, I always said "Yes"). The girl's name was Michelle LeHuede and the man was her father, the local schoolmaster in Romille.

'After some more conversation and their assurances that they would help me, they left. A short time later Michelle and a man I had not seen before, returned, bringing Vic Fleishman with them. Needless to say, we were most happy to see each other. The Frenchman, seeing that I had a bare foot, sat down, took off his own shoes and gave them to me. They were a little tight but okay. I didn't know until later that leather shoes were extremely scarce. I tried to pay him with some of my escape money but he would not take it. (None of these people would ever take money.) When we left weeks later, Vic and I hid the money in a spot where we knew our French hosts would find it after we had gone.

'My spot was now getting crowded so we moved a short distance to another barley field and under an apple tree. They questioned us about our other crew members as they were trying to find them. They left and Michelle returned with a loaf of black bread and two bottles of red wine. The sun was shining and the day was warm and after a few bites of bread and drinks of wine the war seemed far, far away. Michelle left us again and returned later that afternoon with her father. They had found two more of our crew and asked us to go with them to meet them. (Sergeant Robert E. Buck, the 21-year-old tail gunner who was born in Greenville, Maine, in 1923, and Sergeant Ollie Noble Van Horssen, the 20-year-old third engineer, who was born in Chicago, and had enlisted in Kalamazoo, Michigan, in March 1943, had been found hiding in a garden in Romille.) All four of us were taken to a large wood, where we spent the next three days. Michelle came to visit us often, sometimes alone, sometimes with various Frenchmen. Once her mother came with her to meet the Americans. Michelle was 18 and beautiful. We were young warriors that were trying to liberate her country. To us she was a heroine. We all fell in love with her and she with us. (After the war Michelle married Captain Marty of the French Army.)

'We spent the days in the woods eating the food that was brought to us. Each night after dark we moved to a barn loft filled with hay where we slept. We had to be out of the barn by dawn. In June the nights are very short in Brittany and although we got little sleep, we made up for it during the day because we had nothing else to do.

'During this time the LeHuede family were the only people we knew by name. Michelle was the only person we met who could speak English. Vic could speak a little French; the others none at all. We did not want to know names in case we were caught. If you did not know you couldn't tell. During our entire stay in France, we never wrote down a name or address or anything that might be a danger to our benefactors if we were caught.

'Events began to move rather rapidly. We were told we were being moved and were walked to a back road where a lorry was waiting. We bid a tearful goodbye to Michelle and climbed in. We were told to get behind some boxes inside if we were stopped, and off we went. We were stopped twice at German road blocks but no one looked into the back of the lorry. After about an hour we pulled into the courtyard of a rather isolated inn. We entered and met the man who was to take us by boat to England. We went to bed with the expectation of being gone from France the next night but the Germans were moving many troops through the area to the Normandy area so the plans were changed. Our escape photos were taken from us and later in the day we were presented with French identity cards. I was now "Paul Masson", a medical student from Brittany. If I were caught,

I could supposedly get by without speaking French as I was supposed to know only the Breton language.

'We realized we would not be escaping to England in the near future so we stayed at the inn for two days. We watched German troop movements from our upstairs window but no one bothered us. The night we left Vic and I went with several Frenchmen and Buck and Van Horssen went with some others. We were re-billeted at the home of Grandmere Guillot. It was a two-storey stone house and Vic and I were taken to a second-floor room. In the apartment below Grandmere lived with her orphaned granddaughter, Yvonne. This was more or less our permanent home for the remainder of our stay in France.

'About a quarter of a mile away lived Monsieur Rene Guillot, his wife and three children. Monsieur Guillot, who was about fifty, had fought in the First World War and had been wounded and gassed. He had spent some time in an American hospital and still used the US Army Gillette razor he had been given. He stood about 5ft 10in tall with a slender build and had a fierce moustache and usually a home-made cigarette between his lips. An old cap was tilted over his right eye at all times. We could not communicate with the Guillots and we did not know where we were. The Guillots were rather isolated. I can now say we were at Plouasne, Côtes-du-Nord. In 1944 I never saw Plouasne.'

Apart from the crew of *Squat N' Droppit*, other airmen were also hiding in the area. Some of them, like Blaine Barrett, came from the 446th Bomb Group Liberator that was shot down on the same day as the 448th ship. Barrett was the bombardier and had been trapped in his nose turret. The navigator had bailed out and left him. It was almost impossible to get out of the nose turret of a B-24 without someone in the nose to open the doors.

By the time Barrett got out the Liberator was heading earthward and the nose was on fire. Barrett found his chest 'chute, snapped it on, and jumped. Badly burned and wounded in the leg, he remained in a field administering morphine to kill the pain. After a few hours he was unable to see and it was two days before the French found him. They tried to talk him into giving himself up so he could get proper medical attention but Barrett refused. A French doctor later attended him and when Isgrig and Fleishman met him a week later scars were visible around his eyes but he could see and his hands and wounded leg were usable.

Another American in the area was First Lieutenant James Irwin of the 82nd Airborne Division. He had been wounded and captured on D-Day but later escaped. An underground courier arrived at the Guillotts and tried to persuade the Americans to join one of the Resistance groups in the area. Monsieur Guillott told the courier the Americans would not be going. Later, Isgrig and his fellow airmen learned that the group had been betrayed and all were killed by the Germans.

At that time Monsieur Freville, leader of the Resistance movement in Brittany, had finalised plans for uprisings and sabotage to take place once the Allies broke out of the Normandy beachhead. Complete secrecy was needed if the plans were to succeed but eighteen American airmen had literally 'dropped in' on these plans and placed them in jeopardy. Their presence meant that more Germans would be drafted into the area to search for them. There was no communication between Freville's men and the rural Resistance groups so the vicar of Romille acted as a go-between and communications between the two groups were established. The Americans were, by their very presence, responsible for the formation of Freville's main-line Resistance group.

To pass the time before liberation, Isgrig and Fleishman helped with the harvest. For security reasons and probably because the Guillotts needed some relief from feeding the two airmen, Isgrig and Fleishman were moved for short periods of time. The amazingly brave truth is that nearly everyone in Romille knew where at least one of the eighteen Americans was hidden and not a single word was told to German searchers of their whereabouts. One man was held by the Gestapo and tortured. Once he was hung by his heels for twelve hours and since that time had been unable to speak and barely able to walk.

It was under the constant shadow of threats like this that the brave French men and women continued to hide the American fugitives. On 9 August 1944 there was no hint that the day would be any different to the other 57 Isgrig and Fleishman had spent since being shot down over occupied France. However, that night they could hear the unmistakable thunder-like rolling sounds of big guns being fired in the distance. Next day rumours abounded in the village and Grandmere told her Americans, 'The Americans are coming and the Germans are leaving the village!'

Isgrig recalls, 'Monsieur Guillot came running in at noon, highly excited about the events of the morning. Yes, the Germans were retreating. The mighty Wehrmacht were throwing away their guns and helmets as they ran. They had the look of haunted beasts in their eyes, looking back over their shoulders every few steps as if fearing the devil himself was behind them.

'There were still Germans in the vicinity as we went out to meet the Americans so we had to be careful. We walked the back paths and through the fields. Vic and I didn't want to chance capture after waiting this long for liberation. All along the way the Guillots picked red poppies, white daisies and blue cornflowers. By the time we reached the main highway everyone had a corsage of *blu*, *blanc* and *rouge*.

French people lined the road on both sides as far as we could see in either direction. Many flags were being waved, mostly French but a few American flags could be seen among the crowd. We didn't have long to wait and soon heard the rumble of tanks and the mounting cheers of the people as the convoy approached. The first big white star we saw on a tank was a sight I shall never forget. The stirring words of the Marseillaise could be heard among the shouts of the wildly cheering, laughing, crying crowd. The narrow highway was covered by a mantle of red, white and blue flowers as the begrimed but smiling tank men passed slowly by, ever alert for any enemy still in the area. The gallant French had waited four long years for this day.

'As soon as possible Vic and I stopped a Jeep and identified ourselves as Americans; explaining that we were Air Force men shot down eight weeks previously. The soldiers were most surprised to see American airmen in enemy territory dressed as French peasants. They gave us cigarettes, which tasted most delightful after smoking strong French tobacco and plied us with questions. We were so happy we could hardly talk. If only the other members of our crew were alive and well, our happiness would have been complete.

'Later, watching the trucks pass by, I noticed familiar faces in the back of one of them. They were the faces of our pilot, Bill Bailey and our co-pilot, George Cooksey! "George, George!" I screamed. He looked up and saw us, and in an instant, he was off the truck and running towards us. I don't know whether we laughed or cried; we were so deliriously happy. We made our way to the nearest cafe, where with much free wine, we spent several hours exchanging our stories.'

Cooksey had been met by some helpful Frenchmen after landing in a wheat field and had lived with Maurice and Lilly Chauvier and their family for several weeks. Bailey joined them and together they remained out of sight of the Germans. Their escape and evasion photographs were used by their French helpers to make French identity cards. At Pauley's Island, South Carolina, in 1942 Cooksey had met a lovely girl from Columbia, South Carolina, called Justin Derrieux. She had worn her name proudly and Cooksey decided to use it on his ID card. He became 'Georges Derrieux – wine merchant from Dinard'.

The Germans had searched the Chauviers' home, so it was decided that Bailey and Cooksey must be moved to the home of Lilly Chauvier's parents. For thirteen days they had nothing to eat but potatoes. While they were there Cooksey and Bailey survived a bombing raid by 36 A-20 medium bombers. Bombs burst close by and several windows and dishes were broken in the house. They were trying to bomb a railway bridge about a quarter of a mile away but the nearest bomb landed 140ft from the bridge. The French underground thought it must be important so that night they blew it up.

The two American pilots worked in the fields like Frenchmen but the time moved slowly. Their French helpers discouraged escape through Spain and recommended that they stay in the area. It was to pay off because on 31 July they heard the same guns Isgrig and Fleishman had heard. Next day Bailey and Cooksey hurried to a road about a mile away and met the long American column of tanks and trucks. Cooksey had a few tears in his eyes. He recalls, 'The French were cheering the troops along. There were many tears and laughing and crying. I had waited only weeks; the French had been waiting for five years. Flowers were tossed to the troops and wine appeared. *"Vive la France! Vive l'Amerique!"*

'The column stopped and GIs were tossing candy. I asked for a pack of cigarettes and was pitched a pack of "Chesterfields". The GI looked back startled and said, "You speak English pretty well." I told him I used to live in America. Within a matter of minutes, I was taken to a lieutenant colonel riding in a jeep. I identified myself and he asked about Germans in the area. I gave him what information I had picked up from the underground and he asked us to join him. We looked like two of the French Resistance.

'We had joined the 6th Armoured Division of the Third Army. About noon we stopped to shell an area and then waited as troops picked up a few German stragglers. About two hours later I saw a half-track. A man was in it with a shiny helmet and three stars. There were two ivory pistols. The general was standing and holding a Tommy gun. It was General George Patton. About fifteen minutes later I saw another general calmly riding in the right of a jeep. It was General Omar Bradley.'

The excitement continued as Bailey and Cooksey passed through several small villages. More flowers were tossed and French girls kissed their liberators. With dusk approaching Cooksey spotted two figures in the distance waving 'V' for Victory. They looked familiar. It was Isgrig and Fleishman. Cooksey didn't even know if they had made it!

Instead of joining the American troops and making their way out of France and back to England as they were supposed to do, all four decided to spend one more night with the Guillots. Isgrig recalls, 'We returned to the Guillots by way of a number of French cafes and homes, where we were toasted most royally. That night we had a farewell party that none of the participants would ever forget. The only English Monsieur Guillot knew was, "It's a Long Way to Tipperary", learned in World War One. We sang it quite often during the course of the evening. Finally, exhaustion overcame happiness and we retired to our last night in French feather beds.

'The next morning, we said goodbye to our wonderful friends, the French people who had sheltered us from the Germans and risked their lives many times for us. If we had been caught in the Guillot or Chauvier homes the members of the families would have been killed on the spot. These French people had gone barefoot so that we could have shoes; hungry so that we could eat and had slept without blankets so that we could be warm. They had loved us as if we had been their own sons.

'Yes, it was hard to say goodbye. There were tears in our eyes. We had to leave though. We still had a war to fight and we did not know what the future held for us after we returned to England. My last memory of these courageous people is watching Madame Guillot, tears streaming down her cheeks, disappear in the distance as we rode away in a GI truck.

'Not knowing what to do with us, we were sent back to Omaha Beach along with German PoWs. On the way we stopped to pick up Van Horssen and Buck, after we convinced them they had to leave the village before the Germans retook it. Along the way we saw some French women collaborators with their heads shaved.'

At Omaha Beach Isgrig, Fleishman, Van Horssen, Cooksey, Bailey and Buck were put on an LST with a boat load of prisoners for Southampton. Meanwhile, Leslie Fischer had said a tearful goodbye to his helpers, the Morels, and had contacted the American Army in Rennes. 'I was returned to the beachhead in a Jeep with a couple of intelligence officers and was interrogated officially at a PoW cage full of German prisoners. For the first time I learned something of the rest of my crew. According to the GIs at the cage they said some airmen had passed through two days before. They described one as being a "blond, curly headed 2nd lieutenant", which had to be Ben Isgrig.'

Isgrig and his fellow crew members had no money and found great difficulty getting to London from Southampton. Eventually, they were given food and rail tickets at a transit camp. They arrived in the 'spit and polish' capital feeling very shabby, dressed as they were in a mixture of GI uniforms and French peasant clothes. Isgrig was wearing a blue beret, black shoes, an olive drab shirt, and trousers with no insignia. Equally incongruously, he carried a souvenir German Mauser rifle. 'All my companions looked about the same as I did. Some had rifles and others, pistols. We were wandering around when a Jeep filled with MPs spotted us and arrested us for being out of uniform and having no ID cards. The "paddy wagon" was called and we were taken to jail. Some homecoming!

'Finally, we convinced the captain in charge that we were bona fide ex-evadees and he apologized. Released, we eventually found our way to the Army Intelligence Unit at 23 Brook Street. After identification and interrogation, we were quartered at the Red Cross hostel in Jermyn Street near Piccadilly Circus.'

Leslie Fischer, meanwhile, had been flown across the Channel to southern England. He telephoned his base at Seething and they flew down to pick him up. Later, he travelled to London and was reunited with the rest of his crew. Isgrig continues, 'Young airmen and their money are soon parted so after two weeks Cooksey and I took a week's tour to Northern Ireland to give lectures on escape and evasion. Our clothes still hadn't arrived when we returned to London. We were told that they were at Seething. After reporting to Colonel Mason, the Commanding Officer, and our squadron CO, we discovered that most of our belongings had disappeared. Salvaging what we could find, we visited the few friends we had left among the many strange faces and returned to London.'

In September 1944 the crew flew home to the USA via the Azores, arriving in Maine because of a hurricane along the Mid-Atlantic states. The crew travelled on to New York by train for more interrogation and were home for Christmas 1944. Crew celebrations took place and on New Year's Eve a toast was proposed: '*Vive la France! Vive l'Amerique!*'

# Chapter 10

# The Long Walk

*The crew of* Squat N' Droppit *had come to revere their French hosts after being hidden in various French homes following their shooting down on 12 June 1944. Many other American airmen also had to rely on the French civilian population after landing in occupied France. One of them was Staff Sergeant Robert J. Starzynski, who was shot down five days after* Squat N' Droppit, *on 17 June 1944.*

Robert (Bob) Starzynski from Chicago, Illinois, enlisted in the Army on 16 January 1943. He was 18 years old. By June of that year, he was in England assigned to the 4th Station Complement Squadron of the 306th Bombardment Group at Thurleigh near Bedford. When the 306th needed replacements to make up losses sustained on bombing raids, it was to the 4th Station Complement that squadron commanders turned. After numerous requests to transfer to a bomb squadron, Starzynski was sent to gunnery school on the Wash and sent to the 367th 'Clay Pigeon' Squadron (so named because of its high loss rate) in January 1944 as a gunner. His first mission was as a tail gunner on the first American heavy bomber raid on Berlin on 6 March 1944. 'It was,' he said, 'a real rough one.' Although there was a lot of flak en route and on the homeward flight, Starzynski's crew came through the baptism safely. He flew several more missions filling in as a replacement gunner before being assigned to First Lieutenant Virgil W. Dingman's crew, whose tail gunner had been killed in action on the crew's first mission, to Brunswick, and Staff Sergeant Winston W. Burroughs, the ball turret gunner, was wounded. 'We were a very close-knit crew,' says Burroughs, who was born in Charlotte Hall, Maryland, 'and that was by far the worst mission. I thought I was going to finish my tour but on my 23rd mission everything went downhill.'

'The crew had trained together in the States,' Starzynski recalls, 'so it was a little rough getting acquainted but I fitted in and on Saturday, 17 June we were briefed for an early morning mission to France.'

The mission was planned and then scrubbed just before briefing. Then there was a flurry of activity with a briefing at 0900 and a take-off at 0945 hours. To compound the confusion of the hurried last-minute changes, the target weather closed in and the primary was obscured. Forty B-17s had taken off from Thurleigh but seven were forced to return to base after failing to rendezvous with the rest of the formation in the prevailing weather conditions. As luck would have it, the PFF equipment was inoperative, forcing the Group to choose a visual target of opportunity, a bridge at Noyen. The B-17 flown by 2nd Lieutenant Joseph W. Pedersen, flying as deputy lead in the low group, was hit over the coast going in but was able to stay with the formation. Then about 1245, north-east of Le Mans, his Fortress was seen to have an engine on fire. It peeled out of formation, did a 360-degree turn and nine chutes were observed before the aircraft went into a spin. Five members of the crew became evaders and four others met varying fates.[1]

'We encountered several bursts of flak just as we hit the coast of France,' Starzynski said. 'Our B-17 took a direct hit in the No. 3 engine, which started to burn. We dropped out of formation and Dingman asked 1st Lieutenant George Clements, the navigator, for our position. He asked which would be the better action to take; fly back across the Channel or head for the Allied lines in France.

---

1 *First Over Germany: A History of the 306th Bombardment Group* by Russell A. Strong (Hunter Publishing Co., 1982).

Clements replied that they were both the same distance. Several minutes passed and the No. 3 engine was getting worse. Flames were leaping over the nacelle and the slipstream was carrying the fire back towards the tail, and Dingman ordered the crew to bail out. In the bail-out procedure the tail gunner is always the first to go, so I shouted over the intercom that I was jumping. I reached behind to pick up my chest 'chute but it wasn't there! It had apparently slipped down the fuselage to the rear landing wheel compartment. I took off my oxygen mask and crawled back to retrieve my parachute. It was fortunate it was there because there were no spares on board. I crawled to the emergency escape hatch and after a little difficulty, finally got it open. The door blew away and I put my feet out into the slipstream. Hooking on my parachute, I got ready to jump. Luckily, I noticed that one of the hooks was not properly attached. I quickly remedied the situation and put my hands up to grab the top of the escape hatch. As I did so one of the gunners standing in the waist was also getting ready to jump.'

According to an eyewitness account from another B-17 in the formation, Dingman's B-17 was last seen at 1113 hours south-east of Dieppe with the right wing on fire. All nine crew members survived. Dingman; Clements; 1st Lieutenant Robert G. Danknich, bombardier, who was on his 25th mission; Tech Sergeants Wallace P. Powers, engineer and John A. Sheridan, radio operator and Staff Sergeants Robert A. Simonson, waist gunner, and Winston Burroughs, who was on his 23rd mission, were taken prisoner. When Burroughs' chute opened, he was still way above the clouds. 'But,' he said, 'when I came through them, I seemed to hit the ground at the same time very hard, my knees buckled and the wind carried me across a field into a fence. I was able to get out of my chute then and realized I could hardly walk after hitting the ground so hard. I was sure my left knee was broken. then I was picked up by the Germans and put in a truck. At least I didn't have to walk. I never saw the rest of my crew. I was held in a cell in Rouen about a week. My knees stopped hurting. I was put in another truck with other American airmen and transported to Paris. The guard told us if we were attacked by planes we had to stay in the truck while they hid in a ditch. Thankfully, we weren't attacked. It was a scary thing as only Allied fighters were in the air. From Paris prisoners were taken to Brussels at night by bus there we were interrogated and after a few days we went by train to Frankfurt. As we walked from the train to another interrogation unit civilians threw stones and bottles at us.'

Second Lieutenant Wilbur C. Pensinger, co-pilot, who was picked up almost immediately by the underground, was moved three times until being turned over to the Canadian army on 3 September 1944. Starzynski also evaded. 'The next thing I was floating down.' he recalled. 'I had bailed out at about 22,000ft and by the time I had got my oxygen mask off and my 'chute on, I had almost passed out. Apparently, the jerk of the parachute opening made me regain consciousness. I floated down and looked around for the aircraft and any other parachutes. The area was very cloudy and I couldn't make out either. After the roar of the B-17, the stillness was something I will never forget. Only the endless swishing of my white silk parachute disturbed the still, calm air as I continued my steady descent toward the ground with the words, "Pilot to crew, bail out, bail out!" still ringing in my ears and the vision of the fire melting the wing still before me. It seemed like a nightmare. I thought of Petersen's crew and how, on an earlier mission, only two of them got out before the ship exploded.[2]

'It was as if I was suspended; nothing seemed to move. After what seemed to be minutes or so but which were probably seconds, a

---

2  Starzynski is referring to 2nd Lieutenant Walter R. Peterson's crew in the 367th Bomb Squadron that was shot down on 24 April 1944 on the mission to the aircraft assembly and repair works at Oberpfaffenhofen in southern Germany. At 1123 hours the 'Clay Pigeons' lost its first of three B-17s on the mission when over France Peterson's Fortress was hit by meagre but accurate flak. Peterson was a veteran of 11 days in the Group. The No. 4 engine was set on fire and the B-17 peeled out of formation. Three or four parachutes were seen and within a minute the Fortress blew up. Four men survived. Peterson and five crew were killed.

P-51 Mustang appeared and circled several times. I waved to the pilot and he dipped his wings in recognition. He continued on his way. I should think reporting my position as he did so. I kept looking around but I could see no one. As I came through the cloud layers I could at last make out a large farmhouse. What had earlier appeared as flecks of greenery in the distance now emerged as clusters of symmetrically formed trees and hedgerows. I was coming down pretty fast now; probably because my 'chute was the smaller, emergency type.

'It was only a matter of seconds now. I desperately attempted to manoeuvre my 'chute but it was too late. I hurtled towards the ground at an alarming speed. Snap! Crack! Through the branches I crashed, picking up my feet to miss some hedges. By the time I could straighten out again, I was flat on my back on the ground. Fortunately, the ground was soft. I gathered up my 'chute and made for the hedges. I hid my Mae West and parachute under some leaves and rocks so they would not blow away. It was now around 1115 and I decided to stay in the area. I knew that my escape kit contained French francs, maps, a compass, Benzedrine tablets and chocolate. I took stock of these and went through my personal effects, tearing out all addresses; not that any were important. Under the concealment of overhanging foliage, I studied the cloth cap from my escape kit. It was still quiet so I decided to stay a little longer, at least until dark.

'For nine hours I remained hidden not knowing if the German Army had spotted my descent and were, at this moment, searching for me. Now, at about 1130, I decided it was dark enough to start walking. Checking my compass, I decided to walk south. All I had were my flying boots. I had slung my civilian shoes over my shoulder when I had left the plane but they had been whisked away. I began to feel very conspicuous because I was still wearing my flying jacket and suit and my heated flight shoes. I took my clumsy flying boots off and, carefully looking about, I crept across a road and cautiously made my way to a farmhouse with carefully tended grounds. I knocked twice on the door. It was quite late and I assumed that the occupants must be asleep. Eventually though someone answered. *"Aviateur Americane,"* I called.

'Two men looked me up and down and I showed them my dog tags. They let me in and began talking rapidly in French, of which I understood nothing. After checking to see if anyone else was outside, one of the men drew the curtains while the other lit a candle. I pointed to my French phrase card and asked if the enemy was nearby. One of the men, using my map, pointed to the town of Buchy, north-east of Rouen, and said that the Germans were everywhere in the vicinity. Again, I pointed to the card and asked if I might have civilian clothes and something to eat. They responded with cider, ham and hard brown bread. The clothes they brought looked as if they had been worn in the last war but I was in no position to refuse them. They also gave me a pair of shoes, which were exceptionally tight but I put them on. I offered them all the money I had for the shoes but the offer was refused. I guess they were worth more money than I could offer.

'There were too many Germans nearby for the French family to risk hiding me or contacting the Resistance. Pointing again to my map, he indicated that Le Havre, 70km to the west, was a safe place to hide. I might be able to make contact with the underground and slip across the Channel in a boat. I said goodbye to my benefactors wearing an old sweater, cotton jacket, a striped pair of trousers and a pair of shoes two sizes too small.

'It was Sunday, 18 June when I left the farmhouse and strode out into the night. I headed for Buchy, pausing several times after hearing voices. Several German units were camped in the woods by the sides of the road so I did not stop. It was shortly after midnight when I arrived in Buchy. I heard the heavy clump-thump-thump of boots approaching and ducked into a doorway, losing myself in the shadows. Only a moment later two Germans came around the corner and walked right by me. I could have reached out and touched them, they were that close. It was then that I decided to discount earlier intelligence information provided at pre-mission briefings and walk during the daylight hours rather than at night.

'Scouting for a place to hide until dawn, I looked around and noticed a large house, a courtyard and smaller sheds nearby. Upon closer investigation, the shed, containing a hayloft, seemed the safest hideaway. The loft, however, proved inaccessible and I returned to the courtyard. I ducked inside and sat behind a large stone wall. Before I could decide what to do next, I heard heavy footsteps grinding into the gravel path. Were the German soldiers returning? Had I been discovered?

'The door to the nearest shed was partially open. I plunged inside and crouched low in the shadows of a makeshift garage near a camouflaged German staff car. This should have tipped me off where I was but I looked around and discovered a very large barrel of cider. I helped myself. Then I heard the soldiers again so I just sat on the floor, not even daring to look up. The footsteps slowed and then stopped just outside the door. My heart beat faster and faster with each laboured breath sounding like thunder in my ears. Suddenly, two voices – the soldiers had returned. My only hope was to fade into the shadows keeping deathly quiet until dawn. An uneasy silence prevailed throughout the long night.

'Sunlight filtering through narrow slits in the wall announced the break of a new day. Had the Germans left? Recalling a bombed-out house across the courtyard, I decided to make a run for it. I had to take the risk.

'The house was a scene of destruction. Stairs leading to the second floor were a mass of crumpled brick and wood. Using the rubble as a ladder, I hoisted myself to the second floor. The two rooms upstairs had nothing in them. All that remained was an empty shell. Being uninhabited for some time, the house offered little chance of discovery. Some of the bricks in the wall had been knocked out, allowing me a commanding view of the courtyard.

'Lying on the floor, I heard voices of German soldiers once again. Cautiously, I crept nearer the opening. In the courtyard below I could see one soldier showing his rifle to another. I was more fascinated than alarmed. I drew back slowly from the opening fearing they would sense someone watching them. Later I was to discover that the sanctuary I had chosen actually adjoined a German barracks!

'It was still too dangerous to leave because the German soldiers were coming out of the barracks and people were beginning to stir in the streets. Anxiety and restlessness began to mount within me so I left my hideout and headed towards Rouen. My progress would be slow. Lack of rain had made the road dry and dusty. Blazing sun beat down incessantly. The enemy was everywhere.

'Not until late afternoon, did I dare stop in a cafe for a drink of cider. Dusk found me near the town of Barentin, where I decided to spend the night in an open field. By now my feet were really bothering me. The tight shoes were causing my feet to blister. Removing my shoes, I cringed with pain. Blood oozed from my torn flesh and sweat and dirt added to my discomfort. Mindful of the impending swelling, I carefully eased on my shoes. Overturning a few sheaves of wheat, I laid on the ground and scattered them over me for cover. I was awakened several times during the night by field mice rustling in the coarse grain. Tuesday morning, however, brought other visitors. Sharp stinging bites could signify only one thing: lice.

'It seemed like ages that I was on the road and as I limped along each step produced twin bonfires under my painful feet. I had to sit and rest. It must have been my lucky day. An old German guard of about 60 pedalled past me on a bicycle. He was wearing a large leather holster which probably contained a Luger and seemed to be supervising some Frenchmen who were digging trenches alongside the road. Thankfully, he didn't pay me much attention as he cycled past me. Shortly up the road I met him again. Suddenly, I seemed to command all his attention. He came over to me and asked in French where I was going. I answered, "Bolbec, Bolbec" and pointed repeatedly to a road sign indicating the town of Bolbec straight ahead. From what I understood, he said it was a long walk.

'Abruptly, he asked me for my papers. I shook my head. He glared at me once again and looked me over, paying great attention to my old shoes and my clothes. Incredibly, he told me to walk on.

Face unshaven, clothes smelly and filthy; he must have taken me for a tramp. I got away quickly, although he should really have taken me in. Had he tried, he would have had a fight because I was ready to attack him. I didn't have any weapons because we were not issued any for flying. (Some of the boys carried .45 automatics but apparently there was a shortage and we never got any.)

'Shortly thereafter, dusk fell over the countryside. According to my map, I was nearly half the way to Le Havre. How much longer could I continue? Sharp stabs of pain from inflamed feet tormented my sleep. Oh, if only I could reach Le Havre, then cross the Channel to England.

'By the fifth day my bedraggled appearance was beginning to draw people's attention. A short distance from Bolbec, I asked a woman the directions to a barber shop. She understood when I pointed to my hair and used my fingers to imitate the movement of scissors. 'Two kilometres,' she said, pointing up the road.

'I arrived at the little barber shop and looked in. There was only a mother, a young girl and a young boy of about 12 years old. An old barber was giving the girl a haircut as I entered. The younger barber, who was about 16 years of age, directed me to a chair. I removed my jacket and made myself comfortable. As one might expect, halfway through the shave, he nicked me. No sooner had he finished shaving me, than he walked toward the door. I paid little attention, but as I glanced in the mirror to see where he had nicked me, I saw that he was talking with a German soldier. I didn't know what they were saying as they spoke in a muffled tone. Ideas began spinning through my mind. Did the barber know I was American? If he did suspect me, could I escape in any way? Looking about the room for another exit, I noticed their curious glances directed towards me. The soldier mumbled something to the barber and he said something to me in French. Apparently, the German was in a hurry and wanted to know if he could get a haircut before me. I nodded and with that the German soldier left.

'When the barber had finished with the girl the soldier had still not returned, so he motioned me to sit in the chair and began cutting. Almost at once the soldier returned with three other German soldiers. Scowling at me with displeasure, they all sat down a short distance away and I thought, "Boy this is really something." The German who I had promised could go in front of me kept giving me dirty looks.

'About halfway through my haircut the old barber asked me how I wanted my hair cut. I didn't really know what to say so I just motioned him to carry on. In the meantime, I could see in the mirror that the German was looking at me. He was also sitting on the chair where I had left my jacket. In it were all my maps and papers! All he had to do was look down but I didn't give him the chance. I leaped out of the chair, taking the largest Franc note I had and gave it to the barber. My haircut and shave cost me sixteen francs but the experience cost me 16 grey hairs. The barber gave me change and I gave him a tip. I think he was relieved I was finished because he did not want any problems with the Germans. I thankfully grabbed my jacket, left the shop and headed up the road.

'At twilight I was only 16 km from Le Havre. My feet were badly blistered and I had to find a place to hide. I selected a neat, medium-sized farm just off the road. My head was reeling with excitement as I approached the house knowing I had somehow overcome tremendous risks. The farmer and his family listened to my story in disbelief. With the help of an English–French dictionary and broken phrases, I told them I received the clothes from a farmer near Buchy not far from the spot where I had bailed out.

My festered, swollen feet gave evidence of the truth. After providing me with some food, they insisted I bathe my feet.

'Only after resting for a short time, I was informed that the German army had a road block ahead. My long walk had been in vain. I needed identification papers to gain entrance to Le Havre but there was nothing more I could do that night. Taking into consideration my poor physical appearance, they invited me to share one of their beds rather than a hayloft in the barn. After sleeping in fields and haylofts for the past five days, I was most grateful.

'The next morning, I bade a reluctant farewell. Dejectedly, I began retracing my steps. I decided, after checking my map, to return to Bolbec and then head south to Lillebonne.

'Later that morning, after informing some Frenchmen at one cafe in Lillebonne that I was an American aviator, I was refused sanctuary. At another a woman who came to serve me asked me in French what I wanted to order. I could not understand her so I just said, "*Jes Swei, Aviateur American.*" She looked at me oddly and started laughing. She called out to someone in the back room. Everyone thought it was a big joke, so I left hurriedly and starting walking down the road towards the Seine.

'Just south of Lillebonne I came upon a junk peddler pushing a cart. He was a ragged Brazilian who had been stranded in France before the war and had never accumulated enough money to return to Latin America. He was able to speak a few words of English and told me that the Germans had taken over the ferry boat, which was the only way to cross the river. He added that there was a rowing boat, which was operated by the French. He took me to the Frenchmen and told them I was an American airman. What he said must have sounded convincing, for my passage was free. The Frenchmen took me on board the boat and rowed me across the Seine.

'Reaching the opposite shore, we all entered a cafe for sandwiches and beer. We were in Quillebeuf. One of the passengers told me to remain at the cafe. I waited for three hours and nothing happened. I bought some postcards from a stand for some reason, probably to pass the time. Nothing happened and I got up and walked out. Just south of the river I hit the dirt. A sudden burst of machine gun fire and several explosions erupted as two P-38s began their strafing and bombing run in the vicinity of the ferry boat. The ground shook with the bursting of exploding shells. Minutes later it was over.

'Gradually rising to my feet, I hobbled to an abandoned farmhouse. Once inside, I sat down and removed my shoes. My feet were very bad. Unexpectedly, a German soldier walked in and spoke to me. I just muttered, "Oui". He walked over to a wall and took away a home-made ladder. I assume he needed it to repair some of the damage to the telephone lines caused by the bombing. I figured that this was not the greatest place in the world to be so I got ready to leave.

'Before I could get far a voice called out, "What are you doing there?" I didn't, of course, understand French so I replied in my best accent, "Oui". A blue-eyed blond civilian repeated the question and again I answered "Oui". Making little progress in our conversation, he enquired if I spoke English. I confirmed that I did. We conversed for a time and I told him I was an aviator. He looked so much like a German that I thought I had had it. I no longer cared by this time anyway.

'The blond Frenchman, who turned out to be called Charles Lamour, took me outside to an orchard and told me to wait. I thought he must be leaving to get reinforcements but when he returned an hour later, he brought with him a woman who had some food for me. The woman kept asking for assurances that I was an American. They were ultimately convinced I was telling the truth when I kept answering nonchalantly, "Sure I am; what you want?"

'Later, I was to learn that my crossing of the Seine had been well timed. Apparently, the Gestapo had been enquiring about someone fitting my description. The boatman, who was a member of the Resistance, had told them that I had continued walking along the river and had not taken the boat across. Within an hour, they were searching everywhere for me.

'Charles Lamour contacted the French Resistance and they hid me from the Germans. I was taken to another farmhouse in Quillebeuf and only allowed out at night. I stayed in Quillebeuf for ten weeks, hiding in every place imaginable – barns, houses and air-raid shelters.

'During my time in hiding we would carry out some limited acts of sabotage like cutting down telephone lines. Twice we stole a cow from the Germans for food and on other nights we stole beans from the fields. The American Air Force tried repeatedly to blow up the ferry boat. Each time they missed. Towards the end, when the Canadians were approaching, the ferry boat was eventually sunk. Three weeks before the Canadians liberated us my hosts went on a big drinking session. Some German soldiers heard them bragging and they barely got away with their lives. Charles decided to have me moved after this incident. He put me in with a couple who had a small child. I stayed on the second floor of their three-storey house for three weeks. During that time there was incessant noise from artillery barrages and exchanges between the Germans and the advancing Allies. It got so bad on some occasions that we hid in some caves nearby that were used as air-raid shelters.

'I was the first American many of the French townspeople had ever seen. My heart went out to the simple people who had truly saved my life at the risk of their own. Eventually, we were liberated by Canadian troops. They wanted me to hop on their tank and leave the area but I could not because I had to get my ID tags back from the underground. I sent word to the fellow who had them, and £16. He turned out to be the mayor and at first refused to hand the money and tags over to me. The Canadians suggested I tell him that if he did not hand them over, they would drive a tank right through his darn house! That did the trick and I was given back my ID tags and money.

'Word went through about my plight and later a small unit came through to pick me up. They apparently picked up all shot down airmen. I was shipped back to Cherbourg, where we took a C-47 to London and SHEAF headquarters. I was interrogated and after several days I was returned to Thurleigh. There I met Wilbur Pensinger, who had been picked up almost immediately by the underground, but the other seven in my crew had been captured.'

Bob Starzynski returned to the US in September 1944. On 17 March (Saint Patrick's Day) 1945, he celebrated his 21st birthday. Was it Irish luck or Polish luck that helped save his life? After the war he joined the Chicago Police Department and retired after 39 years. In 1982 he travelled to France and was able to thank some of the people who had helped him evade the Germans in 1944.

# Chapter 11

# Special Ops

*In 1944 Flight Sergeant I. W. 'Steve' Bostridge was
the bomb aimer on a 90 Squadron crew flying Stirling
bombers from Tuddenham, a satellite of Mildenhall in
Suffolk. That spring the squadron was flying a mixture
of short-range bombing and Special Duties operations,
delivering supplies to the Resistance in France. Bostridge
had tried to enlist in the RAF in 1941 but he was told 'to
go home and wait'. He thought 'God, I'll never get in.'
But finally, he was accepted and he was sent to the United
States for pilot training, to Georgia in the deep south.*

'We were made very welcome. We liked the coloured lads because
we weren't used to coloured people – we treated them differently
to what the "Yanks" did, especially the Southerners. We always
got best service in the mess – whatever we asked for. We would
eat like horses. You'd call a waiter and say you wanted some more
eggs – they didn't go and get you an egg, they came back with a
great tray full of fried eggs! Same with a piece of melon which was
so big and wide you couldn't get your face into it. But I flunked
the course, so I re-mustered as a bomb aimer in Canada and did
my training there. I came home in June 1943 (with a kitbag full
of cigarettes, nylons and chocolate) and crewed up just before we
went on 'Wimpys'. The engineers and gunners came in and joined
navigators, bomb aimers and pilots who had been together up to
then. We were told to mill around and we just went round and

nattered to people. Are you crewed up? No, I'm not. Well, what about it? I think it was quite a good way of doing it because at least it was your choice. To me, the crew was the most important thing. We became an all-British crew, but the squadron was made up of Aussies, South Africans, New Zealanders, Canadians – we all got on well together.

'Our pilot was Flight Lieutenant Kenneth "Jock" MacDonald. Sergeant James "Jock" Westwood from Dalkeith was the flight engineer, Pilot Officer "Les" Poole, navigator, Sergeant George Jim "Slim" King, wireless op, and the two gunners were Sergeants Peter F. Broadribb and 19-year-old Elwyn "Taff" Healey of Dowlais, Merthyr Tydfil. We were posted to "B" Flight on 90 Squadron in Stirling IIIs at Tuddenham and were not disappointed. I thought it was a marvellous aircraft.

'Our billets were for two crews, fourteen men. The other crew in our billet were a new crew. They took off and we watched them. They slewed off the runway, went across the grass, pulled up over the tops of trees, went round and then there was a great explosion. They went straight into the deck. Another crew went to France and crashed. We heard the Germans captured one of them and shot him! By that time the invasion had started and our blokes were classed as saboteurs because we were dropping stuff to the Resistance.

'Our first op was a "Nickel" leaflet run on Wellingtons – just a training flight at the OTU. You took leaflets over and dropped them somewhere in France just to get used to gunfire and so on. When we were on special duties we did two bombing raids in France on rocket sites and we went with the main force. Once we were used as a decoy for the main force, going up to Bremen. We got recalled when we were still in broad daylight. All we were told was that if you went with the main force, you just kept your head down and watched the stuff going down to the Resistance. We went over singly, one aircraft, not shoals of aircraft, and only in moonlight periods because it was low level, so the rest of the month you were stooging around. You went across to France and then dropped down quickly, low level to your spot, pulled up, dropped the load and then hell for leather out of it!

'My own job – a lot of it – was map reading and navigation. If you flew near enough to the deck you could pick up all the points. You could literally follow a river, the Seine or Somme or whatever, whereas with the main force you had a definite route to take. Our blackout was pretty good, but in France, though the villages were not lit up like London, at night you could pick 'em out. If you got a moon in front of you it was almost daylight. It wasn't so good when the moon was behind you, but when the moon was in front it was so easy; the rivers almost looked black except when the moon caught them and they flashed. You could also pick out towns, fields, bushes quite easily.

'The Resistance lit bonfires and we were told before we went what the code letter would be. They used Aldis lamps, or torches, or whatever they had, that flashed. You'd come over, they'd light the fires when they heard the aircraft; you'd climb up, ready to drop the stuff. You were told how the bonfires were lit. If they were in a straight line of three or four, or a cross or similar, you'd be told what the recognition letter was and once you got that you'd unload. If you didn't get the letter of recognition, you'd take it back.'

Peter Broadribb, the mid-upper gunner, remembers, 'Of these operational flights a number proved to be particularly difficult, through circumstances which cropped up. I recall one mining trip to Kiel, possibly that on 24 February 1944, when we iced up very badly going out over the North Sea and struggled to maintain 8,000ft – in fact we stooged across Denmark without interference until Flensburg, when searchlights and flak left everything above us and concentrated on our aircraft once coned. On that occasion the squadron bombing officer, "Snake", was flying with us as Steve was sick and he virtually took over and dictated the evasive action to be taken. In a steep dive, I understand we reached 400mph and it took three to pull the aircraft out. We got out of a tight spot, although the compass was toppled in the process, which also led to us being lost for a period.

'On one other trip our aircraft was damaged by flak, with a fair proportion of the nose shot away. We came back across France on three engines and a second failed as we neared the English coast. Whilst we got back to Tuddenham, we were not permitted to land, having no undercart. So, we were diverted to Woodbridge. The organisation there was tremendous and we pancaked amidst many sparks from the belly on the runway, to be put most smartly into a blood wagon and rushed away for a quick tot!'

Steve Bostridge recalls, 'We had a super padre on the squadron. He would stand at the end of the runway, late at night and it was cold! He was always there when we came back, with rum and coffee, pouring it out. I never knew him not to be there, whatever time it was. On the first op an electrician came out in his wagon to make sure everything was OK. We were on the ground waiting to take off and he said, "I must have a leak!" So he did, on the tailwheel of the aircraft. The next time he came round he said, "Oh, for luck!" This then became the thing.'

Although this crew had flown on 30 ops, only 26 counted towards their full tour, two having been 'recalls' while two were aborted due to engine trouble. Their op on the night of 2/3 June 1944 therefore was their 27th, a drop to the Resistance at Bayonvillers, a small village south of the main road linking Amiens to Saint-Quentin in the Somme Department. Altogether, 36 aircraft were dispatched on sorties this night, one of which, a Halifax on 138 Squadron at Tempsford on Operation 'Tybalt 29', lost its port inner engine at 100ft after taking off in the half light of dusk. Unable to continue the climb, the pilot made a skilful crash-landing into woods close to the airfield at Sandy. The aircraft caught fire after impact and although the crew survived, four were seriously injured. A second Halifax, which took off from Tempsford on SOE Operation 'Roderigo 1' and 'Osric 77' with a crew of nine and three agents, was shot down over Holland on the southern route to Belgium by a Heinkel He 219 Uhu ('Owl') piloted by Hauptmann Heinz Strüning with the loss of all the crew and two of the agents.

At Tuddenham Jock MacDonald's crew said to their friendly electrician, 'We'll see you this evening, don't forget!' 'He was getting married to a WAAF,' recalled Bostridge, 'and he went into Cambridge or Newmarket, to buy bits and pieces. We were hanging around at the aircraft waiting for him to come but he finally got back about half an hour after we took off without him having peed on the tailwheel. We felt that this was bad luck and got it firmly fixed in our minds.'

It was the crew's seventh trip in EF294, 'G for George'. 'We took a load of empty bottles up with us,' says Bostridge, 'because we understood that if you threw a bottle out from a great height, it comes down whistling like a bomb. "Taff" Healy loaded up the rear turret with the empty beer bottles and he would toss them out over France just for the hell of it.'

As 'G for George' lifted off the runway at Tuddenham 'Taff' Healy checked his watch – the time was 2239 hours. 'It was a successful drop south-east of Paris,' he recalled, 'and we were heading for home at around 300ft when we were hit by flak, one burst putting my rear turret out of action. I tried to inform the pilot, but the intercom was out as well. I then became aware of a red glow behind me and could see the fuselage on fire. I tried to get out of the turret, but the doors had jammed. Eventually I forced my way out with an axe and started fighting the fire with an extinguisher. Just when it seemed I had the fire under control, the bottle ran dry and the flames flared up again.'

Steve Bostridge said, 'We probably had woken a gun crew up – they caught us on the way back. It was only light flak but we were down low on the deck. They shot the two starboard engines and they caught alight. The flames were all on one side of the Stirling and it took both Jock and me all our strength to hold the thing up but she literally ploughed into the ground and very smoothly. (It was 0135 hours on Sunday morning.) We had canisters of some sort, with a spike at the end. If you crashed and the aircraft wasn't alight, you could bang 'em into the side of the fuselage and they would burn. Jock and I climbed out of the top along the other wing and by the time we left it was alight. (We found out afterwards that "Jerry", because they got there so quickly, put it out and hauled the Stirling away.) The rest of the crew went down the back and jumped out.'

'Taff' Healy had decided to jump the fire and inform the skipper of their situation and get another extinguisher. 'Meanwhile I was suffocating from the flames and smoke and could hear the cannon shells still hitting the kite as "Jerry" kept plastering us. On the way up front I told Peter Broadribb, "Slim" King, Les Poole and Jock Westwood, and then carried on forward and told the pilot, who was looking out at the starboard wing. One of the fuel tanks was on fire and the starboard engines had stopped. At that moment Steve Bostridge took up his "crash position" and I ran back to tell the rest of the crew. We had barely taken up ours when we were ploughing our way through a cornfield with thick dust coming in everywhere.'

Peter Broadribb recalled, 'Having made three crash-landings in Stirlings it was, I suppose, unfortunate that the last occasion should be in a ploughed field in France. We had to climb to a safety height of 1,000ft to cross pylons at Saint-Quentin and in dropping back down we had six positions of light ack-ack open up on us – a crossfire! – a searchlight having coned the aircraft. I remember clearly firing from my mid-upper turret down the searchlight beam – one moment my turret was complete and next it had been shattered, with the Perspex blown away and a tremendous gale blowing about me. Two engines were alight and the intercom had broken down. The skipper obviously decided to crash-land the plane, which he did most successfully.'

'Fortunately,' says 'Taff' Healy, '"G-George" was a good aircraft (made by Short & Harland, Belfast) which held together and did not break up or explode on impact. The five of us – Les, Pete, Slim, Jock Westwood and I – got out of the rear exit – Les having set the demolition charges on the H2S – while Steve and the pilot got out of the front. We never saw them again so we assumed they got back to base. It was now around 2 am (3 June) and the aircraft was blazing, so the five of us started walking across country before Jerry arrived to investigate. We walked until dawn and then decided to hide in a bean field. We were soaking wet and lay there shivering with cold until the sun came out and then we started to roast with the heat. It was a boiling hot day and we did not have any water or cover, so it was very uncomfortable.

'When night came, we walked for about ten miles, then Pete said he could not go any further, as his back was giving him a lot of trouble. We lay down in a corn field to wait for dawn and when daylight came, we had a look at his back and saw he had been hit by the flak and the area around the wound had turned green. That day we came to a farmhouse, where we were given some food and bathed Pete's back. We were then taken to a derelict chateau by the farmer and told to hide there until evening, when we would have to move on to Paris. But Pete was too ill to move, so we stayed there all night and the following day (5 June) until about 4 pm.

'Then some Jerry soldiers came in the house and we started our careers as PoWs. We were taken to a Luftwaffe camp in Rosières-en-Santerre, then searched and put in solitary confinement. Pete was taken to a hospital in Amiens and Les was kept guarded in the office as he was an officer. Slim, Jock Westwood and myself were locked in separate cells – about 7 ft x 4 ft x 10 ft with one little glazed window high up and soundproof walls, one light in the ceiling and a bunk bed with straw palliasse. Under the corner of the palliasse was a set of playing cards someone had made out of crepe toilet paper – they were only about the size of postage stamps but were carefully marked out in pencil.'

Broadribb says, 'Whilst I knew I had been hit quite heavily in the back, I did not appreciate until at the escape hatch by my turret that I was partially paralysed. Fortunately for me two of the lads pushed me through the escape hatch. Once we were out of the aircraft, the five of us who had escaped through the mid-hatch got as far as possible away from the burning plane. I was able to shuffle but not raise my feet from the ground; in consequence as we moved away and kept to the fields, the other lads manhandled me over or around hedges. Whilst my memory is not too distinct as to the time, I recall that it was around 2 to 2.30 am when we came to grief. I also remember seeing two or three other aircraft and thinking that before long they would be on the right side of the Channel.

'However, we kept moving until daylight, when we hid in a field of flax. During that Saturday, 3 June, we kept our heads down and "Slim", our wireless operator, a qualified St John's Ambulance man, did all he could in applying dressings to my back wounds. Throughout the period from being shot down we were aware that "Jerry" was searching for us. Once dusk descended, we got on the move again, moving inland, hopefully towards the Maquis areas where we had been involved previously.

'Sunday I was in rather a bad way and on reflection I have always felt the other lads should have left me, as I was in urgent need of proper medical attention and delaying their progress. Late that day it was decided to approach the French for help. We were taken to a farm and contact made with the underground movement; the schoolboy French of three of us proved better than the English of a French school teacher. The message we had was that if I was attended by a doctor, they would need to give me over to "Jerry". In the event, we were given food and taken to a nearby chateau at Beaucourt-en-Santerre, which, whilst empty, had been used by the Germans as a barracks. We stayed overnight and through the Monday, it being a wet day. Food was provided, but shortly after midday Germans were seen outside and eventually as they moved into and searched the building we were found on the top floor; however, we did conceal in a chimney food given to us by the French.

'Having been taken out of the chateau, we were placed against a wall and each of the five of us was covered by German field police but, fortunately, the intention was merely to search us. In due time we were taken by the army to Rosières, where we were interrogated in a straightforward manner, but prior to leaving the grounds of the chateau a German officer had examined my wounds which, in the words of the lads, had turned green. Having been searched and all valuables removed, they were placed in an envelope, which was sealed in my presence; these were later returned to me at Wetzlar. I was then taken to a nearby airfield and placed in sickbay; the other lads, I gather, stayed in Rosières.

'I was running a considerable temperature and clearly the Germans wanted this reduced before moving me elsewhere. I stayed in the sickbay until the Tuesday evening of 6 June, when I was taken out to a half-track vehicle and placed in the rear on my back. My first shock was when being helped into the vehicle an American Thunderbolt flew down the road and, to this day, I do not know why he did not open fire, yet French people nearby were waving.

'From here I was taken to Amiens, but when on the outskirts of the town the half-track pulled off the road – I knew why when the bombs started to whistle down unpleasantly close. However, I managed to scramble from the back of the vehicle and join my German escort already in the ditch – we were opposite the marshalling yards being raided by American Mitchells. After the first wave I was taken to air-raid shelters and but for my German corporal guard pulling a pistol I would have been lynched by Todt workers[1] in the marshalling yard who pointed to the bombers above.

'When the journey was resumed after the raid ended, I was taken to the Military Hospital in Amiens. As I was taken up the drive my corporal guard, who spoke very good English, told me the invasion had started that morning, in his words "at Cherbourg and Le Havre". On entering the hospital, I was handed over to a German doctor, who told me he had been in practice in Hampstead before the war. However, I received only limited treatment, bandages being of paper. I was placed in a room at the top of the building with an American pilot who had lost a leg. On telling him the invasion news this went round the top floor at great speed and all the airmen prisoners' morale was greatly boosted.'

---

1 Organisation Todt was a civil and military engineering organisation in Nazi Germany from 1933 to 1945, named for its founder, Fritz Todt, an engineer and senior Nazi.

Taff Healy was taken out of his cell on 11 June and, to his relief, put on a bus along with Slim, Jock Westwood and Les. (Their skipper, meanwhile, had evaded and Les Poole was sent to Stalag Luft III.) 'On the coach we met Pete, who told us they had not done anything to his back, as they did not have any drugs or medicines. After a journey of about eight hours, we arrived in Brussels and Pete was taken away for treatment. We were put in an old jail in solitary confinement on bread and water. They interrogated us again (12 June) and told us we would be moving. On the morning of the 13th, we were taken to Brussels railway station and put on a train, passing through Cologne – where there was an air-raid alarm, but nothing happened – and Frankfurt. After a journey of 28 hours, we arrived at Oberursel about 4 am on 15 June, where we were searched and put in solitary confinement. Jock and Slim were taken away on 16 June.

'At 0600 hours on the morning of the 17th the guards took us to a transit camp (Wetzlar), which was a journey of about six hours. There we were given a suitcase with a pair of pants, one vest, two bars of soap, sixty cigarettes (American), ten packets of chewing gum, two towels, one pair of boots, a tin of boot polish, one belt, one pullover, a brush and comb, a razor, toothpaste and a US Army greatcoat. All of this was given as a gift by the American Red Cross. Then we had a shave and a shower-bath, the first for two weeks, and given a meal of tinned salmon potatoes, bread and butter and jam. This was the first time my stomach was full since we left England. Jock and Slim had been waiting for me at the camp gates and they took me to a bed space they had reserved for me, where I had a good night's rest.

'On the morning of 18 June, we were given a Red Cross food parcel for your journey to a permanent camp. We travelled by rail in cattle truck, but who cared as long as we had someone to talk to after eleven days of talking to yourself in solitary confinement. When we arrived at this camp (Luft VII on 20 June) the fellows who were already there had a cup of hot cocoa ready. Then six of us got together and came to Hut 82, which was to be our home for who knew how long. The six of us, all sergeants, were John Hamilton (of Truro, Cornwall), Len W. Cook

(Blakeney, Norfolk), Jock Westwood and Robert S. 'Bob' Hall RCAF (of Normal, Illinois, in the USA) and Walter S. 'Scotty' Rowan from Gowkshill, Scotland [who were 2nd pilot and wireless operator respectively on a 432 Squadron RCAF Halifax shot down on Bourg Leopold on 27/28 May. Rowan was arrested in Antwerp on 6 June]. 'They were a good set of boys and we got along quite well.

'The next morning, we got up at 0730, had breakfast, which was porridge and cocoa. Then played about until dinner time when we had soup and tea. Then we had a Red Cross food parcel and a bread ration – ⅙th of a loaf. We made up what we liked for tea, so we had tinned salmon, bread and butter and tea. For supper we had some bread and butter and jam and cocoa. At 9 pm the curfew sounded and we had to go to bed. We sang songs and talked about our different adventures for a while. Then when it got dark, we went to sleep.'

Pete Broadribb wrote, 'After a night when I truly thought I would die in the absence of medical attention I was taken for interrogation and had a phoney Red Cross form placed in front of me, which I could not complete in any event, being unable to write. However, after giving my number, rank and name, I eventually also gave my home address and civilian occupation. I was told consistently that without answers to the remaining questions I could not have hospital treatment; nevertheless, in the absence of further response on my part a telephone call was made which resulted in the interrogators determining I had been flying in a Stirling and not a Lancaster or a Halifax as they had suggested originally. I was staggered when they referred to an indexed filing cabinet and subsequently told me of the squadron, the wing co's name, the fact he picked his trips and correctly with one exception the names of the members of the crew.

'Following this I was taken by lorry to Ste Gilles Hospital in the suburbs, used exclusively by the Luftwaffe. From this moment I was treated splendidly. I owe much to the wonderful surgery and good luck, as part of the transverse process of my spine was sheared off by flak which was two inches inside me; suffice to say I lived to tell the tale! After six weeks plus in hospital, once I was on my feet

I was returned to the barracks and from there shipped to Dulag Luft at Frankfurt-on-Main, thence to Wetzlar transit camp and so to Stalag Luft VII (arrived 5 August). Although handicapped to a degree, the sojourn at Luft VII was a period of my life when I learnt lessons which one could not learn other than in adversity. The odd Red Cross food parcel was received from time to time to supplement the meagre German rations and we fared reasonably well until January 1945.'

Though the five crew members had assumed that their skipper and Steve Bostridge had made it back to base after they had run in one direction and the rest of the crew had run in the other, it was premature, as Bostridge recalls. 'We heard dogs barking and all I know is that the other five got captured almost immediately, but Jock and I managed to get away with it for three and a half months. We spent the first three nights hiding out in woods. On Sunday we walked further because we heard church bells. We sat in some woods and we could see the church. We thought we ought to be able to get some help there but decided it was a bit too dicey. We'd had first-class training on escape at Feltwell in Suffolk for about three days and told all the things we should or shouldn't do. Finally, they took you out in crew buses into the countryside and dropped you off, one at a time. Your job was to get back to a given point in the camp without being caught. It did teach us a lot, including simple things like "Never go to knock at a door for help, unless one of you remains hidden and one goes – you can both get caught". Once or twice, we knocked at a farm – Jock usually went and I stayed hidden in case he was jumped upon so I'd come to his help. No one offered any help at all. It wasn't because they were anti-British; they were just too frightened. Our uniform looked much like a German uniform. We'd still got flying boots on.

'We walked eastwards, towards Vervins, where we knew there were Resistance there so we might be able to contact them. On the Sunday we spent the night in a haystack, got inside it; got bitten to blazes! We were in a little clearing and in the morning, we shook all the filth and wetness off after being woken up by a woman with a pail. She turned out to be Polish. (Don't ask me how we found that out.) She could hardly speak any French, nor could we. She milked the cows in the field and gave us a drink of milk. It was warm milk straight from the cow and it was horrible!

'Told to go back and wait in the clearing, she would bring help. Shortly after, two men arrived. They didn't speak to us. Jock and I sat in the middle of this little clearing, only about 25ft across with a tree in the middle. We sat with our backs to the tree and these two men went round and round with sickles pretending to chop. They were really watching us though we didn't realize at the time. Then a big woman who'd lived in the Channel Islands and could speak English came, saying she'd be back that evening with some clothes. She took our flying boots, gave me this old pair of boots tied up with string and Jock got a pair of shoes. We kept our trousers. She also gave me an old jacket and Jock an old zipped cycling jacket and bloody old caps! She took our flying sweaters, which were jolly nice wool, and gave us a haversack each with a bottle of water and some bread and then we pushed off.

'We'd got our escape kit with us, a plastic pack with a razor, a rubber water bottle. You could tie it on to your belt and put it down inside your trousers so it couldn't be seen. There were maps of the area which you could be used as silk scarves, Wakey-Wakey pills, which you could take if you were in a real emergency and odd things like that. There was also a bit of chocolate, nuts and raisins.

'This woman said, "Wait in the clearing. A youngster will be along from the village later on this evening and you should follow him. He doesn't speak English but he'll make signs and you do exactly whatever he does and what he says." So, later that evening at about six or seven – it wasn't dark – this lad arrived and beckoned us and we followed him and we came to a big country house with walls round it and gates. He motioned us to be quiet. We jumped into the ditch because we heard the clattering of boots and then we heard guard changing and German voices. We lay doggo in this ditch and the lad said "*doucement*!" (follow), which we did. He wriggled forward to go and get the lie of the land. We waited there for about an hour or more and he never returned. My belief is that this was deliberate. We didn't know who they were. We didn't know where we were, they'd got our clobber from us, they'd got no love for us and they'd deliberately taken us out and dumped us right beside a German headquarters of some sort, wriggled off and that was it. When it dawned on us this was probably what had happened, we well and truly shot off!

'Later, we saw an old girl picking up ears of corn. She was about sixty or seventy, a typical little French peasant woman. She'd got a barrow and was collecting greenery and putting it in it. We went up and spoke to her and she realized what we were. Jock spoke better French than I did but I could listen to it better. That was how we worked it. After three days we were getting a bit desperate. I think we would almost have approached Hitler himself and asked for help. We thought, she couldn't lay us out! If she'd started hollering, we could have run, but she didn't, she was very good, very good indeed. She made it clear that we were to follow her so we did with about twenty yards between. She took us back into Saint-Quentin and into her house. She gave us these super omelettes, which she prepared on a stove with broken twigs for heating, and she put us up in the front bedroom of the house. There were shutters on the windows. And right opposite we could hear the Jerries going in and out of what I imagine was either a mess or a canteen. We would look through the cracks in the shutters and watch them going by. We must have spent a week with her. The poor woman tried to contact the Resistance and eventually she found a schoolmistress who spoke English and she got us out. We had to follow a man in a white mac. If he was stopped, we weren't to do anything, we were to keep going and move on. He took us to the railway station, where we had to look at the train timetable. We hadn't a clue what all this was about. We just stood there looking at the timetables which we couldn't understand. Two women came up to us, caught hold of our arms and they got tickets and took us to the train.

'We went to another town and there we were put up by Jean-Marc and Claude, who had a little girl named Françoise, for a week or so, but I think they decided it was dangerous so they moved us two or three doors away into a house owned by a chap named Gilles. The house consisted of a front bedroom, a front sitting room which we never went into and never saw, a back bedroom and a kitchen. At the back was a yard with a small barn at the bottom where they kept chickens. Gilles disappeared and we had the house to ourselves, but Claude or one of her sisters would come and give us food and we could take eggs from the chickens and so on. We were told exactly what would happen if there was banging on the front door – we had to leap out of the window – and which direction to go.

'They moved us several more times and on one occasion we were put up in a house for a short time. There was a husband and wife and we had the bedroom of their son who was about our age and a prisoner of war in Germany. We opened a drawer one night and inside were shirts and rolled up socks – loads of them. I said to Jock, "Look at this lot, my God!" This was dreadful really. I was going to nick a pair of these socks because mine were absolutely ruined! Eventually, we moved off into the woods with the Resistance. There was a lot of arguing among the crowd and they kept looking us over. The argument was about whether they should put a bullet in me! At one time we had to run for our lives because the Germans were supposed to have surrounded the village. We got into the woods and we saw three figures coming towards us. They turned out to be an American pilot, navigator and gunner. From then on, the five of us stayed together. We hid up in a barn for a long time and people brought food to us every day. One of them took us out once on bicycles to get a breather.

'When we heard that Paris was liberated, we accompanied the Resistance on bicycles to the American lines. They took the three "Yanks" off separately and shoved us in a wire compound for the night. Next day we were taken by jeep into Paris. Jock and I were wearing civvy clothes so every time we stopped in a village, the villagers shook their fists as they thought we were Germans or collaborators because we'd got an armed guard in the jeep! Instead of getting feted as we hoped, as heroes, they were threatening to kill us! It was rather funny.

'We came back to England in a motor torpedo boat. I was scared to death because I thought that having got this far, with my luck I was going to drown. I stayed on deck all the time. We landed at Peacehaven and were whipped through to London for debriefing, still in rags and tatters. A corporal said, "We can't do anything about it tonight because we're all knocking off, it's 5 o'clock' – war on, mind you! Make yourselves scarce and find somewhere to kip and we'll see you back here tomorrow morning." We'd got damn all, no money, nothing, so we made our way to the Strand Palace where the crew used to meet when on leave and we met a whole crowd of our bods on a night out! We were welcomed, still in rags, boots tied up with string and dungaree trousers. They said, "Telegram home to say that you're OK." My wife was expecting our first child. She couldn't believe I was home safe and couldn't stop crying. I went up to the RAF nuthouse (rehabilitation centre) in Scotland for psychoanalysing. We had our teeth pulled and we all acted daft deliberately. The CO who was as nuts as any of us had a car and invariably about half a dozen of us used to clamber all over it, on the running boards, in the back and he would take us into town and dump us somewhere and we went drinking. I didn't go on ops again. I was posted to Canada on Liberators to go to the Far East, but they lost my papers and the war ended before I could be sent.

In 1965 Phil and his wife went to France for a holiday and retraced his steps, visiting the brave French people who had saved them from the clutches of the Germans. A woman who had given him a pair of trousers that had belonged to her husband who was a prisoner of war took only a couple of seconds to open the kitchen window and shout, 'Philippe! Philippe!' They met the husband whose trousers he wore! The whole family were there – it was a very drunken day! 'I thought they'd probably dealt with dozens of airmen, but for that particular village Jock and I were their big war story. We met the grandchildren and the aunts and the uncles – they cried over us and kept pouring out more wine! Wherever we went there was a tray of wine! It was a fantastic holiday!'

# Chapter 12

# Full Moon, Cloudless Sky[1]

*On D-Day+1 – 7/8 June 1944 – road and rail targets at Achères, Juvisy, Massy Palaiseau and Versailles were bombed accurately by 337 aircraft of Bomber Command but because the targets were mostly more distant from the battle front than those recently attacked the German night fighters had more time to intercept the bomb forces and 17 Lancasters and 11 Halifaxes were lost.*

The target for the Lancasters on 115 Squadron at Witchford was a major road bridge between Chevreuse and Massy-Palaiseau, barely 25km south of the centre of Paris. To avoid loss of French civilian life, the orders were to wait for the Master Bomber to verify that the markers were correct before any bombing took place. There was thick ground haze and the Master Bomber went u/s. The deputy took some time to get it all together and in the meantime the force of 337 bombers sent to various targets around Paris waited. It was a clear night and the night fighters descended. 'J-Jig', piloted by 28-year-old Flight Sergeant John Edward Todd RAAF, was shot down and crashed at Montchauvet (Yvelines). Todd and five of his crew were killed. A seventh member of the crew was taken prisoner. 'A4-H2', flown by 21-year-old Pilot Officer Ronald Peter Maude, crashed near Giverny

---

1 Adapted from a story written by Archibald Russell's son from his father's dictation quoted in *Memories of Witchford* by Barry and Sue Aldridge (Milton Contact Ltd, 2013).

with the loss of all seven crew. Before the war Maude was training to be an accountant, having left school in Gloucester in 1939. 'K-King', flown by 28-year-old Pilot Officer Charles Henry Quinton exploded over Paris killing all the crew. 'C-Charlie' piloted by Flight Lieutenant Peter Wingate Norbury, crashed at les Bréviaries (Yvelines) with all seven crew being killed. 'H-Harry', flown by Pilot Officer Sydney Frederick Francis, crashed at Houdan (Yvelines). There were no survivors.

'W-William', skippered by Pilot Officer Eric Aubrey Law RAAF, was attacked by two German fighters, Sergeant Harry Newton, the 35-year-old rear gunner, was wounded and all the engines set on fire. Flight Sergeant Archibald Russell, the flight engineer, went to the rear of the aircraft to check on Newton and saw that he had bailed out. The rear gunner died later. 'Archie' extinguished the fire in the fuselage, spoke to the skipper on the intercom and was told to return to the cockpit and assist him to put on his parachute. They then both bailed out at 700ft. On the way down, Archie saw the wings of the aircraft break off and the fuselage nose dive into the ground at Massy (Essonne). Flight Sergeant John Rowland Nurse, the Australian wireless operator, recalled that the aircraft was attacked by two fighters when commencing the run into the target. The port engine caught fire but was extinguished. The starboard inner engine was also hit and a fire started in the starboard wing. Efforts to extinguish were ineffective. The abandon order was given. Nurse bailed out at about 6,000ft and after landing safely was unable to contact any other member of his crew, except his pilot, who informed him that Sergeant J. E. Parkinson, the navigator, Flight Sergeant Gordon Washbourne, the 20-year-old bomb aimer, who was from Perth in Western Australia, and Russell, had all bailed out. Their pilot would successfully evade capture.

Archie Russell realised on landing that he had lost a flying boot. He took his parachute to a nearby house, retraced his footsteps and jumped into a bed of nettles about 100 yards from the burning aircraft to gather his thoughts together. He heard German vehicles and troops arrive and decided when the panic was at its height to move out of the nettles and commenced walking down the road. He took off his battledress tunic and tossed it over a hedge; the verges on both sides of the road were lined with poplar trees, which gave excellent cover from oncoming vehicles.

As dawn broke, he left the road and went into a forest intending to hide. Fortunately, he saw a cottage and decided to contact the occupants. A man opened the door and Archie explained in schoolboy French that he was a sergeant in the Royal Air Force. The forester spoke to his wife and then took him into the forest to hide and await his return. At this point, Archie had no idea whether the forester would assist him or notify the Germans. Within the hour, the man returned bringing a mug of goat's milk and explained that he would try to contact the Resistance and have Archie moved from the forest before the Germans launched a full-scale hunt for surviving aircrew. The forest was near a German airfield, Villacoublay, and the Germans searched for the aircrew for two whole days. At about 7 o'clock that evening, the forester returned and asked if Archie could ride a bicycle. He said that he had contacted the Resistance and two men arrived and gave Archie a pair of shoes and a jacket. They took him along a track where there were three bicycles and said that he was to follow the front man, not to talk to anyone and that the second man would bring up the rear. Before long, they came to the main gate to the German aerodrome and passed without trouble. Shortly after, Archie was taken into a house at Villacoublay, given a meal and afterwards moved into what appeared to be a garden summer house to remain there until contacted.

The next day, Archie was visited by a young woman wanting information about his crew and the aircraft. The only information she got from him was name, rank and service number. The people who were looking after him said that she would come back again and must be given answers to her questions. Upon her return, she gave 'Archie' a full run-down on the crew by name, the type of aircraft, his name and the information that the rear gunner was dead. This information convinced Archie that he was with the Resistance.

Approximately two weeks later, Archie was escorted to Paris on the Metro. As he emerged from the Metro, he saw a large swastika flag over the entrance to an imposing building. As they came opposite the entrance to the building, they turned at right angles down a road and entered a café, where they went into a back room and met four or five people. A lot of talking took place and before long, Archie was taken over the road into the headquarters of the Garde Republique, where he was reunited with Sergeant P. Murphy the mid-upper gunner, and was informed that Sergeant J. E. Parkinson was also in Paris. When Parkinson enlisted in the RAF at 29 years of age, leaving behind his poultry farm business at Appley Bridge near Wigan in Lancashire, he could never have known that after being shot down into a French potato field early on the morning of 8 June 1944 a broken bone would save his life. Having buried his equipment in the potato field, despite a badly cracked ankle he had hobbled barely 2km towards Paris when he was accosted by two members of the French Resistance. Five minutes later they met Gordon Washbourne. The two airmen were taken to Châtenay-Malabry on the south-west outskirts of Paris, where Parkinson's ankle was bandaged.[2] While he rested, Washbourne went into Paris the following morning in civilian clothes along with armed Resistance members. There they were stopped by a German patrol and Washbourne endeavoured to run away, resulting in his being shot and killed.

The Commandant of the Garde Republique and his wife, Madeleine, were both members of the Resistance (he was later to be arrested and sent to a concentration camp, but survived) and it was she who took Archie Russell to his first accommodation in Paris and supplied him with a false documentation, identity card and ration card. From that moment, he became 'Jean Cartier', although he was unable to speak much French! In order to obtain a photograph for his identity card,

---

2  *RAF Evaders* by Oliver Clutton-Brock (Grub Street, 2009).

he was taken to a booth in one of the Paris railway stations. While waiting to be picked up by the Resistance, he was approached by two German officers, who asked him questions, presumably about the train service. He knew that if he opened his mouth, all would be lost. With incredible presence of mind, he pretended to be both deaf and dumb, touching his ears and mouth and making gurgling noises. The officers retreated in disgust! In all, he was hidden in three separate flats in Paris; first at Saint-Denis, then Saint-Germain and finally, near the Jardin Zoologique.

On leaving Paris, he was brought together with the two other crew members and moved by the Resistance to a farm north of Paris. That evening, just about everybody from the village called to see the RAF airmen, which did not seem to them to be very good for their security. Later in the week, they were visited by an escape route organiser, but nothing came from this, although he returned two days later and asked them what they wanted to do. The Resistance had discussed the idea of taking the airmen through the German lines to reunite them with Allied troops. But it was not possible. After some discussion, they agreed to make for Dieppe, hoping to get back to England via the Channel. The next thing was that two youngsters, a boy of 12 and a girl of 10, arrived at the farm with bicycles and escorted them to Beauvais. This was an uneventful journey thanks to the capability of the youngsters. Years later, the boy and girl married and Archie was given a copy of their wedding photograph.

On arrival at Beauvais, they were housed with the le Cure family consisting of husband, wife and niece. The crewmen were reluctant to stay put and await liberation and they explained that they wanted to get to Dieppe. Monsieur le Cure said that he would organise bicycles and escort them there, which he did ten days later. When they arrived in Dieppe, they took cover in a cave in the chalk cliffs, where they were told to await instructions. After about two hours, Monsieur le Cure took them to a house in Dieppe, belonging to Madame Malige. By then they had realised that the town was full of Germans. Shortly after they arrived at the house, a German soldier knocked at the door demanding a room for an officer. Madame Malige told the soldier that she did not have an air-raid shelter and that it would be better for the soldier to look for a room elsewhere. The crewmen spent that night on the roof of the house in order to protect Madame Malige in the event of their being caught by the Germans. It was clear that the crewmen could not stay in Dieppe. The Maliges and their friends organised a hay cart in which the airmen hid. The driver of the hay cart took them through three German checkpoints before they were clear of Dieppe's restricted area. Then they were on their own and they decided to return to Beauvais on foot.

Their first encounter came when they walked into a wood to get out of the sun and have a rest, only to find a number of German tanks and their crews were already there. They therefore walked straight on through the wood and did not meet any trouble. Later in the day, they discovered a hay barn and decided to spend the night there. The following morning when they got up, they were covered with insects so they plunged into a nearby pond to get rid of them. As they got out of the pond, they saw a number of Germans having what looked like breakfast. The crewmen gave them a wave, to which they responded and carried on. Later that day, they saw a convoy of farm wagons driven by children under the guidance of two elderly people. The youngsters made signs that they had cigarettes, but wanted matches. They gave the children a light and were given three cigarettes. The wagons appeared to be transporting V-weapons! Their next encounter was with a German staff car, which was endeavouring to pinpoint a fighter aircraft that had been shot down. They pointed back towards Dieppe; the staff car turned and drove away.

By now their feet were feeling the effects of the walk and their mouths were extremely dry. By the time they arrived back at Beauvais, at the same house as before, they needed a few days' rest to get their feet back into shape.

They were then taken to Les Andelys, just north of the Seine, to stay with an elderly couple who were looking after another RAF airman, not part of their crew, who had been wounded. The man was a Jesuit who had been a missionary in Algeria before the war and who could not return because of the war. The Jesuit had nursed the wounded airman and he had almost recovered. 'Archie' and his crewmates stayed at the house in Les Andelys for about a week. The Germans were now in retreat. A Canadian officer arrived at the house as part of an advance party and the next morning British soldiers arrived in tanks and the RAF men were able to make contact with them. Later, they were escorted to Lisieux, debriefed by English officers and flown back to England from Saint-Lô. They had been on the run for three months, with the help of the Resistance.

On the night of 9/10 June, Parkinson was moved to another house in Châtenay-Malabry, where he stayed for approximately four days before going 'to the barracks of a guard and from there to a warehouse of another member' in Paris. With his ankle mending well, he enquired as to how he might regain the Allied lines, but was told that that was quite impossible. On 5 July he went to Feucherolles planning to escape from his benefactors and was joined by his flight engineer, Sergeant 'Archie' Russell, and by his mid-upper gunner, Sergeant P. Murphy. On 6 July they contacted another Resistance group at Poissy, across the River Seine to the west of Paris but, still unable to get away, went to Élancourt three days later 'to await the arrival of an intelligence agent ('Maquis') to journey to the lines in Normandy.

After waiting for a further ten days, they were informed that the agent had been killed at Saint-Lô owing to there being German agents among the aviators. Accordingly, on 19 July they were passed on to another organisation, at Gournay-en-Bray, where they learned that the heads of the Resistance had been arrested two months earlier. Growing ever impatient, they were given an address in Puys, a couple of kilometres north of Dieppe, where they understood that they would be able to get away by fishing boat. They left on 21 July but, with no boat, transport was arranged some days later to take them back to Paris. Before they could leave, however, it was discovered that Paris was now a 'closed' city. Russell and Murphy left anyway on 17 August in the hope of getting through to the Allied lines. Parkinson stayed behind and after a close encounter with some German soldiers who appropriated a couple of bicycles and demanded food and drink, was liberated on 20 August barely three hours after Russell and Murphy.[3]

Meanwhile, the family waited back home. Archie's wife, Ena, knew where he was stationed and that he was on operational duties, but never knew just when he would be flying on a mission. The first she even knew that he was flying on the night of 7/8 June was when the telegram arrived with the news that his plane had been shot down and he was reported missing. At that stage Ena had no idea whether her husband was dead or alive, whether he had escaped or was a PoW. The telegram was followed up by a letter from Archie's commanding officer, but still no definite news one way or the other. All she knew was that the plane had come down in France. There then followed weeks of waiting for news at the same time as trying to lead as normal a life as possible, caring for their young son. The days turned into weeks and weeks into months and still no news.

Then, in September 1944 Ena received two letters. The first was from the Commander of the 8th Canadian Reconnaissance Regiment with the news that Archie's name had been passed on to him by the French underground and that he was alive and well. The second, from a major in the Royal Artillery, who had promised the Frenchwoman who had sheltered 'Archie' and two of his crew members for eight days that he would get news through that Archie was OK. For the safety of the French underground, neither letter could give many details. Ena didn't know how recent the news of Archie's survival was, but the letters gave her hope. Not long after these letters, the long-awaited telegram from the Air Ministry arrived with the news that 'Archie' was safe and well and in England. In fact, Archie had beaten them to it. He arrived home to Ena the day before the official telegram arrived.

---

3  *RAF Evaders* by Oliver Clutton-Brock (Grub Street, 2009).

After some leave at home, Flight Sergeant Russell joined another bomber aircrew. Their task was to drop equipment and supplies to the Resistance in France and other parts of Europe. Fifty years on from 'VE Day', Archie was able to go back to France and visit Madame Malige, who, by then was living in the small village of Crillon-le-Brave in Provence near Mont Ventoux. She had kept in touch with some of the airmen whom she had helped and had written to Archie the previous Christmas with an invitation to visit her if at all possible. Madame Malige was living on a smallholding, growing olive trees and living with her was Monsieur le Cure, who was her brother-in-law. By then, her husband was dead. There was chance for a long conversation and Madame Malige took Archie into her study where she was proud to show him a letter from General Eisenhower thanking her for the help she had given to American airmen. She had also been presented with the Légion d'Honneur. The Mayor of Crillon gave a civic reception for Archie and spoke of his war exploits.

# Chapter 13

# 'Ursula'

*Donald Meese worked in the Sheffield steel works prior to volunteering and joining the RAF in 1943. While still in Sheffield he helped with firefighting and assisting people to shelters after raids had caused explosions at the gas works. Donald completed initial training in Torquay and London in 1943 and was then posted to 615 Squadron at Chedburgh. He eventually joined 622 Squadron at Mildenhall in Suffolk. While waiting to fly his first operation he learned to fly on simulators in his spare time. As a flight engineer, he was very aware that in the event of a pilot being injured or killed, another crew member would be needed to be able to fly the aircraft.*

Donald Meese and his crew's first operational flight took place on Friday/Saturday, 23/24 June 1944. Donald, who was only 19 years old, was the flight engineer/2nd pilot on Lancaster I LM138 'N-Nuts' that was part of a bombing operation to a flying bomb site in the Pas de Calais. His pilot, 24-year-old Flight Sergeant Wilfred Harold Cooke RNZAF of Te Awamutu, New Zealand, had been posted to 622 Squadron on 24 May. 'Harry', as he was known, had flown his first operation as a 'second dickey' on the night of 17/18 June in a raid on the Montdidier marshalling yards. His crew on his second operation, on 23/24 June, consisted of Flight Sergeant R. J. Hansford; Warrant Officer Richard John Chapman RAAF; Flying Officer Albert William Simmonds; Sergeant Fred Oliver, the 22-year-old mid-upper gunner, whose wife Kathleen Oliver, lived at Beech Hill, Wigan; and Flight Sergeant Thirlstone Durrant RNZAF. Lancasters had recently been adapted to take a greater bomb load, with some guns removed on the underside. In the early hours of the morning they flew into clouds after releasing their load and were attacked from below by a German fighter flown by Unteroffizier Konrad Beyer of 1./NJG 4 at 0028 hours. The Lancaster was hit in the wings, which caught fire and the controls were badly affected. The crew literally had seconds to get out when the call came from the pilot, 'Emergency, bail out!' Meese and four of the crew bailed out and all were taken prisoner. However, Harry Cooke and Fred Oliver were killed when they bailed out too late for their 'chutes to fully deploy. Their bodies would have been thrown into the flames of the Lancaster, which came down in a corn field just outside the village of Socx near Saint-Omer but for the courageous intervention of the mayor, who forcibly argued that the airmen were only carrying out their duty and deserved a proper burial. He arranged for them to be buried in his village churchyard the following day.

Meese recalled jumping out, pulling the ripcord and nothing happening but at some point, he says he straightened out, the plywood front of his chute came up, the webbing hit the sides of his face, but his 'chute opened. He landed in 10/10ths pitch darkness in a field and promptly buried his parachute and set off through the fields. At one point he lay down in a corn field to collect his thoughts and then realised that in getting to the centre of the field he would have left a trail that the Germans could spot from the air. He stuck to the fields, going along the hedges and as it became light started to head for a church. He met up with four Frenchmen, two of whom ran away when they realised that he was an English flier; the other two sent him in a direction that they said would take him through an area where there were no Germans. After blundering into an area of minefield, Meese realised that the lanes were probably safer. He turned his flying jacket inside out and cut his flying boots down and began walking down a lane, which was bordered by high hedges. He decided that his best hope in being mistaken for a Frenchman was to sing the only French song he knew: *Clair de lune*. However, at around 0730 he became aware of someone emerging from the hedges behind him, felt a tap on his shoulder and was taken into custody by four Wehrmacht soldiers. He had been at large for just eight hours.

Meese was taken in a 'massive German car' to a castle and after a wait of three days he was reunited with the other surviving members of the crew. He was offered coffee, which he spat out, and he refused to eat any of the food offered. At some point he was taken to identify the wreckage of his Lancaster at the crash site and the two crew members who had died. He confirmed the identity of Cooke, whom he said was the pilot, and further identified the other body as Oliver, in front of whom he burst into tears and said that he was his best friend. Meese and the other crew members were taken to a Gestapo jail in Lille and over a number of weeks subjected to varying degrees of torture, mainly psychological, but also physical.

It was while in solitary confinement in Lille prison that Meese experienced a kind act from a young German that was to change his opinion of all Germans being bad. A young lad came in singing *Lilli Marlene* and shared his food and some cigarettes with them. Donald finished up as a prisoner in Stalag Luft VII in Upper Silesia in German Poland. Towards the end of 1944, with the Russians advancing from the East, the Nazis started moving PoWs back toward the German lines and the River Oder.

In January, with snow thick on the ground, prisoners were taken from the PoW camp and embarked on a 650-mile walk towards Darmstadt. At the time they had no idea where they were going and Meese, who had managed to keep fairly fit, had no intention of marching west towards Germany. Together with Sergeant Tom Greene, it was decided they would hide behind a woodpile when the prisoners were halted in a brick works. Establishing they had 16 seconds when their sentry guards turned during their furthest time apart, the two men gradually ran desperately towards the forest. Greene was recaptured in the afternoon of the following day by a

German patrol and taken to Brieg, but when the town was evacuated a few days later he hid under a kind of stage with several others. The Germans did not discover them and they remained in Brieg until the Russians liberated the town on 6 February 1945.[4]

Using the night sky to navigate, Donald Meese spent eight days trekking through snowbound forest in soviet-liberated Poland. At night he listened to air and artillery barrages around him. The cold was so intense that his boots were frozen in the morning. He was on the point of giving up when a Russian plane flew over as he attempted to enter a village the Russians had fought over the previous night. A jeep full of Russians were initially unconvinced that Donald was an escaped PoW, but using sign language he managed to convince the commanding officer and the Russians took him away and fed him.

During his time on the run, Meese was discovered hiding in a barn by 19-year-old Fräulein Ursula Hosier of Kreuzburg, Upper Silesia, collecting eggs. She persuaded the farmer not to give him up and to let him rest before setting off again for the Russian lines. Donald was later to meet up with this young German girl in Czestochowa and to save her from the liberating Russians, he married her in Cracow while en route to Odessa and brought her to England as his wife. Donald was the only British soldier to escape through Russian lines and the only Englishman to marry a German girl in the course of the war.

In Sheffield on Monday, 16 April 1945 Mrs Sarah Meese embraced and kissed her new daughter-in-law. In 1945 Donald and their marriage was front-page news in all the national newspapers and Mai Zetterling starred in a play at the Sheffield Royal, based on their story, which in 1947 was turned into a film version called *Frieda*, starring Swedish actress Mai Zetterling in the title role, David Farrar, Glynis Johns and Flora Robson. In it RAF pilot 'Robert Dawson' (Farrar)

---

4 See *The Long Road: Trials and Tribulations of Airmen Prisoners from Stalag Luft VII (Bankou) to Berlin, June 1944–May 1945* by Oliver Clutton-Brock (Grub Street, 2013).

returns home from the war with his new bride, Frieda, the German girl who helped him escape from a prisoner-of-war camp. Frieda has to deal with the venomous bigotry of both Robert's family and neighbours, however just when the small town's prejudice against her begins to subside, her brother Richard (Albert Lieven), a closet Nazi sympathizer, arrives for a visit, causing even Robert's faith in his wife to be tested. The film was re-released in 1948 to excellent box office results.

In reality, what had started out as a marriage of convenience became a long-lasting love story.[5]

---

5 Donald Meese died on 24 March 2010 in the East Surrey Hospital, aged 86 years.

# Chapter 14

# Market Garden Mass Evasion

*From Sunday 17 to 21 September 1944 British, US and Polish airborne troops made a gallant attempt to seize and hold bridges across the Lower Rhine at Arnhem in Holland as a springboard for crossing into Germany, 'Market', the airborne part of the operation, was at the same time the largest in history. If successful the war could be over by Christmas. Lulled into a false sense of security, many were of the opinion: 'What could go wrong?' But it did and on such a massive scale, from its over-optimistic beginning to the tragic conclusion. During seven days of bitter fighting the gallantry shown by the troops on the ground and by the RAF and American air crews, the glider serials and the American, British, Canadian and Polish paratroopers, who tried so desperately to wrest victory from inevitable defeat, was unprecedented. British casualties were the highest, at 13,226 men. In all, 1,485 British and Polish airborne troops were killed or died of wounds and 6,525 more became prisoners of war. From a combined force of 1,438 C-47/Dakota transports (1,274 USAAF and 164 RAF) and 321 converted RAF bombers (mainly Stirlings), 932 aircraft were damaged or destroyed. RAF pilot and crew losses totalled 294. A handful (42 air crew and 17 RASC air dispatchers/ drivers on 38 Group Dakotas and 46 Group Stirling aircraft) evaded capture or escaped. Among them were*

*Flight Lieutenant Jimmy Edwards and Pilot Officer Christie, both Dakota pilots in 46 Group, and Sergeant Walter T. Simpson, a Stirling air gunner on 299 Squadron.*

'Arnhem began with the best intentions,' recalled Flight Lieutenant 'Jimmy' Edwards on 271 Squadron at Down Ampney, who towed a glider on 17 September and flew on successive days from the 18th to the 21st. Born in Barnes, London (then Surrey), on 23 March 1920, the son of a professor of mathematics, James Keith O'Neill Edwards was educated at St Paul's Cathedral School, at King's College School in Wimbledon and at St John's College, Cambridge, where he acquired a taste for comedy and the stage while performing in the 'Footlights Revues'. His aptitude for the footlights was confirmed with the staging of concert parties at Down Ampney. He had nicknamed his Dakota (KG444) *The Pie-eyed Piper of Barnes*, the name of which was painted in large yellow lettering on the nose in the style used by the Americans and it certainly gave him 'much more interest and pride in the job'.

'More men were going to be dropped than ever before and were going further into enemy territory than ever before,' he recalled. 'The first glimpse of that map in the briefing room brought whistles of incredulity from many of us. Clearly, the moguls had gone mad. It seemed to many of us that the generals were determined to use this massive airborne force simply because it was there and all their previous plans had been thwarted. It was all made to sound so simple at the briefing. "You will take off and fly in pairs to Aldeburgh on the Suffolk coast, where all the other aircraft involved will join you in a steady stream as you set course for the Dutch coast. It has all been worked out with split-second timing so that a continuous flow of gliders will arrive at exactly the right time over the dropping zone the other side of the river at Arnhem."

'All well and good. But it didn't happen like that. For one thing, the "other aircraft" involved were not all Dakotas. By this time, the lumbering, stolid Stirling bomber had been relegated to this humble

179

task of dragging three-ply and piano wire through the sky and so had the Albemarle, a medium-sized bomber that had done very little to commend itself up to now. The snag was that they all flew at different airspeeds, so that even with the most immaculate precision flying, the 'steady stream' was just a briefing officer's pipe dream. In the event, it was more like a dog's dinner ... Treble Four's days were numbered.'[1]

During the drop at LZ 'L' on 18 September most of the Stirlings had been hit by AA fire and fourteen aircraft in the formation, including three on 570 Squadron from Harwell, were damaged, one fatally. LK555, flown by Squadron Leader J. Stewart, was hit by flak but returned to base. LJ944, piloted by Acting Squadron Leader Hudson, crash-landed at Ghent. Flight Lieutenant Dennis Liddle and crew, flying LJ913, were thought to have been hit repeatedly by anti-aircraft fire in the area of the DZ and crash-landed at Schaarsbergen. Liddle pressed on and dropped his load of supplies on the DZ before the aircraft was seen to crash-land to the north-west of Arnhem. All the crew bailed out and were taken prisoner.

In the region of Stampersgat, Stirling AJ594 flown by Pilot Officer D. H. Balmer RCAF, a 25-year-old lumberman from Comox, British Columbia, was severely hit by flak. Balmer recalled, 'The aircraft immediately caught fire and I gave the order to bail out. Rear gunner Flight Sergeant J. T. Archer, passenger Sergeant R. W. Crabb, bomb aimer Pilot Officer E. G. Blight, flight engineer Sergeant T. Ireland

---

1 On 21 September Jimmy was shot down and, badly wounded, crash-landed in Belgium, saving the lives of his crew and subsequently evading with his wireless operator. Flight Sergeant 'Bill' Randall was hospitalised in Brussels until 24 September, when he was flown home to Down Ampney. Badly wounded, Edwards was treated for serious burns to his face at a field hospital and a few days later he was taken to Brussels and a special burns ward. He stayed there until the 27th, when he was flown back to Down Ampney. For his brave action Jim received the DFC. Post-war, 'Jimmy' Edwards became famous as a comedic script writer and comedy actor on both radio and television. He was best known as 'Pa Glum' in *Take it From Here* and as the headmaster 'Professor' James Edwards in *Whack-O*.

and navigator Flying Officer V. C. Keag all bailed out, but as the aircraft was by this time too low for a safe jump, I told the remaining members of the crew that I was going to make a crash-landing and that they should assume emergency positions. (Ireland and Archer were subsequently taken prisoner.) The 2nd pilot, Flying Officer Mombrun, at great risk to himself strapped me into my seat, using his arm as a strap, realising that if this was not done, I stood a grave risk of being killed on landing. By doing so he thereby jeopardised his own chance of escape. I landed the aircraft in a grass field at Zegge near Bosschenhoofd, badly bruised and shaken but otherwise unhurt. Mombrun and wireless operator Flight Sergeant R. J. Kempton were in the same state.' (Driver W. H. Bridgeman sustained a dislocated shoulder and was taken prisoner. Thirty-one-year-old Corporal A. E. Barker, who was from Braintree, Essex, had a serious head wound and was taken to hospital at Roosendaal en Nispen, where he died.) Balmer continued, 'The aircraft, which was burning, was immediately surrounded by Dutch people and Father Pater Raseroms, a Catholic priest who spoke English, took us to a nearby house where a young girl tended our wounds. From there on my movements were arranged for me.' For nine days Balmer, Kempton, Flying Officer Geoffrey Adrian Mombrun, Blight, Keag, Crabb and Bridgeman remained in hiding with a downed American Dakota crew and Sergeant Fitzpatrick of the Royal Armoured Corps, who had been taken prisoner and had escaped from the Germans at Breda railway station. Then, on 3 October, they were dispersed to different addresses. Balmer stayed in Breda until Polish troops entered the town on 31 October.

Meanwhile, on Tuesday, 19 September Dakota KG428 on 48 Squadron was flown by Pilot Officer Valentine Brock Christie RCAF. As Christie approached DZ 'V' the space around them was full of puffs of smoke the size of footballs; 20mm light flak, Christie thought they called it. When it hit the aircraft halfway through the drop it sounded like gravel hitting a tin roof. Ahead of him two Dakotas were on fire. Just seconds after giving the signal to the four air dispatchers from 63 Airborne, the starboard engine was hit and seconds later the port engine spluttered and stopped. Fortunately, the Dakota did not catch fire but in Christie's opinion they now had had a very heavy glider and at less than 1,000ft altitude, so there was nothing to do but put down full flaps, glide straight ahead and try to crash-land in an opening between trees. At 100ft a rifle shot from 10 o'clock entered the port window and grazed Christie's left shoulder, which felt hot like a branding iron. A second or so later and it would have been through his heart.

Christie alerted the co-pilot, Flight Sergeant Frank Fuller, but still kept control of the aircraft. They bellied in, sliding over a single-track railway north of Arnhem and avoiding crashing into trees at the far end thanks only to a small railway embankment that had been built to haul ammunition trucks from a dump in the forest. The nose of the Dakota came to a halt only feet away from the trees, 12in in diameter. There was now no Plexiglas left in the windscreen and the force of the impact had thrown all the radio and radar instruments into the doorway through which Christie and Fuller entered the crew compartment, so this exit was unavailable to them but on the starboard side of the cockpit the Dakota had split apart and they were able to squeeze through and jump only a few feet to the ground.

The navigator, Warrant Officer A. P. Anderson RCAF, and wireless operator, Warrant Officer A. R. Fulmore RCAF, survived the rough landing but Fulmore had a few cuts from flying cockpit glass. Driver H. W. Thompson was wounded and died in the aircraft. The three other dispatchers had all been injured by flak and crushed by the supplies on the roller conveyer, and were seen to be bleeding. Driver R. Ollerton had a broken leg. Corporal R. C. Balloch had been wounded in the leg and by a bullet in the left arm and a piece of shell in the left shoulder. Christie, Fuller and Anderson carried them out as there was still a danger of fire, and made them as comfortable as possible. As they were doing so a group of German soldiers came from the far side of the clearing and began firing. Knowing the injured men urgently needed medical attention they had to leave the soldiers and dash into the wood. After capture

Ollerton, Balloch and Lance Corporal R. Bradley were subsequently incarcerated in Stalag XIB.

The navigation maps were buried with their revolvers in the woods as they felt being unarmed if captured would be in their best interests. They soon discovered that the battle was too fierce and confused for them to head for Arnhem and after lying low for a day or two set out north, out of the battle zone, with the idea of contacting the Resistance. The airmen and their dispatchers spent the night of 19/20th in the woods and used the contents of their water bottles and lunch packs. As they moved through the woods during the day, they saw odd groups of Germans and so decided to wait for nightfall before moving on. 'Just as it was getting dark,' recounted Frank Fuller 'two Jerry soldiers came walking along the edge of the woods towards our concealed position. They were laughing and talking to one another; when immediately opposite, one handed his rifle to the other, walked into wood a little distance and stopped about a yard or so from us; another couple of paces and he would have stood on us. We hardly dared to breathe – it was a toilet call and we were almost the Jerry's lavatory! The next few minutes seemed like hours and after the Germans had gone, we all swore we had heard each other's hearts beating.' Darkness came without and further surprises and they continued on their way.

At dawn they hurried over a field, climbing a fence and found themselves on a road, where a signpost told them they were near Hoenderloo, a small farming village, so they decided to call at the nearest farm. Everything turned out well and they were soon in the farmhouse drinking milk and eating some very welcome toast and eggs. The head of the household was Gerard Bloem, a forester. Nobody on the farm could speak English, but one of Bloem's sons went off on his cycle and soon came back with an underground worker, Jort Frans Smit, who was the schoolteacher and who could speak English. For the next two months they were moved from place to place by Dutch people, living in barns, chicken huts and goat houses, but spending most of the time hidden in underground hiding places that had been dug for them in the sandy soil of a young pine plantation on a local estate. They often had to be moved when the Dutch gamekeeper received news of the German officers' shooting sprees. On one occasion they spent the day in the attic of a woodman's unused house – on the very day the Germans chose it as a meeting place and remained there all day beneath them. It meant keeping still and quiet for the whole day and they were glad to get back to their hole in the forest that night.

Among their helpers at this time were Cornelius Van der Kooj at Hoog, Jan Oosterbroek, Mr Kerscherre, and Jon Obbink at Arnhem. The evading party increased to six on 2 October when a paratroops major and glider pilot sergeant were brought in by the Resistance to share the 'digs'. The party now began to get a little restless, but were then told of the Pegasus plan that had been carefully worked out by the Dutch Resistance and MI9 over the past few weeks. There were by now hundreds of Allied personnel in hiding and the Resistance decided that a mass escape should be tried. The Resistance had reconnoitred the route from northern Holland down to the Rhine. They had checked the route chosen thoroughly, and the risk was worth taking. Dates had been fixed, and Allied forces, still on the southern bank of the Rhine, would be sending amphibious craft across at a certain spot at a certain time. A supply of Sten guns had been dropped by the RAF especially for this show. One such mass crossing had already successfully taken place.

The first task was to gather together the whole party from a widespread area to one convenient spot, which the Resistance achieved without any trouble and in magnificent style. Fuller's party were actually packed tight into a motor van and taken to a particular farm. On three or four occasions the van was stopped and German voices were heard questioning the driver, but they seemed satisfied and the van went on. Later, in the dim light of a barn Fuller noticed both British and American airmen and even Navy personnel. The senior Army officer in charge was a British colonel, and he organised the marching formation of the party with the Dutch guides. The fighting men, mostly paratroopers, had the Sten guns and were positioned in front, to the sides and at the rear of the column. There were about ninety men in all. Those who had lost their uniform or part of their uniform were fitted out with new ones, so as not to be shot as spies if captured. When the time came to move off they were to march for two nights and rest for two days and then on the third night they were due at the appointed spot on the Rhine.

'All went well,' recalled Frank Fuller 'until we were within 45 minutes of our rendezvous, when we were challenged by a German sentry whose voice wavered as he stammered, "Halt, who goes there?" The column halted and there was silence for a few seconds, then the sentry repeated his challenge and started firing. The whole area was soon alive with Germans, machine guns chattered and the escort of paratroopers returned the fire. The Germans were also firing flares to light up the place.' The time had come to put an emergency plan into action, as Fuller explains, 'We had made plans for such an eventuality; I would partner Anderson and Christie would go with Fulmore. We would split up and try to make our way to the appointed place on the Rhine.' Fuller and Anderson soon came to a main road running east and west, but it proved to be hopeless as there were hundreds of Germans around, so they decided to head north. They had only gone a short distance when they were challenged by another sentry who, when they did not answer his challenge, once again began firing. Fuller shouted to Anderson to run and that was the last he saw of him until the end of the war, for he was later taken prisoner, along with Fulmore, on 19 November.

Fuller ran as hard as he could. A dog was chasing him, but gradually the barking stopped and he fell down completely exhausted in a field of tall wet grass. As he lay there, he saw the red Very lights coming up from the south bank of the Rhine. This was the signal that the amphibious craft was at the allotted spot to pick the evaders up. At that moment he felt very disappointed, but was so tired that nothing much mattered and he soon fell asleep. When he awoke it was light, and he was soaked to the skin and so stiff that he could hardly stand up. It took him an hour to get himself walking again. He had no idea where he was and was not so successful this time in contacting friendly Dutch people and had several doors shut in his face, before being taken in at a small cottage in Utrecht by a Dutchman called A. J. W. Hilhorst. Here he was given food and drink and allowed to take his clothes off to dry them by the fire after the family had gone to bed. They were naturally very nervous because of the number of Germans around, and asked him to leave by dawn the next morning. This he did, but the Dutchman must have got word in the meantime to the local Resistance, for he was approached in the woods nearby and guided to a hiding place where several RAF airmen were already in residence. The guide's name was Van Eyden and this was at Amersfoort.

Two days later Christie was brought to the hiding place, but not Fulmore, as he also had been taken prisoner. For the next five months until April 1945, just after the Allies crossed the Rhine into northern Holland, this was to be 'home' to Fuller and Christie. The Canadian pilot was awarded the Distinguished Flying Cross. Thanks to the 'Rhine Crossing Group – Leek' of the Dutch Resistance, headed by Klass Heiboer of Groot Amersfort, 49 allied soldiers and airmen were led to freedom. Of the 90 men who set out in the march of September 1944, sixty were killed, wounded or taken prisoner. Fuller believes a few managed to reach the appointed spot on the Rhine, and the remainder succeeded in getting back into northern Holland to rejoin the Resistance.

On 19 September 20-year-old Sergeant Walter T. Simpson, an air gunner on Stirling LJ868/R piloted by Flight Lieutenant Geoff C. Liggins, was en route across south-east England to Arnhem to resupply the 1st Airborne dropped during Sunday and Monday. LJ868 was one of 17 Stirlings that took part in a resupply flight that took off from Keevil at 1245 carrying 24 containers and panniers. A further seven Stirlings on 299 Squadron towed Horsa gliders. 'Having been briefed to fly at some given height and in "V" formation of three aircraft,' recalled 'Wally', 'this had to be given up during flight as a bad job due to poor visibility, so we climbed above it and reached blue sky and sunshine. All was quiet crossing the coast, not even a shot fired in anger. That was until we crossed over into enemy-held territory. Then all hell let loose; big stuff, little stuff; everything including the kitchen sink. The war virtually stopped on the ground and all guns were pointed skywards. You could hear it hitting the aircraft and could smell the cordite fumes of the exploding shells.

'The pilot was trying to take evasive action but as we had now regained our "V" formation, we could only move to the right and back again. The closer we moved to our target the more we were hit. One shell burst somewhere near my turret as shrapnel passed through the top of my turret and the blast forced me over onto my right shoulder. I regained my position and blasted away at anything that moved. We were now getting closer to our dropping zone and I could hear the bomb aimer giving instructions to the pilot. Sergeant Rudsdale, the WOp, came down the fuselage and gave Corporal Prior and Driver Braid, the two dispatchers, a hand and gave them the signal to drop the baskets which would be pushed out through the well in the fuselage floor. Bomb doors opened, we were nearly there and still in one piece.

'Flight Sergeant Ken Crowther, the bomb aimer, was still giving the pilot instructions and then I heard "Hold it!" and away went our supply load beneath my turret. With bomb doors closing and heading for home, a turn to port and bingo, we had it; the swine's set our port wing on fire. As I rotated my turret to see if I could see anything, the pilot told us to take up our crash positions. He was going to put her down. I acknowledged that I was leaving my turret to take up my crash position. I indicated to the WOp and the two RASC dispatchers from 253 Airborne RASC that we were going to crash and by movement of my hands suggested that they got down. I took up my position, knees up, hands behind my head, elbows forward and waited. Waited for what? Would it be the end for some of us, or all of us? We couldn't and wouldn't know until it was all over. If we survived, we were going to be very, very lucky indeed. We waited, engines throttled back, a change of note, a bump, engines picked up and then by the time I came to, it was all over, so I thought.'

The aircraft, which had broken in half and was on fire, had landed in the river behind the church at Oosterbeek. The two air dispatchers, Corporal Prior and Driver Braid, along with Walter Simpson were unhurt. Sergeant William Alan Rudsdale, the 23-year-old WOp from Middlesbrough who had been a clerk in civvy street, and Sergeant Donald George Gaskin, the 18-year-old flight engineer from Edmonton in London who had been a fitter's mate, were hurt and unable to get out of the aircraft, so Simpson went back to help them out. He then realised that Crowther was also missing, so he went back in and got him out. The pilot, Liggins, and navigator, Flight Sergeant Frank Henry Humphrey, were rescued by Prior and Braid. Liggins was in great pain and given morphine by Braid.

'There's a fire,' continues 'Wally' Simpson. 'Someone screamed from up front. I found that my legs were trapped underneath the WOp's body. I moved, he shouted out with pain, he had sustained a back injury. I couldn't open the fuselage door. I assisted him to the rear escape hatch, only to find it missing and my parachute gone with it. We got ourselves out and took up a sheltered position near the aircraft. The water of the Rhine was almost lapping the aircraft's tail. Our sheltered spot was a breakwater bank which shielded us from the blazing aircraft and the German snipers. Only then did I realise that Gaskin and Crowther were still in the aircraft and were trapped due to their injuries. I re-entered the bomber and brought out the flight engineer, who had a broken leg. I then returned for the bomb aimer. The snipers were still having a go at us. I reached him and brought him to safety. His injuries included both arms broken and a partly severed foot. Some thirty seconds later the aircraft blew up and burnt itself out.

'By now the local Dutch people had arrived to help us, they had come from the village of Driel. After attending the wounded as best they could, it was decided to take them into the village. Anything that could be used for a stretcher was used. I recall a ladder being used.

I was told by one of the Dutch ladies who could speak English that they would come back for me and my two dispatchers when it got dark, but due to a misunderstanding we missed each other.'

At 2000 hours Dutch civilians arrived, with them, a lady doctor and two nursing sisters, the wounded were taken to a barn for immediate first aid treatment. Here they stayed until the 20th. The whole time they were under sniper and 88mm cannon shellfire that was being aimed at the stricken aircraft while the injured men were carried on makeshift stretchers made out of ladders and an open cart to the vicarage in Driel. There they were tended by a Mr Hendrick, a first aid man, and Cora and Reat Baltussen. Hendrick had a special pass issued by the Germans that enabled him to carry out his duties and so he could tell the Germans that the wounded were too ill to move, although much of the dressings were 'window dressing'. For the next three days Prior, Braid and Simpson were hidden in a drainage tunnel let into the riverbank. The food they had was from Walter's air box and 24-hour ration pack from the aircraft's dinghy. It contained Horlicks' tablets, sweets and chocolate, but they had no water and going down to the river would mean exposing their position to the German patrols in the area. But as it happened, it was not a German patrol they heard but a friendly one. A farmer came and brought someone who could speak English but all he could say was that the British were expected on the 23rd. He came from Driel and said that the people there were nervous. It was not unexpected as five had been shot a few days ago for helping evaders. The British arrived on the 21st but owing to a lack of transport they had to stay there until the 24th. On the 21st a Polish patrol got into the village and fought with the Germans, with the result being the Polish had to retire. They left behind a Polish doctor to treat Liggins, who had burns to his hands and face and had also injured his back in the crash-landing, and the other injured crew men. The Polish doctor had to amputate part of Crowther's foot due to gangrene setting into his heel. He had also broken both arms, and sustained a fractured skull and shrapnel wounds. Flight Sergeant Humphrey had a badly cut left leg, Rudsdale had a broken back and

Sergeant Gaskin a broken leg. On the 24th the wounded were taken by ambulance to Nijmegen and put into a casualty clearing station.[2]

'With my crew gone to receive medical attention,' continues 'Wally' Simpson, 'I was left with my two dispatchers. It was decided that we should leave the crash site and move away from the direction where the snipers were firing from. We had not moved many yards when a single shot whined through the air in our direction. In no time at all we were flat on our bellies not daring to move. By now it was getting dusk, so we crawled forward until we reached the next breakwater. We made a quick dash, up and over and stayed put. We now found that we had cover from three sides so we were fairly safe from surprise (we hoped). During the hours of darkness, a patrol passed within 30ft of where we were lying. We froze, not knowing if they were friend or foe. (Only four years later did I find out that they were friends and they were out looking for us.) It was a cold, damp, long night. Would daylight ever come? A river meadow was not the best of places to spend a night under the stars. We went into hiding for three days and managed to survive on my 24-hour ration pack.

'On Friday, 22 September we were able to join up with a patrol of the Polish Parachute Brigade and were taken to their headquarters in Driel. We were there for approximately 36 hours, in which time we had been shelled and nearly killed. During the short stay in Driel I was able to see the five members of my crew. The staff at the medical centre did not know if the bomb aimer was going to pull through as his leg had been amputated because gangrene had set in. Pull through he did and was returned to Wharton Military Hospital (Wiltshire) three weeks later, where further amputations took place. Geoff Liggins, Braid, Prior and Simpson were taken by jeep to Nijmegen and stayed there for two days. They were taken to the Reichswald Forest for three days under canvas. They then ran the gauntlet on a transport column down a two-mile corridor known as "Hell's Highway". They finally arrived in Brussels and MI9. The crew survived their ordeal

---

2 *Air Battle For Arnhem* by Alan W. Cooper (Pen & Sword, 2012).

but did not return to the squadron.'[3] On the 29th 'Wally' Simpson arrived back home in Coventry.

After Geoff Liggins visited his old airfield at RAF Keevil and had given his version of events, he was recommended for the Conspicuous Gallantry Medal (Flying), an inappropriate decoration as all the action was on the ground so the air officer commanding 38 Group deemed the Military Medal a more fitting award. Liggins returned to duties with 299 Squadron. Sadly, he was killed in a car crash in 1955.

On 20 September Stirling LK556 on 196 Squadron from Keevil was hit by flak and Flying Officer J. W. McOmie was forced to crash-land at Elst-Lijnden (Valburgseweg). Sergeant David Nicholson Clough, the 22-year-old flight engineer who was from Coventry, was found dead in a field and Drivers' Robert Frank Pragnell, aged 39, and 38-year-old Corporal A. W. J. Pescodd of 63 Airborne RASC also died. Driver Pragnell has no known grave and is remembered on the Groesbeek Memorial. Corporal Pescodd and Sergeant Clough are buried in Jonkerbos War Cemetery, Nijmegen. The five survivors, McOmie, Flight Sergeant S. R. Brooks, Flying Officers' George Murray Cairns, J. L. Patterson and G.F. Talbot, who possessed a total of three pistols between them, were soon surrounded by Dutch peasants, who told them that there were Germans all around and that they should go north with a view to crossing the river and joining up with the airborne troops at Arnhem. McOmie was dressed as a Dutchman in a cap, clogs and overalls over his uniform, furiously pedalling a child's bicycle. They started to stroll across an open field; but sniper fire drove them to take shelter in a ditch before they were taken to a tactical headquarters. On the 23rd a farmer told them that British troops were in Valburg, so they walked back and reported to the HQ and from there they hitch-hiked to Brussels, arriving on the 25th.

---

3 Quoted in *Winged Victory: The Story of a Bomber Command Air Gunner* by Jim Davis (R. J. Leach & Co., London, 1995).

It was on 20 September that Edmund 'Teddy' Townshend of the *Daily Telegraph* flew to Arnhem in Stirling EF260 'R for Roger' on 190 Squadron piloted by 22-year-old Flying Officer John Douglas Le Bouvier, an engineering student in peacetime. Townshend, born on 28 May 1912 at Bourneville, Birmingham, when he was a child, had often seen George Cadbury, the chocolate magnate, walking home. After matriculating at King's Norton secondary school, 'Teddy' started work with a chartered accountancy firm but soon found a job, at ten shillings a week, with a local weekly newspaper. He progressed to the *Birmingham Mail* and then the *Daily Mail* in London before joining the *Telegraph* in 1944. As the invasion of Normandy was about to begin, he was attached to the Merchant Navy and given blue battledress, with a war correspondent's shoulder tabs and a big 'MN' on the chest, 'I don't envy you, old man,' said the news editor. On the morning of 'D-Day' Townshend was in a troopship in the Strait of Dover, watching a ship astern take a direct hit that cost twenty lives. When he looked from the bridge at a clock tower on land to check the time for his dispatch, he saw a shell from a British battleship neatly remove it. Later, in another ship, which was loaded with 800 tons of high explosive ammunition, the chief officer observed, 'One enemy shell into this lot and you won't know where to look for your typewriter.'

'We took off from Fairford at about 1510 hrs,' Flying Officer Le Bouvier recalled. 'We were scheduled to drop supplies to the First Airborne Division but about 1530 hours we were hit by flak near Oosterbeek. We were then flying at about 900ft and were hit in the port wing. I came in, dropped the supplies and then climbed. At about 2,000ft the crew bailed out. After they had gone, I got out and landed a few miles north-east of Elst. I was immediately picked up by Dutch peasants, given an overall and hidden in a ditch. At about 2100 hours a Dutchman came back and took me to a farm on the northern outskirts of Elst on the main Elst–Arnhem road. There I met Private Stephen Danby of the First Airborne Division, who had reached Elst the day before from Arnhem. We were given civilian clothes and hidden in the farm. The Germans were concentrating in the area and there was a sort of advanced HQ on the other side of the road.'

'R for Roger' had just dropped its supplies to troops on the ground amid heavy flak and 'Teddy' Townshend was watching from Flying Officer 'Tom' Oliver's co-pilot's seat. Oliver, who was 30 years of age, had been a policeman in the City of London before the war. Townshend saw the coloured parachutes floating down like autumn leaves when he heard over the intercom: 'Weave, skipper, weave … Keep weaving.'

'Engineer officer,' called the pilot, 'come forward and take a look at the port outer motor on fire.'

'What port outer motor on fire?' asked the engineer officer.

'Bail out,' came the order and, after clipping on his parachute, Townshend found himself being bundled to the open hatch in the nose.

'Gripping the parachute release handle to make sure I had it, I leapt into space too eager to escape from the blazing plane to feel fear at the drop,' he wrote in his front-page story. 'For minutes like hours, dreading attack by machine-gunners below, I swayed slowly to earth. Breathlessly I watched the Stirling roar away in flames, losing height. With relief I saw other parachutes opening in its wake.'

On landing in a ploughed field south of the Rhine, Townshend was immediately met by members of the Dutch underground, who gave him food and drink and buried his parachute and Mae West. They were disappointed that he carried nothing more dangerous than a pencil and notebook, but escorted him along dykes and behind hedges to meet up with nine fliers, including four of the crew and one of the dispatchers on 'R for Roger' (Flight Sergeants D. Martin, bomb aimer, and G. Kershaw and the other dispatcher, Driver H. S. Hill, having been taken prisoner), whom they made lie down in a beech wood in silence for fear of enemy patrols.

At dawn the underground returned with hot milk and sandwiches. German ack-ack fire whistled through the tops of the trees as another supply flight passed overhead in the afternoon and the group ended the day crouching in a tunnel as the artillery of both sides exchanged shells. A farmer's family invited all of them into their house, where 'Tom' Oliver sat down at the harmonium to play the Dutch national anthem and a picture of Queen Wilhelmina was pinned on the wall. A dozen more fleeing airmen appeared – one had landed in the river and swum 100 yards to the Dutch side as the Germans fired at the floating body of his co-pilot; others had watched the enemy retreating without shoes. Setting out at dusk with a map, compass and hard rations, they found the roads too dangerous and the dykes too wide and deep to cross. They encountered their first Allied patrol the next morning.

On 22 September the farm where John Le Bouvier had been hiding came under fire from British artillery and that night the family decided to evacuate and advised their guests to do the same, preferably in the opposite direction. On 23 September the British party was all ready to go, when at 0715 hours a German platoon turned up at the farm. 'We managed to get away through a cellar corridor in the back of the farm,' wrote Le Bouvier, 'and headed roughly due west in an attempt to reach the bridgehead west of Nijmegen. At about 1130 hours we met an advanced platoon of the Worcesters on reconnaissance. We were sent to HQ and I was able to tell them the position of the German concentrations near Elst, which they immediately attacked by artillery. At the HQ I was told that Flight Sergeant S. F. Saunders, the wireless operator, Sergeant C. Ryan and the two Army dispatchers and Mr Townshend were reported to be safe further to the north.'

'Teddy' Townshend hitched a lift to Brussels to phone over his story. When he submitted his expenses back in London they included 'replacement of splinter-proof spectacles swept away by an involuntary parachute exit' and 'rewards to Dutch underground workers for protection from enemy search parties'. The news editor paid up with a wry grin.

Le Bouvier's party was sent to Nijmegen, where he left Private Danby and then continued to Eindhoven, where he spent the night. On 24 September he flew to Brussels and from there to England. John Le Bouvier was awarded the DFC.

194

On 21 September 17 aircrew on 196 Squadron at Keevil had been killed on the dropping mission that day. Ten Stirling crews were detailed and of these six were successful and three aircraft failed to return. It being Yom Kippur, 22-year-old Pilot Officer Mark Azouz DFC could have taken leave on the 21st but he refused as men at Arnhem were waiting for supplies. He had earned his DFC for his action on the night of 2/3 August 1944 when a warrant officer. He was detailed for Operation 'Horace 8' for SOE (Special Operations Executive) over the Brest Peninsula. In the run-in to the target the aircraft was hit by anti-aircraft fire. The propeller and reduction gear of the starboard outer engine were shot away. The ailerons were damaged and other parts of the aircraft were struck by fragments of shell. Despite this, Azouz successfully completed his mission and returned safely to base.

Azouz and crew by now had made four supply flights to Arnhem: on the 17th, from Wethersfield on the 18th, on the 19th, when they dropped 24 containers and four panniers but sustained 27 holes from light and heavy flak at the TRV and LZ; and on the 20th. On the 21st, in LJ810, they left Keevil at noon with a similar load for Arnhem. Arriving twenty minutes late owing to engine trouble, after dropping his supplies, Azouz's Stirling was hit by flak over the DZ, but he got away and took the transport up to 4,000ft. 'The natives were hostile,' wrote 'Bert' Turner, the flight engineer, 'and they threw everything at us but we got through badly damaged. As we flew out of the target area, Mark asked the navigator, "Ginger" Greenwell, for a course to Brussels. Before we could do anything else we were attacked by three to five Fw 190s. Flight Sergeant Peter Harold Bode, the 21-year-old rear gunner, shot one down.'

At 1415 the fighters set the Stirling's tail and both wings on fire and the aircraft was going down when Mark Azouz gave the order to abandon. Everyone answered except for 'Pete' Bode, who was dead. Spitfires and Thunderbolts then appeared and covered their descent. Flight Sergeant Leo Hartman, air bomber, having bailed out, landed by a farm near Wijchen and sprained his ankle. Some farmers who had seen him bail out of his aircraft took him in and a member of the underground arrived and took away his parachute and Mae West.

'When we landed,' says 'Bert' Turner, 'we were taken to a Dutch farmhouse, where we were treated like royalty. There were now only six of us, we had somehow lost Mark.' 'Ginger' Greenwell, John McQuiggan, 'Bert' Turner and their two army dispatchers, Lance Corporal Day and 43-year-old Driver A. E. Norton, evaded. All arrived in the UK on the 27th. Greenwell was recommended and awarded the DFM.[4] Lance Corporal Day, a member of 63 Airborne RASC, was awarded the Military Medal.

On 21 September one of the 117 resupply sorties of that day was flown by 33-year-old Flight Lieutenant Reginald Thomas Frederick ('Reg') Turner DFC, a Stirling pilot on 299 Squadron at Keevil. He had previously served on 120 Squadron in 1942–43 and on 15 February 1942 had made three attacks on surfaced U-boats, one of which, U-225, was credited as 'sunk' after he dropped six depth charges. Turner had flown Stirling LJ971 to Arnhem on the 17th but he had to abort shortly after take-off with outer engine problems. After casting his glider off over the airfield, he had then landed safely and the glider was taken by another crew. His flight on the 21st was his third to Arnhem, this time at the controls of LK545 'T-Tommy' carrying 24 containers to be dropped near the Hartenstein Hotel.

'Our journey had been quiet until we crossed the Rhine over the DZ,' recalled Turner, 'when heavy, light and medium flak concentration opened up, followed by enemy fighters who were waiting outside the DZ area to catch who dodged to get in. We had no fighter cover, so enemy aircraft were able to attack in numbers, until air cover arrived later and the enemy dispersed. While over the DZ we were hit by flak and the tail caught fire, forcing Flying Officer J. S. Sutton DFM,

---

4 'Ginger' Greenwell had flown 30 operations as a navigator on 196 Squadron and on 2 August had navigated his aircraft on two engines and the third failing, back from the Brest Peninsula to Colerne; his aircraft had been hit on the final run into the DZ.

the rear gunner, who was wounded, to bail out, after attempts had been made to get him out. I continued course, but the fire got out of control, so I chose a position in or near our territory and crash-landed. No one was hurt and the secret equipment was destroyed.'

Over the DZ the two air dispatchers, Corporal Clemont Burton Sproston and Driver Brackman of 253 Airborne Divisional Composite Company RASC, 49 Air Despatch Group, were given orders to despatch the load. Although the aircraft was well ablaze and the rear gunner's ammunition was exploding inside the fuselage, Sproston continued to despatch the load, which consisted of high explosives, at the right moment. It was entirely due to his coolness and courage in despatching this extremely dangerous load, that Turner was able to crash-land the bomber in open country without loss of life. Flight Sergeant J. E. Price, the navigator; Flight Sergeant Sedgwick, the bomb aimer; and Flying Officer Sutton were captured. Turner and Warrant Officer Bernard H. Harvey, the flight engineer, and the two dispatchers, helped by Dutch civilians and the Resistance, evaded capture and were taken to a village by the local inhabitants. They were then picked up by a Dutch policeman in a car and they proceeded to XXX Corps' headquarters HQ near Nijmegen, where they remained throughout the night. Next morning transport was provided for Eindhoven. Between Uden and Veghel the party was held up because the road ahead was under shell fire. They were informed by a Dutchman that four Tiger tanks were ahead, and these immediately engaged their vehicles. A number of British trucks were knocked out, but a small party from the group took up a position in a nearby house. Sproston took charge of a forward observation post and directed fire from a Bofors gun, which succeeded in fending off the attack. The party turned around and proceeded in the direction from which they had come. After a mile and a half, they met two more Tiger tanks. One of the tanks opened fire on the lorry and the party took to the ditch, where they remained for fifteen minutes, but as the tank got closer it was decided to make for a house.

Edmund Townshend wrote up the epic story thus: 'F/Lt R. Turner, a Londoner, had gone ahead of us to the road south between Uden and Veghel and had run into a road blocked by German tanks and had fought his own private battle on the ground for 28 hours to get back out of the trap. He took command of 30 men, four of them his own crew and the others Bofors gunners. They destroyed a Tiger tank and an Armed Car and held on with the loss of four killed and eight wounded until British tanks relieved them.'

'In the general confusion,' reported Turner, 'I lost sight of the rest of the crew.' When the tank concentrated its fire on the house, Turner, Sergeant W. Moss the WOp/AG and Driver Brackman made for another ditch further away from the tank. 'After proceeding from ditch to ditch for three hours we met an American Airborne patrol with four jeeps. They took us into Veghel and here we remained until 1400 hours on Saturday, 23rd September, when an Army officer gave us a lift into Brussels. We then went from Brussels to Northolt in a DC 3.' For his actions this day Sproston was awarded a well-deserved Military Medal on 5 April 1945. On 13 July 1945 Acting Wing Commander 'Reg' Turner was awarded the Military Cross.

The fighting north of the Rhine in September forced the 1st British Airborne Division to withdraw, leaving several thousand men behind. Several hundred of these were able to evade capture and go into hiding with the assistance of the Dutch Resistance. Initially the men hoped to be able to wait for the British 2nd Army to resume its advance and thus rescue them, but when it became clear that the Allies would not cross the Rhine that year the men decided to escape back to Allied territory. In 'Pegasus I', the first escape operation, overnight on 22/23 October over the Rhine near Renkum, the Allied military forces, MI9 (the British intelligence organisation) and the Dutch Resistance successfully evacuated approximately 130 Allied soldiers (about 120 airborne troops, supplemented by flight crews) and 18 Dutch civilians, trapped in German-occupied territory who had been in hiding since the Battle of Arnhem. 'Pegasus I' was the largest escape from occupied territory during the Second World War.

But for 'Pegasus II' on 18 November the security of the operation was unfortunately compromised early on when a reporter impersonated an intelligence officer and interviewed several escapees from the first operation. The subsequent news story alerted the Germans, who strengthened their patrols along the river and only seven out of about a hundred soldiers managed to reach the south bank of the Rhine. About 30 men were captured and about 50 escaped from German hands. Despite this, over the winter the Resistance continued to help the evaders and many more men were able to escape in small groups.

# Chapter 15

# End Game

*The Light Night Striking Force, which operated Mosquitoes, acted as night bombers and as diversion raiders for the main force squadrons. On 14 October 1944, when 993 Lancasters and Halifaxes were dispatched to bomb Duisburg for the first of two raids on the city in 24 hours as part of Operation 'Hurricane', 36 Mosquitoes were included in two of the four diversionary sweeps; 20 to Hamburg and 16 to Berlin. According to the directive issued to Sir Arthur Harris, Hurricane's purpose was, 'In order to demonstrate to the enemy in Germany generally the overwhelming superiority of the Allied Air Forces in this theatre ... the intention is to apply within the shortest practical period the maximum effort of the RAF Bomber Command and the US 8th Bomber Command against objectives in the densely populated Ruhr.' Thirteen Lancasters and a Halifax failed to return and also lost was an outbound Mosquito on 692 (Fellowship of the Bellows) Squadron (an Anglo-Argentine group that raised funds to buy aircraft) detailed for the diversionary strike on Berlin. This was attributed to Unteroffizier Hans Dürscheidt of 1./Nachtjagdgruppe 10 flying a Focke Wulf Fw 190A from Bonn-Hangelar. Dürscheidt was killed on 24/25 October 1944 in a crash at his airfield.*

Flying Officer Francis Humphrey Dell and his 21-year-old navigator, Flying Officer Ronald Arthur Naiff of Hartshill, Stoke-on-Trent, had taken off in Mosquito B.IV MM184 from their 692 Squadron base at Graveley, Huntingdonshire, at 0130 hours. In the area of Münster the fighters managed to get in among the Mosquito force and mark the route their crews were taking. 'As we came over Münster,' related Frank Dell, 'up came the searchlights when suddenly we got hit from behind. In any event I lost control. I think the elevators were shot off and we stood up on our nose and fell away into a spiral dive. We were both forced down in our seats with little hope of getting out. My navigator had less chance, as his 'chute was still on the shelf. In a short while the aircraft broke up and I found myself out in the fresh air. I had my seat pack on and pulled the rip-cord and the 'chute opened successfully, but at a height of 24,000ft it was going to take an age for me to get down. It took about twenty minutes before I saw a dark shape. I thought it was a wood but it was a newly ploughed field. I hid my 'chute in a ditch and made for a cart track, which I started to walk along, when suddenly I heard an engine sound and, looking back, I saw torchlights and heard voices. I assumed they were looking for me, so I got off the track and around the back of them and then followed their progress up the road.

'1 then turned off the track into a wood and spent the night there until daybreak. I was only wearing my battledress jacket, under which was my polo-neck sweater. The sleeve of my jacket was torn, and my face was cut and grazed and I was feeling very sore, just as you do after a hard game of rugby.

'I opened my escape pack to see what it contained. The first thing I saw was a cellophane packet which contained tablets. Two were missing, the two I had taken when I first landed on the ground. I thought they were Benzedrine tablets to keep me alert, but as I now found out they were water-purifying tablets, so it just shows you that in the main taking tablets was all in the mind. In the pack was a needle and thread which enabled me to repair the sleeve of my jacket. One might as well be a tidy evader.

'I had a compass but no silk map. (This was because when Brussels had been liberated in September crews were landing there on the way back from ops for a bit of a binge and the escape packs were coming back without the foreign money and the silk maps.) With no map I decided to make tracks in a westerly direction towards Holland, a 100-mile journey I estimated. In the wood I became very lonely and sad at losing my navigator, Ron Naiff, but in a way, it helped me as I became determined to get back to visit his parents.

'In the middle of the day, quite suddenly, there was a horrendous noise. It was ear-splitting. The trees shook and dead leaves came down all around me. What the devil could it have been – I had not heard anything in the war as yet like it. Then suddenly I realised that a vehicle I had just followed was not looking for me but was a V-2 rocket carrier. At that time, we had heard only rumours of rockets and explosions in the East End of London.'

After hiding during the day, Dell walked a further 20 miles. 'Just before daybreak I came upon a farmhouse and another shelter and spent the whole day there while outside the usual activities of a farm were going on. They had no idea I was there, but in this situation, animals are a problem with their sense of smell. Each time the horse and cart came by the horse would look around at the shelter. Small children and dogs were also a problem, but no one came too near and I was okay in that respect but I was getting very cold and started to shake badly. I decided to get out and walk about to get my circulation going.

'I set off down the road. It was pitch black and I bumped into a man repairing his bike. He grabbed my arm and spoke in German. My reply, also in German, was that he should strike a match to see what he was doing. Then, making suitable grunting noises I carried on my way. Suddenly ahead I saw a small hut, like a sentry box, which could be the frontier or border between Germany and Holland. It was raining now and I made a detour around the post, then I saw another little farm with a chicken house at the back, but thankfully for me there were no chickens, so this became my lair for a while, but I was unsure if I was in Holland or still in Germany. I looked for the telltale signs like windmills. By now I was getting a little low and needed some help.

'I moved on and found another farm. This one had a welcome straw-covered loft in a barn, so I took off my wet uniform and hung it up to dry and lay down and fell into a deep sleep.

'I awoke to the sound of aircraft overhead and then machine-gun fire. I heard footsteps on the stairs of the loft, then excited voices. It was two 16-year-old boys, they both saw my uniform. One, in broken English asked, "You are Tommy Pilot?"

'I said, "Yes."

'The boy replied, "Be still. We have German soldiers in the farmhouse."

It turned out that a German truck had been strafed, hence the machine-gun fire. They had jumped out of their truck to seek shelter in the farmhouse. The two boys themselves were on the run, in a sense, as all men between 16 and 60 had to register for forced labour. The only alternative, if you did not register, was to go into hiding, which they had done. One of the boys was the farmer's son and the other, who spoke a little English, was the son of the local schoolmaster. He said he would speak to his father that night, for he might well know someone who could help. The farmer's name was M. Breukelaar and the farm was near Aalten.

'The farmer's wife gave me a cup of milk,' remembers Frank. 'Wisely she told me to drink it slowly, having not eaten or drunk anything for some time. When I looked in a mirror for the first time, I had two black eyes and a five-day growth of beard. I stayed for 24 hours at this farm and then another man came for me on a bike. He told me to sit on the front of the bike and off we went. We arrived at another farm, which had a beehive at the back, under which was a trapdoor which led to an old disused bread oven about 8ft by 4ft and 6ft high in one part. I could sit up but not in the main part of the oven. The ventilation came from the chimney, so I would not suffocate. I was given a blanket, milk and bread and then the trapdoor was closed again.

'At meal times it was the farmer's wife who brought me food. On one occasion she put her hand on my head in a motherly way, and this did it for me. Up till then I had put on a proud front and had not dropped my guard but when she did this I burst into tears. It was a sort of anticlimax, having bottled the whole thing up. A candle was left for me and matches so I could, if I needed to, have a light. In all I spent about two days and nights in the oven.

'After two days they came and took me out and gave me a pair of gym shoes so we would not be heard walking along the road. I still, however, kept my flying boots, which I had cut off at the ankle to make them look like shoes. The pieces I had cut off were lined with sheepskin and so I put one piece up the front of my battledress and the other up the back for extra warmth.

'They took me to yet another farm and this time my home was to be an attic. All the time I had been holed up they were checking with London that I was who I said I was. The farmer here was Henrick and the name of the farm was Klein Entink. During the day I helped with the many chores there are on a farm.

'Then one day we heard an aircraft flying very low and obviously in trouble, as it had smoke trailing from it. It was an American P-51 Mustang. All of a sudden, up came the nose and out came the pilot. This soon brought a lot of Germans into the area, while the Resistance men went out to look for him. When I saw them coming back, I foolishly went out to greet them and as we walked back to the farmhouse along came two German soldiers on bikes. I saw them but I don't think they saw me. Just beside me was a haystack and it was this that I was shunted into by one of the Resistance men. The Germans stopped and asked the Resistance men questions but soon went on their way unaware I was around the other side listening.

'When night came the American pilot had still not been found, so I was asked by the Resistance to teach them a phrase in English which the American would know if they called it out in the woods. I got them to repeat over and over, "Come out, you silly bugger. We are your friends." When they had got it off fairly well, they left once again to look for him, but as before they returned without him.

'After about three days he was eventually found and brought in. His name was Joe Davies. I asked him where he had been hiding and he replied, "Well, all night the Germans were walking up and down shouting 'Come out, you silly bugger,' so I stayed hidden. I had also hurt my knee in baling out so I could not walk far."

'It was then decided to move both of us on as the area was too dangerous, so we were moved to a farm owned by the marvellous Bernhardt Prinzen. He had ten children and his farm was at IJzerlo. In the area, because of his name, he was known as 'Prince Bernhardt'. I was told that Jan Kett was controlling the Resistance movements in this area.

'At first the children were a little nervous of us and on one occasion when we were washing as best we could everything went quiet. When we looked up there were ten pairs of eyes looking at us through a window. They were anxious to know if we were white all over.'

It was at that time that the former Humphrey Dell became Frank. Jan Kett found Humphrey unpronounceable, and his second name Francis became abbreviated to Frank. This name stuck in RAF circles and in Frank's post-war service in the civilian airlines when it became known that he was called Frank by the Dutch. His family, however, called him 'Humph'.

'When liberation came, things were a little tricky as a party of German parachutists were billeted in the farmhouse, but during the night they left and Bernhardt came to say to me that he thought a Tommy tank was at the bottom of the road. Being the only Englishman there, I was elected to go and speak to them. It proved to be an advance armoured car of the 2nd Canadian Army and as I walked towards it, its gun followed me. I banged on the side and said I was an English airman, a pilot. With that the turret lid opened and what I first saw was a handlebar moustache, complete with steel helmet. He gave me a broad grin and in a deep voice said, "Jolly good show, old boy." We were soon away, hardly having time to say our goodbyes. On our way to Tilburg, we saw the largest traffic jam we had ever seen or are likely to see. It stretched for 80 miles, bumper to bumper.

'I will always remember, while on the run, the sound of singing voices coming from a train. A solo tenor voice would then be taken up by hundreds of voices, to the tune of the "Hebrew Slave" chorus. It gave me a most uneasy feeling. Many years later, when driving along in my car, I heard this tune and suddenly realised what they were singing. The line the train was on led to Belsen.

'Ron Naiff was never found but his name along with 20,000 other airmen and airwomen who have no known graves is recorded on panel 208 on the Runnymede Memorial.'[1]

---

1 See *Free to Fight Again: RAF Escapes and Evasions 1940–45* by Alan W. Cooper (Pen & Sword, 2009).

# Index

–